FEAR NO ART

Michelle, Gene
Nicole, GiANNA

ALWAYS REMEMBER,
NEVER FORGET

" IN THE LAND OF THE SWINE
THE ONE-EYED PIG IS
KiNG!! "

PEACE & CHICKENS
COUSIN —

Published by BLAZO!!
www.blazo.com
103 Pleasant Ave Suite 2
Upper Saddle River, NJ 07458

Design by james campion

Cover Idea & Design by Eric Knight Holbrook

Photograph by Erin D. Moore

ISBN 0-9679296-0-1

Library of Congress Cataloging-in-Publication Data is
available upon request.

www.jamescampion.com

FEAR NO ART

(observations on the death of the american century)

james campion

for my partner, my sweetness, my wife,

erin

Any man who inflicts the human race with ideas must be prepared to see them misunderstood.

- H.L. Mencken

CONTENTS:

FOREWORD

Though technically this is considered a "Foreword," in this particular case I think a forewarning is more appropriate. Like the ominous surgeon general warning emblazoning the box of your cancer sticks of choice, this message is better served as a warning of the potentially brain damaging effects prolonged exposure to this mad, political analyst/ satirist/absurdist/ genius (?— it's a very fine line...), dropping verbal grenades on all accountable from his bunker somewhere up in Fort Putnam (the only records of his specific whereabouts were in that "misplaced" multi-million dollar Mars probe drifting deeper into the black abyss — slap a Lojack on these things for chrissakes).

Delivering the hard-line in his weekly Aquarian column "Reality Check," Colonel Campion has illustrated a consistent objectivity in the dispensing of his ire. No one is sacred, no punches are pulled. One week he'll piss off the conservatives, the next the liberals, and the next both. But hey, fair is fair and if you're going to lift up that rock, you'd better expose all the slugs. Though this isn't to say there isn't a fully functioning, blood-pumping, chest thumping aortic muscle beneath the hardened exterior that over the years has deflected more bullets than Rambo in the jungles of 'Nam (hell, his reader mail routinely outnumbers exponentially that of the rest of the entire paper!). When not dropping bombs on the camps of the latest clan of depraved politicos, this crusader of truth isn't afraid to stop and smell the freshly cut Yankee Stadium grass, to ponder the profound impact our culture's heroes do possess. As the amorphous bodies of celebrity and leader continue to mesh into one frighteningly blurred amalgam, perhaps it is this appreciation and respect of this impact our political, economical and social leaders possess, that so strikes a nerve when he observes this massive power being abused and misused.

So to those guilty parties and, more importantly, those courageous enough to read on, once again, consider yourself forewarned.....

Chris Uhl
Managing Editor, Aquarian Weekly

INTRODUCTION

"Who is that kid?" I asked the half-soused singer of a rock band back in the blistering hot summer 1996, mere moments after spotting a fresh face in the crowd at one of my local haunts. "Oh, that's Jim," the singer replied. "He's writing a book about us," one of the guitarists answered. "Writing a book?" I asked in a complete state of shock. "About you?" I asked even more perplexed. "He looks like he's too young to even be in here, let alone master the fine art of being a wordsmith! And what the hell is he going to write about? You guys are a fucking cover band, for chrissakes!"

Well, I don't know if those were the exact words I used, but it went something like that. Here I was, the Managing Editor for the biggest rock and roll publication in New Jersey. I had my proverbial finger on the pulse of the club-going public. Why was an obvious authority on the music scene such as myself not asked to write a biography on these hacks? Come to think of it, why would I want to?

Jealousy was not the issue, only skepticism. So I did what any journalist would do; I got a fresh drink and went over to meet this little shit. It was during that brief conversation over the pounding din that I first recognized Mr. Campion's infectious personality and stylish intellect, which made him forever endearing. It was either "endearing" or "disturbing", I honestly cannot recall. I decided that he was one of the few people on the circuit I could tolerate with less than four drinks in me, but still had no idea what the hell he was doing there.

Not long after, I began building the staff for a satellite sports publication. When every avenue was exhausted, including my sixth grade gym teacher and the janitor of our building, I called Jim and asked if he would like to contribute a column. He reluctantly agreed, at first complaining of spasms brought on by being exposed to certain intense levels of testosterone. Yet, when I received his first piece, I knew this guy was the writer I someday hoped to be.

So it came to be in these crude, but poignant literal forays that I discovered Campion had already been a sports journalist and part-time broadcaster. This fucking imp had my dream job and threw it away to write some ridiculous book about New Jersey rock bands. I was stuck with articles about second-rate bands making first-rate dollars, while he was sitting in press boxes of major sporting events. Now I was jealous!

Months later over drinks in a smoky nightclub Jim handed me a pre-

press version of his first book, "Deep Tank Jersey." All those months running around those dank halls of iniquity was apparently no ruse. It was certainly a book. And I was honored to be one of the lucky few to read it first. I finished it in a couple of days and loved every page. The imagery, emotions, fun and harsh realities of living the rock and roll life were captured in an incredible hybrid of "Spinal Tap" meets "On The Road." James Campion, had done what I thought was undoable!

As fast as I could, I tried to think of new and exciting editorial ideas to throw Jim's way, and every damn time I did he came through with flying colors. A few people at the paper once complained to me that they thought his work was a little too highbrow for our beer-guzzling, shot-slamming, "I want to rock" audience. So what if some of this stuff was over the heads of our readership, the ones I'd affectionately dubbed, "Darwin's Waiting Room?" I didn't care. Simply, Campion's articles were fun to read!

But it wasn't until I checked the fax machine one day when I realized Campion's true calling. It was a curious piece of hyperbole that began, "Dearest Dan, King of the Wild Frontier." It wasn't an assignment I'd given him, but a letter sparked from the temporary banning of a Marylin Manson show at Giants Stadium. I perused it, laughed my ass off, and called Jim up. "I can't run this," I said. But he said he'd only written it in the an attempt to "re-educate me on the wretched abuse of democracy." That, and he had an hour to kill. This guy was truly amazing, and according to the man himself, that letter started it all for *Fear No Art.*

James Campion keeps amazing me. He is one of the few demented souls our industry has produced. We've shared drinks, cigars, and a pretty damn good Yankees baseball run. We have woken up at the crack of dawn, hung over on chilly Sundays, only to be trounced by 105 points in a cheap Jersey basketball league. For godsakes we lost a fucking basketball game by 105 points! I brought his extraordinary writing skills from my former post for that regional music paper to my present one as the editor of a national men's magazine. The best of that work appears as part of this incredibly entertaining compendium.

Today, I proudly call that fresh-faced kid friend. But I have warned him more than once if I get one more phone call in the middle of the night begging for plane fare to D.C. in order to find kidnapped journalists I will shoot him.

Dan Davis
11/3/99

Dan Davis
Managing Editor
Aquarian Weekly

Dearest Dan,
King of the Wild Frontier,

What in the name of that long-dead, loudmouthed patriot, John Adams is going on in that goddamn state
of yours? Has the chemical reek from out at the
airport set the brain waves to stun for the summer?
Perhaps that governor of yours finally sold her soul
to the right-wing religious Mafia roaming around the
gin joints of Trenton. Because for one sad, soiled,
rotten moment I thought I'd read in the New York
Times that some New Jersey state commission had decided to ban that putrid excuse for a rock act,
Marylin Manson from performing at the Meadowlands
Complex next month.

Of course, the only time I can gear myself up to
peruse the local papers these days is after four or
five straight belts of vodka. So there might have
been some booze clouds dragging this insane gibberish to my already muddled eight percent, but then
some monotone freak from CNN corroborated the story
during my t.v. dinner; and we both know that no
amount of bottled spirits could rescue any of us from
that kind of reality check.

Exactly when did they start hanging papers in Jersey,
Dan? Did I miss some fascist insurrection or pooling
of the deranged? What kind of feckless claptrap sells
for real news down there anyway? Sounds to me like
the kind of low-rent garbage being peddled in Alabama
after a meeting of the Birch Society reunion club.
You know those guys, don't you, Dan? Bald, fat,
white, angry males, throwing back a few while making

Grade-A decisions on things like art and women before running amok through the local bars screaming about property values and Andy Warhol's effect on 20th century hunting fashions and pro football.

What sort of constitution are you guys using down there these days? Don't read me wrong here. I'm a proud, former citizen of the Garden State. This ain't a Jersey thing. This here's about old-fashioned American rights. You remember them, don't you, Dan? Before Nixon and the Red Scare, before the A bomb and the discussions to take cocaine out of Coca-Cola. And don't get me wrong, this ain't no rock n' roll freedom trip either. I'm talking about good old-fashioned freedom here, my boy. This is about THE revolution. And not the mind-dumb sixties version, but the Big One, Dan; the American Revolution.

Oh, those guys knew how to fight then; rusty muskets and all. You don't think those ornery bastards who were holed up at Concord gave a rat's ass about Marylin Mansion, do you? But you know they took the buck shot just the same. I imagine there's little else more terrifying than dealing with a heavy ball of flaming hot metal in your body, Dan. That's the type of archaic weapon that will tear huge pieces off you. Man, some guys play for keeps, like the Rabbi's at Massada or those last few hardy souls at the Alamo. Nobody likes their freedom screwed with; least of all, the desperate. And that's what's left of this, or any other generation, Dan; desperation.

You know why, my friend? Because all the other generations of the American century have failed to get the point of this freedom thing. What is so difficult about interpreting the First Amendment? It's not exactly the Koran. And I ain't talking about no "shouting fire in a crowded theater" crappola, either. It's the principle of the thing we're playing with these days. It's our job, (the last remaining peeved) to inform those who find it abhorrent to recall the dark ages; when the tube was the source of destruction and everything that spewed from the evil "Negro Music" was the work of Communists and Beelzebub.

You do realize there are still people in this country who believe the very foundation of civilization was shattered by the sight of Elvis shaking his ass on the "Ed Sullivan Show". And this is not some fanatical band of Waco dissidents clogging the Internet with delusions of hostile takeovers and bake-offs. These are voters, Dan. They own rifles and union cards and play bridge on the weekends with Margie and Hank. This isn't just the great unwashed. These types are in our schools, churches, and the Lincoln bedroom, hanging with Oprah and Geraldo, and apparently sitting in judgment over there at the N.J. council of the misguided.

This reminds me of the time a Senator from Wisconsin was scheduled to speak at some ladies function in West Virginia and went off the rails with stories of informant lists and an underbelly of crackpots who sold a cup of java for prices too good to believe. I know you remember Joseph McCarthy, Dan. But what about the rest of them? What of this infamous council waving Bibles at ol' Marylin Manson? Do you think they remember that raving lunatic? There's a special corner of hell for a monster like McCarthy, but what of his ideas, Dan? What of his methods?

Ah, but this is neither the time or place to recount such blatant disregard for the Bill of Rights, Danny Boy. But, you know all too well, that unless we STUDY history we're doomed to SUFFER from it. Listen, I'd sooner jab a flaming spike through my right eye than go to a Marylin Mandson affair, Dan; but you know what? Nobody asked me. And that's a good thing, because if anybody had consulted me on who's allowed to entertain the greater populace Frank Sinatra wouldhave been shining shoes in front of the old Copa before 1970.

One last thing Dan, before you take action on this egregious mockery of civil liberty. I must inform you of the type of human mucus we're dealing with here. Beware of anyone bringing Satan into the fray. When all else fails they'll throw Satan against the wall and see if it sticks. And when they do, you tell them that Satan is an angel of God who never did fall from grace, and that people didn't even start jamming that name down our throats until at least the year 200 ce. So before we start misinterpreting the Bible, let's stick to things which are more legally binding.

This is, after all, music; however drowned in distortion and clown make-up. They didn't like Beethoven all that much in Vienna, Dan; thought he was a sex fiend and a revolutionary lout. They tried to kill Charlie Parker; thought he was dangerous with that saxophone hanging from his face. They drummed John Lennon out of this country back in '66 for comparing the Fab Four to Jesus Christ. And the funny thing is that at least those guys WERE envelope pushers. Those were the days of wine and agitators. But not Marylin Manson, Dan. Let us pray this mess doesn't amalgamate into some living poster for the First Amendment, like O.J. Simpson suddenly becoming Rosa Parks because he couldn't control his tempestuous libido.

But hey, Dan, if the world does come to a screeching halt because of a rock concert I think we could sell the formula to Hollywood, alert the military, crack open a Heineken, and wait for "Bay Watch" to start.

Never Surrender,

jc

CHAOS IN MOTION

Hypocrisy is a basic human trait.

Love is optional.
Need is involuntary.
Want is crucial.
Hate is constant.

P.T. Barnum was right

Eve of destruction.
The papers print the daily instructions.

There is no color in racism.

Comedy need not apologize.

Significance is subjective.

To be human is to sin.

More people should listen to Warren Zevon.

Make the line, then cross it.

Industry put a hole in the sky.

Safety is overrated.

Shakespeare needed the money.

Every book is in the dictionary.

MORALITY IS NOBODY'S BUSINESS.

Black salvation.
The news at eleven has the rotation.

Freedom is freedom.

Pay the teachers.

World War II: 1939 -1945
Viet Nam Conflict: 1959 - Present
Sex sells everything.

GEORGE ORWELL WAS WRONG.

Farmers are starving.

Earn your faith.

Poetry is mental masturbation.

Fast talk/No Solution.

Blind ambition.
It's the university admission.

The earth is trying to tell us something.

There is only real change from within.

Use Words.

8/24/97

THE MANIC, THE CORPULENT, AND THE E COLI SHUFFLE

Naugatuck, Connecticut

At the first sign of any trouble with the "beef people", those in the know attend a meeting of the First Order of Rabid Vegetarians. The FORVgathers weekly in an abandoned firehouse on the bucolic outskirts of quiet Naugatuck, Connecticut. It's only been six weeks since the great "All-Beef Patty Scare of '97" pulsed from the suburbs of balmy New Mexico and already their rowdy celebrations burn until dawn.

A crowd of over 200 strong raised their full mugs of V-8 to the cob-webbed rafters with unbridled jubilation on this night. As expected, it was impossible to find a single person without his or her eyes wide with anticipation for another report of tainted Whoppers shipped from Nebraska and stacked in the refrigerated excess of a Hudson Foods truck rolling across Highway 61.

"This is a true sign of the Apocalypse," bellowed a rather chunky fellow standing on a teetering chair just to my left. "It is written in the Scriptures!" he managed to cough out—all the while continually claiming that his considerable weight was a result of having been a vegetarian for only 48 hours, with the strong stipulation that lobster didn't count. When I left his boorish rant he wasn't sure that poultry should be included either.

The women of the FORV do not play those type of vacillating games with their diets. Less than 24 hours after the local Burger King heard rumor of recalls on beef, and harried managers balked futilely at panic, nearly 30 Naugatuck women were out front swinging their fists and raising signs which read, "Scares The Beef," and "Beef Is Suicide." Despite suffering sizable fines, their clever protest has not gone unnoticed. As of press time the U.S. Department of Agriculture has issued warnings to all plants churning out the government approved 100% beef, which by moral standards registers in at about 12%.

Feeling uncomfortable among this rabble of unfettered passion I felt compelled to remind the less volatile that almost 20,000 Americans are stricken with infections due to the bacterium known as Escherichia coli every year. "E. coli," I preached, "is a malady that can't only be derived from uncooked beef!"

"Flesh off the bone!" cried one skinny young girl in a pony tail. "Would you like some fries with that?!"

8/31/97

HALT THE SCOUNDRELS

"I always believed the media would kill her in the end."
- Earl Charles Spencer

So claimed the brother of the late Princess Diana less than 24 hours after the tragic accident which took her life. On the heels of similar sentiments from such notable celebrities as Tom Cruise and Andre Agassi it is only fitting that all of us in the fourth estate take a hard look at ourselves and begin to weigh the true nature and importance of our business. After all, when a rich guy, superstar hunk actor, and a dude that hits a tennis ball real hard begin pontificating it's time to rearrange the furniture.

So I am here to proclaim that all paparazzi—those stealthy photo-crazed miscreants who follow around these narcissistic louts—be banned from society. And while we're banning, let's just ban the use of cameras all together; the continued abuse of video cameras especially. Seems today all one has to do is plunk down a few bucks and focus the damn things and —whammo— it's "Let's play CNN time!"

Now it's my understanding that the fatal car crash happened in a tunnel. Doesn't anyone realize the inherent danger in driving into one of these things? Particularly at night? So, there is no logical need for using them. All tunnels should be closed. In fact the original concept of the Roman arch is downright evil. If this publication could afford to run a poll I'd bet we'd conjure up enough evidence to support a rise in "tunnel accidents."

Before you rip this out and send it to your local congressman please remember I'm here to save lives.

Finally, what caused the "accident" in the first place? Men on motorcycles, that's who. I believe an anti-bike rally is in order. All humans riding these highly dangerous vehicles should be taken away and given psychological treatment. Who in their right mind wants to ride unprotected, screaming metal death machines, at top speeds, on the same byways as two-ton cars and massive trucks? Why we'd be saving these poor souls from themselves.

As for the media, I move to ban Oprah, the WNBA, and anything with Pauley Shore involved.

Next week we'll discuss the burning of books to reduce the harmful cancer-causing rays of the sun.

9/8/97

BIG BROTHER CONDOM

"Don't need a weatherman to know which way the wind blows."
- Bob Dylan

Received a rather interesting call last week from my Georgetown friend. The man said the Republican-owned House of Representatives quietly passed a bill allowing federal health clinics to distribute condoms and birth control pills to children as young as 13 without parental notification. Then he was silent for a few eerie minutes.

Although he sounded like he was weeping, I could tell after a while he was quite drunk. Figuring I'd take advantage of his weakened state by grilling him for further information I was only able to get numbers. Apparently it was a final approval count of 220 (46 of which were of the GOP variety) to 201, in a rather smooth victory for *the frightened*.

My friend, a staunch conservative with one eye on the television and the other on his semiautomatic rifle, didn't quite understand what I meant by *the frightened*.

"Get with the times," I blurted. "There are far too many humans already!" He remained eerily silent, and when I was almost sure he would start quoting from the Bible, he began stammering on about freedom. "You silly man," I sighed. "Freedom died with Beavis and Butt-Head!"

You see, Georgetown couldn't grasp the notion of an America failing to trust the modern family. He is obviously living in the dark ages when people raised children. We traded that right in for a new pair of shoes and a warning label on Ice T. records. Now it's the government's job.

There's a great hush in Washington D.C. these days about the next steps that are to be taken in order to relieve the responsibility of future parents. The government started measuring this insidious plot while everyone was busy doing the Macarena. It's the kind of backdoor politics that once had Ed Meese salivating. "We've done it this time," I calmly told him. "We cannot control ourselves any longer."

"It is a robot race!" he screamed before hanging up.

Not even I understood what that meant. Sadly, he was nothing more than a burgeoning attorney, not quite used to being reduced to an innocent bystander; and he was quite definitely soused. Besides, it was too close to Jerry Springer time, and there were far more important freedoms to exercise. The way I figure it, even the concept of sex has been lost on us. We are a people mired in the degradation of wit; slow to understand the intricacies of government. The brain-dead have the wheels and the frightened must pay the bill. After all, there is no doom in a fast lane that's been closed. It's only when the traffic is backed up that we complain.

Anyone got a horn?

9/15/97

THE MULTI-BILLION DOLLAR TOBACCO LIE or HOW THE FAT RATS LEFT THE SINKING SHIP

"And he cried out with a mighty voice, saying, 'She has fallen, she has fallen, Babylon the great; and has become a habitation, a stronghold of every un- clean spirit and hateful bird; because all the nations have drunk of the wrath of her immorality, and the kings of the earth have committed fornication with her, and by the power of her wantonness the merchants of the earth have grown rich."

- Revelation 18:2

Nothing quite stirs the juices of the rabid hounds inhabiting the journalism trade as a huge industrial parasite cracking under the weight of public pressure and government investigation. The only comparable high is the final results of such an implosion. The latest tease in the always sexy romp of sinking dollar signs is the Clinton Administration vs. the Tobacco Industry. The P.R. Chief vs. the Cough Trade.

Yee-hah!

It's this type of crazed barn dance which once inspired the writing of "God Bless America" and can fire up any round of the PTA. If one puts an ear to the tracks it's easy to hear the rumble of the gravy train screeching to a nauseating halt, for there is no sweeter sound to the vocation of the printed word than the conductor's faint cry as he hurls himself off. It is a thing of brutal beauty, like the smoky crumble of a skyscraper sucked under by streams of dynamite. The legend of the Ma Bell breakup still triggers fond memories and rowdy celebrations when mentioned in network news circles.

Every tragedy has its King Lear, and every cancer-inducing product has its pusher. Last week the Philip Morris Agency, whose U.S. tobacco division accounts for half the country's retail sales of cigarettes including Marlboro, Merit, Benson & Hedges, Parliament, Virginia Slims, and Basic received word of a prominent defector. One James Morgan decided it might be as good a time as any to retire from the front lines and get off at the next station.

You might remember Mr. Morgan, Philip Morris' top tobacco executive, who had most of us media whores rolling in the aisles last year with his sworn testimony that the product he's peddled like ice pops at the beach for 28 years was "no more addicting than Gummy Bears." Before leaving this tribunal of the absurd Mr. Morgan promised, with somewhat of a straight demeanor, that he wouldn't beg out of the tobacco business even if he were totally convinced the stuff caused cancer. It was a fitting denouement to the lunacy of greed and deceit on parade, and certainly the kind of statement which would make P.T. Barnum and the authors of the Warren Commission Report proud; but, as it turned out, hardly the truth.

Because if it's the truth you crave, then Philip Morris may be the wrong place to search. The world of advertising and big business rolls out the red carpet of mighty horse dung riding on the fumes of large breasts and white teeth tipping their cup of Joe in a pleasant salute to ignorance. It's not their job to measure danger against the bottom line. That's your gig, Mr. and Mrs. Consumer. They present the dagger. You drive it home.

The battle between the president and the cigarette industry over roping kids into the butt binge has put a damper on the "ching-ching" picnic for the boys over at Philip Morris. Threats of $1.50 packs within the fortnight has made enough suits nervous to bring a battalion of lawyers to the table. Morgan wants no part of it. He and his buddies in the song-and-dance troop, all of whom joined in on making a mockery of scientific fact, are leaving the premises like rats from a burning wreck. These are the clear signs of an A-1, full scale, supercharged panic, and anyone who misses the ecstasy in this just ain't living.

Smokers on life support are suing left and right, and every public establishment outside of gin joints are hanging "No Smoking" signs at every turn. Let's face it, the minute Al Gore wrapped up his now infamous pedantic swill-speech at the Democratic Convention, in which he nearly wept over his sister who died of cancer, jokers like Morgan had to know the jig was up. Sure, the vice president made countless pro-tobacco speeches for almost four years after her death, but as evidenced in all political blather, the wind shifts. That type of low-rent hypocrisy never evades a career snake-oil salesman worth his salt. Now Mr. Morgan runs and hides. His swaying Tower of Babel looks awfully shaky. But the writ of vengeance says the jackal must have his day. The harvest has indeed come in. Put that in your pipe and smoke it.

Yee-hah.

9/23/97

DEATH TO THE MESSENGER

I should never watch CNN while sober. This is a dangerous proposition even for the normal and centered among us; but for the really jolted, the truly mangled minds of a wilted generation, it is folly. Yet, I cannot help but slide by in a fruitless surf through the channels. It is the bane of cable television to be faced with so many choices. People such as myself should not be privy to this kind of "entertainment" if not fully prepared to take on the consequences.

It is the case of a program called "Impact" of which I speak specifically. Hosted by veteran news-master, and ubiquitous network point man, Bernard Shaw, it runs intermittently on CNN for those lucky enough to have initially been spared its ugly truth. You may be able to endure tabloid shows, and the human freak-parade afternoon panel shows, but when top news studs like John Camp start rolling out economists, graphs, and high profile sources in order to better illustrate the wealth of human leeches, there is every reason to start praying for an apocalypse.

So here I am, perfectly willing to numb my brain with a sitcom or Larry King, and I'm faced with the sickening specter of a Jimmy Swaggart comeback. It isn't enough that this redneck slug, who has bilked the feeble and the scared out of their hard-earned greenbacks by promising some dime-store salvation, survived the soliciting of a prostitute because of a pathetic public weeping for the forgiveness of the Lord, but here he is again staining my television screen.

Does Camp have to tell me about Swaggart's $4 million mansion and annual six-figure tax-exempt salary complete with graphic pictures of his spanking new Mercedes? Does CNN have to show the highlights of the song-and-dance brimstone hyperbole Swaggart has been selling as religious deity for decades? Does anyone even have to bother to beg for the slightest bit of mercy after this barrage of disgust? Then, when hatred has been lifted to dangerous levels inside the bile of my stomach, Swaggart speaks. Like a man being fit for a suit of martyr in the bowels of Louisiana he prances through a land mine of inquiry; claiming poverty and asking for love. Camp smirks and presses him further. Then Swaggart's wife, made-up like a parade float, clamors for justice against the nasty, prying media. "We've checked your tax records," Camp tells her. "This is what you do all day, poke around people's lives?" Mrs. Swaggart snaps back.

Before the credits roll you only hope there is a special corner of hell saved for these mutants.

Now, I realize it stretches the credibility of complaint to say that televangilists are despicable con men. The equivalent would be decrying starvation and reminding everyone that war is bad. But at the risk of coming off as some 60s' granola head, it is only fitting that we should be warned about television news shows who inform us that there is such a creature as Jimmy Swaggart breathing our air, and that by some genetic malfunction in our brains, we allow his lifetime party to continue. Then we can get back to the sit coms and Larry King.

9/30/97

THE RESURRECTION REVIEW

What is now being billed as The Rolling Stones will be coming through here soon, and I, for one, see nothing wrong with that. Sure the core of the band are all pushing 60 and converge for a studio recording every couple of years as an excuse to hit the road—the same way you and I would crank out a letter to a friend we haven't spoken to in some time in order to break the ice for a visit. But just like all those infernal Grateful Dead jaunts of yore there is something patently nostalgic, yet clear, about the reminder of rock n' roll as originally intended.

There is simply no blueprint for a rock band today without The Rolling Stones. The future must be shown the roots while there is still some branches remaining alive. All the great blues men are shuffling into the history books, (John Lee Hooker, B.B. King), or are long dead, (Leadbelly, Muddy Waters), but the residue of their efforts still beats in the Stones. And not just the new incarnation without Bill Wyman (retired) and Ian Stewart (dead since 1985), but the living memory of its collective rampage.

One can still smell 60s' rebellion or the stench of 70s' excess with the very mention of The Rolling Stones. And who could recall those lovely traits of the absurd if the band became a museum exhibit like The Beatles, pulled from the mist every few decades for moneymaking revivals in culture shock? This has never been the track record of Mick and Keith. They stay too long and make terrible noise doing it. This is not especially exciting now, but what a road has been paved. Only when the Stones appear from the dust of time can we relive it.

When one considers that the The Rolling Stones have been in existence longer than founding member, Brian Jones was alive, a splash of perspective washes over the clock. As long as the Grunge and Hip-hop minions continue to delve into living history, can there be any true connection with its source? The time of pushing the envelope to dangerous levels is long gone, drifted away with the echo of Altamont. But once, not too long ago, there was a hint of anarchy in the riffs, and mischief in the lyrics; unlike the contrived anger and wit passing for passion now.

When I first saw The Stones in 1978, 16 years after it's inaugural club gig, the word was that things were getting silly. I can assure you that for a boy of the same age there was only awe. It was the same reason I dragged my tired ass miles into the thick to see the brilliant Muddy Waters and sit through Bob Dylan's incoherent show a few years later. It is the beating heart from which a genre was built, and somewhere in all the succeeding bombast, it still beats.

Sure The Stones seem like a traveling Vegas revue motivated by the almighty buck in a vain attempt to appear like the real deal. But there was a time when this was the "real deal." For that alone it must live and breathe and return this novice planet back to the primitive age of the back-street boogie and its devil rhythms. Lest we forget where we've come from, we'll be doomed to delete it.

10/7/97

SOCIAL INSECURITY

If you were born sometime after the Korean War you have a better chance of being hit by lightening twice on a clear day than seeing a return on the weekly chunk of money you sacrifice for Social Security. It is a fantasy money pit, and the white rabbit will disappear all too soon. What you are paying for now is the love of your parents and the good people who put Hitler away. When the Baby Boomers are done mopping up you will be lucky if you can scrape a subway token out of the Federal Government.

For those of us mired in the lost generation, and the wonderfully positive souls who make up this Generation X thing, it's every sucker for themselves. All those beautiful people who flocked to Woodstock are entering the second part of their own century; and in the fashion they have stomped through tulips, they will stomp on unimpeded. The Boomers have used up cultural boundaries and left the fumes of regret, and like the gray suit custodians after a parade, we shall clean it up.

The well dries during the eventual ride on the inflation highway, and with every cost-of-living raise there is another bucket-full dumped. We're paying on credit now. Every dollar is sucked into some kind of insatiable vacuum with no conscience about where it might end up. But we can be sure it isn't any trust fund for our wrinkled days. They'll be thawing Walt Disney's head long before that.

Those elders you can't pass on narrow roads? You know, the ones who refuse to use the turn-signal? They laugh at you. Then, as an extra perk, they screw your kids by voting against the school system to save two bucks a month in taxes. By the time your little bundles are trotting off to kindergarten, the school system, as you have come to know it, will deteriorate past the point of fair recognition. Remember when you were a tike and imagined school as some tortuous prison run by ego-inflated power mongers who were kicked out of decent society just to run your fragile id into the dirt? That will one day pass for the good old days.

If FDR could see the mess his cute plan has wrought 75 years later, he might have pissed the Japanese off sooner. The man knew a world war was the only solution for a fractured economy. But this was a country inhabited by a majority of people far too concerned about who Charlie Chaplin might be humping then facing any nasty world war. So, old Frankie had to push some buttons. Besides, it gave him something to talk about during those fireside chats. But now the shiny perk of "The New Deal" is burning up on its own fuel, and you won't get the government to admit it. Call your congressman, ask him what might be in the coffers in 20, 30 years, and listen carefully for the response. If it is followed by a snicker you'll see things clearer.

This is not an economy column, and I'm not about to fill up an entertainment publication with boring statistics, but if the sign of the times tells us anything about personal investment, there will be some angry old folks living in the next century. For it is written that there are only two things Americans are willing to pay for and not receive: education and Social Security. We have seen Bill Clinton's bridge to the next century, and it boasts an awfully large toll.

e-mail mania

Date: 9/17/97 12:52 PM

James,

In a recent conversation with you concerning my one-man show, we discussed how much you enjoyed my making fun of angst-ridden poets. Following your highly entertaining, but obviously drunken, rant about the framing of Lenny Bruce you had the audacity to refer to rap as being the only real poetry left. If this is true, then I'm John Keats. I buy that line of shit like I would buy a 1978 Buick with no engine. Poets my ass. Only to those in their environment. And I suppose they're musicians too? And Charlie Parker was a plumber.

Quacky

Date: 9/18/97 12:32 AM

Sir,

Rap is the only true poetry left. Join us in the 20th century.

jc

Date: 9/19/97 11:23 PM

Mr. Campion,

Having just completed the rousing abuse of your answering machine, I will only compromise enough to agree that rap is a form of poetry. Not the only one.

What made Charlie Parker great was that he could blow jazz and also play "God Bless America" on a kazoo. The problem I have with a great deal of this "music" is that the people can only do that one thing, and musically, it's not very good. However, I can understand the lyric part of it being considered poetic in so far as it is a description of what's going on in the time frame and some of it is written OK. However, it is not what is going on in my life. And their message is, and it rings through loud and clear my friend: "If you ain't into this, you ain't happening." And I am happening, so fuck 'em. And it is not a viewfinder into everyone's existence. Only certain people.

While I'm not sitting around under trees writing poems about flowers to Elizabeth Barrett Browning, I'm also not "gettin' jiggy" in the hood with the bros. I need to write poems about cars breaking down and having no money. That's my viewfinder into the universe.

My friend Toni, who came to see our comedy show last week, is quite an excellent poet. I was supposed to go see her do a reading last night, and as per usual, became financially strapped at the last minute. Toni, who happens to like rap, but does not write poetry that is rap. However, it mirrors everything that has gone on in her life. I will see a man tomorrow night whom I'm friends with who, along with his wife, is a published poet. He's excellent, and so is she. They don't write rap. Does that make them less poets? No. Besides which, both wear well-tailored pants. It pisses me off that that "pants" look is a paean to guys in the joint, who shouldn't be lauded. Not every cop is a good guy. And not every guy in Sing Sing is innocent, either. I guess there's room for everybody.

Quacky

Date: 9/20/97   2:04 PM

Q Man,

Lighten up, homey. Life is short, but apparently not as short as your tolerance. Beyond your ramble on cops and pants, I was able to comprehend most of your points.

This Toni and her husband; are they black? What would be the point in bringing up their poetic influences, and excluding rap, if they're middle class white people? There is little point to poetry culled from scenic Scarsdale, or 17th century England. Rap is the only poetry that counts now. Great poets of their generation spoke to the masses, revealed the plight and passion of the common man. There were people in Shakespeare's day who considered him a hack and a fad. The man was just trying to make a buck writing off drunks and whores.

I'm not comparing rap to great literature of the world, but one man's ceiling is another man's floor. Let's face it, today's pop is tomorrow's classic. It wasn't too long ago when the Beatles were mocked as flash in the pan teenage music. And where the hell exactly does Charlie Parker fit in here?

By the way, there are poems about cars breaking down and having no money; it's called country music.

When do the hip lessons start?

jc

Date: 9/20/97   2:31 PM

James,

I will now take each part of your reply and respond to it.

"Are these poets you know black? All I'm saying is that no poetry today speaks to a mass audience the way rap does."

A couple of them are. Some are Caucasian. Some are Latino. They are not writing rap-like poetry. You are correct. Rap does speak to a mass audience. However, it is not an audience that echoes my life experience. Nor does it echo yours, in my estimation. I had a girlfriend who saw an episode of "Cops" and all of a sudden thought everyone was oppressed and she was "down with the cause." Of course that's h——sh—t. You, I and her, are white middle class kids. We did not grow up in the environment that is being portrayed.   So, I don't relate it as the only poetry. However, I will admit that rap speaks to that audience, and it is poetry for them. One of my biggest problems with this "poetry" is what I consider to be the constant degradation of women and police officers. I am friends with many police officers. I know many others through these friends. Some are great guys, and some are total assholes. However, they're not all terrible people who beat you and kill you. I also realize that not every guy wears his pants halfway to the floor and dons a huge hat is a bad guy. And not everyone who sings a rap song and claims oppression at the hands of a so-called "police state" is innocent. Some of these people are criminals, plain and simple. And we laud them. FUCK THAT. And they tell me if I don't "hear them" I'm an asshole. Yeah, they're speaking about their environment to their masses. But, while they're not totally at fault, they play a part in creating that environment. There needs to be better understanding on all sides. In plain Shakespearean English.

"Remember there were people in Shakespeare's day who considered him a hack and a fad. The man was trying to make a buck writing for the masses."

That's true. He was writing the language of the common man. And people did consider him a hack and a fad. However, there is something 1000 times more eloquent about the writing style. Maybe I'm just saying that because it sounds eloquent in this time since its a different vernacular. Also, it's so much more varied in subject matter. Two centuries from now, I don't think people are going to be saying "Hey man, remember that rap (and I use the term loosely) "song," by Humpty Dumpty Snoopy Doopy — "Fuck the Cops!" That always reminds me of the "Merchant of Venice."

"I'm not comparing rap to great literature of the world, but one man's ceiling is another's floor and today's pop is tomorrow's classic. there was also a time when people mocked the Beatles as flash in the pan teenage music."

The Beatles, James? Please. Why don't you go buy a box of straws, attach them on the ceiling way above your head, and start grabbing at them. The Beatles wrote "Yesterday" and "Michelle". When John Lennon wanted a better blow job he sang "Come on, Come on, Please Please Me." And people said "wow that's great, cute, etc..." without realizing what he meant. Genius. These guys just sing "Hey baby, give me a fuckin' blowjob." There's no subtlety, unless of course you consider it subtle when someone drops an anvil on your head. Then: "Michelle, my bell, these are words that go together well, my Michelle. (sung by Paul McCartney, plaintively over a beautiful melody) Today: "Yo, Michelle, baby, come on over here and suck my dick, yo." ("sung" loudly and flat by a guy with fourteen ridiculous, insular nicknames over a "melody" that sounds like bowling balls being rolled in the Holland Tunnel at rush hour) My father, who never cared for the Beatles, said to me on his deathbed, "You know Al, now that I've heard rap, I'm getting an appreciation for the Beatles."

"Where does Charlie Parker fit in here?"

Wise ass. I realize I wasn't very clear. Today, if you're conservative and don't care for this stuff, everyone calls you a racist. I have many African-American heroes, Charlie, Dizzy and Monk being three of them. And Bird and Monk were total fuckin' drug addicts (Monk was pschizo) but were brilliant. I wanted to make the point that this isn't a black/white thing with me and that there are African-American musicians that are so brilliant and wonderful, yet these other guys get all this credit. And I just don't think they are as talented. And, I don't think its music.

Hip lessons, you can't afford.

Quacky

Date: 9/22/97 3:31 AM

Q.,

Speak for yourself, white boy. I grew up in the boogie down — Bronx. We were taught to look out for separatists like you. And I defy you to ever use "Merchant of Venice" and the Beatles again in another analogy. Remember the credo, FEAR NO ART. The truth will set you free.

jc

10/14/97

TAO JONES

Wall Street

The week that was. Standing in the pits with the big boys during the ping pong Bull Market down the corridors of Black Monday II where the weak and feeble take a dive and the *certain* become fodder for the ages. When it's strife-time baby nobody knows it like the dollar; greener than the pastures after 554 points drop off the board. The brave stood in silent awe for minutes as the numbers plummeted in a sick dive toward Satan's lair. "God help us all!" one cried. "The demons have stolen our soul!"

Before 3:00 p.m. the grinding sound reached the floor as a nattily dressed man started to yank what hair was left on his temples and began screaming like a school girl. It was time to own up to all the smiling. Things were rosy here only 24 hours ago. "For weeks we've been sweating the inevitable," said a man named Elsworth. "We will die in here before this thing goes above 400!" And those would be the lucky ones.

Can you hear the horrid screech of recession, chum? It is the bane of the middle class two step. There will be fire sales at Macy's before the world is right again. When crushed between sweating miscreants howling to sell like banshees on a fiesta there is a sense of the real. It is not unlike being injected with elephant adrenaline glands while guzzling a gooey mixture of Surge and Jolt. You will see God while kneeling in a pile of discarded slips; far too late to save the planet.

Then comes twisted Tuesday, when the cheap roll over like Auntie May's poodle. The suckers hit the wall and the losers take the walk. No one is free of madness in the pits. Here the planet trades life like the back alley deals in Memphis which awake the souls of the greedy. The slanted road to Lower Manhattan raises eyebrows in Japan where the bargain is king and there is no man alive who wouldn't purchase the rock bottom even if it meant trading his first born. 'Cause Mamma the pulse is back!

The United States government knows when to keep its collective mouth shut. Even above this wretched din one can still hear Herbert Hoover choking. Long before the ugly crash, and the night the dead walked in a field of no names, we cranked out the gold and pressed the money to the pedal. Remember, here in the pit there is always a tomorrow. And like the song says, there will be sun. But daddy needs a brand new pair of shoes, and the further the rubber band bends the more likely it will return to its original form. It is on this dangerous curve that the high rollers survive on gasoline and the mere dabblers burn on their fumes. This is the landscape we choose to stroll. On a clear day standing on the stacks of mammon you can see the streets of tin. They are paved with the American Dream.

10/29/97

THE ART OF RELIGION

The word out of Tinseltown lately is that we are to expect several new films on the subject of religion. The latest surge on Tibet and Buddhism aside, those practicing the Judeo-Christian standby can be assured that their take will be less than honorary, or, at the least, hardly stagnant. This already has the puritanical fear-mongers raising their collective ire for the usual protests and shakedowns.

Among the films in the midst of production, or settling in the proverbial can, is Warner Bros. "The Butcher Boy." This tale of Irish angst and misguided faith stars the dreaded bane of Catholicism, Sinead O'Connor, who will play the Virgin Mary. Not only do the concerned want to put the kibosh on this thing because O'Connor was last seen ripping up a picture of Pope John Paul on an ancient episode of Saturday Night Live, but apparently the Holy Mother spends her film time convincing an adolescent boy to kill.

Now admittedly, this is stretching the bounds of fictitious credibility, but it is a movie, and it is, in fact, fiction. Traditionally, Hollywood's interpretation of Biblical characters have towed the line and gone the way of one-dimensional creatures completely devoid of sympathy or compassion save for their own inflated egos. For the most part, unless you were willing to throw together four-hour epics with no teeth, present Charlton Heston in all his bombastic glory, or stick some bland, handsome blue-eyed guy with long hair in the Jesus role, you were getting crap from someone somewhere.

During the last decade such films as "Last Temptation of Christ" and "Priest" have been met with lashes without any of the back. Far more times than not churches and their rabid minions don't even bother to see the work, but nevertheless spend all their time working to stop the artists from finishing the films, or preventing them from being distributed. These charlatans of the First Amendment predictably use the argument that certain subjects and articles of faith must be left untouched with no room for interpretation or rediscovery. And folks, this speaks volumes on what is wrong with religion in the latter half of millennium number two.

The concept of spirituality has been so wounded by the fumes of the Enlightenment and the mushroom cloud of modern science that people have packed their faith away like pictures from their third birthday party. More than 90% of Americans believe there is a God, almost 85% attend a weekly service, and a frightening portion watch "Touched By An Angel;" but how many live the philosophy to they subscribe? Those who laud the beauty of faith would rather leave the icons of lore in glass cases with Elvis' 70s' garb and bow with thoughtless reverence. So it's not terribly surprising when these fanatics leap from the bushes to howl at the moon when these icons are dusted off and given a new coat of metaphoric paint. However, just because there is over 1,500 years of bully dogma behind you, doesn't mean you own the store.

Since when should the boundless gift of spiritual creativity be policed by the atavistic few who choose to keep the wonder of the universe under some museum lock and key for no one to revisit but those who run the company line? If a country was run with this much mindless tyranny we'd be bombing it in no time. Yet, because religion has become more about frozen images in time and less about vibrant spiritual and creative progress, we shudder like ignorant children at the sight of a breathing thought. Which, if you gave it any thought, would be something to protest.

11/4/97

PARTISAN SUICIDE

This just in: Christie Todd Whitman is politically dead. It is not the result of her narrow victory over Jim McGreevey—keeping her in the New Jersey governor's seat—but the present standing within her own party. It is now, and forever shall be, impossible for a member of the two-party system to dare stray from the stagnant Republican or Democratic policies, or they will be dust. Whitman is not the first victim, and won't be the last.

Whitman will be starting her second term come January. This came very close to not happening. You know why? Christie Todd Whitman is a Republican who happens to also be Pro-Choice. This is the political landscape the two-party system has wrought. It is the dance of the damned. Everyone step left. Everyone hop right. Never the twain shall mix. Four short years ago Whitman was the darling of the Grand Old Party, mentioned in the same breath with Jack Kemp and Colin Powell to save the failing '96 presidential ticket. Tough talking campaign monster and P.R. queen, she could do no wrong, and was projected as a serious contender for the presidency herself. Now she is a pariah. No one in the party will touch her. This almost killed her chances to be re-elected, and clearly means that Whitman will never again be elected to another office as a Republican.

Rudy Giuliani is the best mayor New York City has had in over 30 years. He has cleaned up the streets, revitalized tourist traffic, and, most importantly, significantly cut down on crime. He has breezed to re-election. Uncle Rudy has shown little desire to move into the national arena. He is too ethnic, too much a classic New Yorker, to make the grade in the heartland or the Bible Belt. He is the Italian Ed Koch. But not even the big gun in the country's most influential city was allowed to speak at the Republican Convention in '96. You know why? Because Uncle Rudy backed a Democrat for governor. Giuliani put his constituency and the interest of New York City before the Republican party. He did not like a country bumpkin like George Pataki swooping in and complaining about how much of a money pit the Big Apple has become. Uncle Rudy liked the city boy, Mario Cuomo. Cuomo was defeated. Now Giuliani is ostracized from the tree house. Uncle Rudy would be lucky to get his parking validated on Capitol Hill.

If you choose pro-choice in the Elephant party you will lose your massive right wing, conservative, religious fanatic voter base. If you are anti-affirmative action or a fourth amendment shrill and you hail to the donkey you will alienate the leftist, activist, gay, minority vote. Look to the White House for evidence. Bill Clinton can smoke all the pot and screw all the secretaries he likes as long as he keeps paying the piper by kowtowing to the vacillating popularity polls. The president has survived because he stands for everything and nothing. He is a political weather vane pointing in the direction of the pressure wind.

It is the way of the two-party system now, this tainted Constitution: "We the special interest groups in order to form this imperfect disassociation salute you." Listen to the blustering pundits, talking heads, and scribes tell you that property tax and car insurance hikes are the reasons Christie Todd Whitman had Jim McGreevey on her ass for the duration of election day. Then think about the percentage of her votes which slid on down to the "Right To Life" candidate. Christie Todd Whitman is a lame duck governor. She is doomed in this narrow tank of piranha swimming in their own filth. Not because the people say so, the system says so. She is politically deceased. She should be glad.

11/11/97

GEORGE BUSH LEFTOVERS

For all the pictures painted of the President of the United States as some bleeding heart hippie draft dodger who never fingered a rifle in his Commie Pinko life, it is ironic how he is left to pick up the bitter pieces of the failed "Desert Storm" from a man who held the office before him. Bill Clinton has inherited the residue of the big, bad Armed Forces, CIA alumnus, George Bush, and, with apologies to those who did some inhaling; what a long strange trip this has been.

Saddam Hussein is still kicking, and once again, thumbing his nose at the West. This is George Bush's fault. Back in his wine-and-roses days, when he was riding approval numbers that would have King Solomon blushing, Bush sold the American public a pile of horse manure so thick it was impossible to ignore.

It was a good old-fashioned slice of violent patriotism in the great tradition of John Wayne, available hourly on CNN. It had a cool name, "Desert Storm," chilling everyone with the kind of pride which raps yellow ribbons around everything. It was skud missiles and stealth bombers deployed on strategic "humane" targets, and before long had frightened Iraqis surrendering to Dan Rather. But, in the end, it was innocuous and stupid; and it was less about wiping out a madman with nuclear capabilities then it was about the price of gas.

The fact that Hussein still threatens the world with this tired backwater act of his is living proof.

When the oil was safe and American business interests were back and running Bush pulled the plug on his Gulf War. Despite the better judgment of his military advisors, the commander in chief left Hussein in charge to massacre innocents and rebuild his stockpile of death toys. By then Bush was well-ensconced in his ill-fated excuse for a re-election campaign, and who could blame him for half-assing a second term run. He'd carried out the fable to its apex and did it with less casualties than Kent State. Ironically, by the end of 1992 a drowning George Bush attacked his laughable opponent as a man who could not protect us in times of world crisis. This desperate swipe served as nothing more than an empty serenade into oblivion for the man whose political meal ticket, Ronald Reagan, had once called "a wimp."

Bill Clinton wiped the floor with George Bush in every facet of show biz politics earning him a place on the hot seat across from a third-rate crazy man. Seven years later Bush is a trivia-question president, and his once "laughable opponent" is left to try and clean up his mess. This may be a scary prospect for those of us in the know, but one thing is for sure: not even a blowhard shill for the tough wing like Rush Limbaugh can put a happy spin on that.

11/18/97

NY TOLL MADNESS

A '79 Mercury Cougar, a six pack of Bud cans, warm raspberry Margaritas, three $12 cigars, and an EZ-Pass; for two long hours it was all we had, my burly friend, Willie and myself. We were stuck in a major traffic jam on the approach to the Whitestone Bridge against a backdrop of snow flurries and an angry Mexican on our tail laying on his horn as if a battle ship were about to ram him. It was an education in patience and the art of the swerve. We did not surrender our wits, but sold the better part of our senses to the highest bidder, and it was not the Transit Police.

"Goddammit!" Willie yelled over the pumping radio noise. "What is the fucking point of this EZ-Pass if we have to sit here like trapped rats?!" He had conveniently forgotten he was the one who insisted on driving earlier that day. "You have no cassette deck," was his reasoning. I did not argue.

"We might as well start on the beer," I suggested, following closely the agitated tone in Willie's voice and carefully placing it within the parameters of my own growing rancor.

Yes, of course, drink beer in a traffic jam. This seemed like the right thing to do at the time. It was just a bridge, and, after all, we were crawling. There was little we could do in the way of real damage. Desperate times call for desperate measures. The only problem, I was to learn, was that Willie did not handle pressure like the rest of us weary New York travelers.

That's when we decided to hit the tepid Margaritas.

The Mexican was still leaning down on his horn. Willie rolled down his window. I can still hear its droning squeak. "How about I get out of this car and cram that fucking horn up your ass?!" Willie screamed. The Mexican could not hear him over the horn and the distortion blaring from the overworked speakers in our dashboard. Unfortunately, two sharply dressed black guys in the left lane heard him. They jerked back, immediately thinking the expletive-driven tirade was directed toward them. Down came their window.

By now a yellow-haired woman with thick glasses, driving a blood red Toyota of some kind, began waving her EZ-Pass at us, and started to edge her way in front of the Cougar. Willie did not see her. He had other concerns. "What did you say, fat boy?" the black guy in the passenger seat yelled as steam rose from his gritting teeth. "I'm not talking to you, asshole!" Willie yelled back, flailing his arms and causing his beer to spill about the front seat. I quietly sipped my Margarita, chased it with a cold shot of Bud, and sparked a cigar for us both. It was becoming painfully apparent we were not moving toward any bridge.

"Willie?" I called.

"What?" he blurted, refusing to take his eyes from the two angered black guys.

"What do you think that woman's doing up there?"

Eyeing the woman in the Toyota slipping ahead just inches from our bumper, Willie was incensed. Just as I asked the question, his head turned to watch the wave of her EZ-Pass in thanks for letting her in. It was then that events became hazy.

It took the Mexican 45 minutes to stop blowing his horn, but far less for one of the black guys to exit his car and start pounding on our roof. By now Willie's bravado had peaked and appeared to take on the mellowing effect of mainlined Prozac. The two of them must have discussed the "asshole" thing and decided it needed physical restitution. But by the looks of the man's face it would not be without the sacrifice of pain on someone's part. My cigar was almost done, and through a slight afternoon buzz, I could not think of one solid reason for saving Willie from his own stupid anger. And, most importantly, I could not help but think why in hell we needed an EZ-Pass in the first place?

Willie offered the riled black guy a beer if he'd smack the Mexican, who was back to leaning on his horn.

He accepted.

Willie smiled.

It was time for another Margarita and one last drag on my $12 cigar. I didn't know anything about an EZ-Pass, but there was nothing hard about this.

11/25/97

MERRY MERRY

'Tis the season to shop like the guilty, paranoid robots we have become; wandering aimlessly through malls in a march of pathetic fusion. It is a holiday ritual, after all; burnt into our brains like the branded cattle being lead to some slaughterhouse on 5th Avenue. There is no escaping. Your parents did it, and so did theirs, and theirs before that. You will wear out your credit, push through the hordes, and wrack your constitution until it screams for mercy. Somewhere along this heinous odyssey you will search for the perfect tree for trimming with lights, gnarled and uneven, and bulbs that cannot decide if they are blinking or dormant. You will seek out your neighbor's advice on turning your home into a fairyland of ostentatious delight. Perhaps, if you are unlucky enough to have a lawn, you will litter it with enough decorations to motivate the confused to drag their children to your door demanding to see Santa.

If you are brave you will have parties and invite family. Those you truly love and cherish, and others you would not feel comfortable speaking to through glass on a phone with a state trooper standing behind them. You will open your home to the leeches of cheer, and they will eat your carrot cake and guzzle all the eggnog; boring you to tears with stories of holiday bonuses and their child's first tooth. You will wish for the type of mercy killings allowed in countries where holidays mean a cease fire.

Perhaps you will attend the religious service of your choice, looking around to wonder if these poor saps go all the time or just on the holidays like you. A man will stand in front of the congregation and regale you with images of love and God and the spirit of caring for humankind. You may chuckle at this world of wonderful fantasy and decide if there is truly a purpose to this suffering, simply because the calendar deems it so.

Then when you begin to relate to the alarming rise in suicides during this time of year, you recall a far-off time and close your eyes with the thought that you may wake up and get that electric football game you always wanted. And on the way to Grandma's house you look up and see a star so magnificent that it glows through the deep black sky like the sudden warmth in your chest. You might recall your dad squeezing his hand over yours, and how you felt safe and alive, so full of a joy unexplained in text books, shopping carts and television ads and jingling all the way. Then you will smile and be happy that something is left for you to believe in while the planet spins again.

12/2/97

THIS IS THE YEAR

"O generation of vipers, who hath warned you to flee from the wrath to come?"
- Matthew 3:7

"I'll sleep when I'm dead."
- Warren Zevon

It is at year's end that we become melancholy and retrospective; sleepy with memory and a hint of regret. It is at year's end when what we are not comes to the fore, and we wish for better and promise to enact it. It is especially at year's end when we are expected to denote the curious and promote the stagnant, and remember all the good a life could be when allowed to continue unabated with a comforting consistency.

However, this should be the year we fight all that. This should be the year of the exploding light burning the tradition of fear. This should be the year for personal madness, clarity, and an absurd trip to the bitter end; to live like John the Baptist on the kind of caffeine binge that would scare Friedrich Nietzsche down to his war-torn Calvin's. A tattered voice echoing through the wilderness; rabid and crazed in the most severe of definitions. This should be the year of the wild Phoenix rising from the ashes of faceless banality, breaking the scroll of Jung's Synchronicity by dancing on the hearts of the placid.

After all, aren't we finally weary of the status control which has taken the minutes and squeezed them like tired vessels screaming for relief? Things could be worse. Things could be better. Things will change with the wind, and the rain, and that sickening twisted feeling we get whenever we are pounded with relentless TV ads for long distance companies and collect call numbers. When did the idea of phone calls get away from us? When did we decide to buy a car, get married, have 2.3 children, escape the nest? What will we do when the devil music comes down and we're left without our boogie shoes?

We are the degenerate numb fumbling toward a goal line painted by those who laughed at the Dali image dripping from the trees. Remember their voices. Forget their crap. Run until the breath leaves for good. Thank yourself.

FREAK DOMAIN REVISITED: THE SAD AND TERRIBLE TRUTH ABOUT DOGVOICES

It has been three years since my world was sent sideways on a wing, a prayer, and something resembling sleep after four months on the road with a band called DogVoices. It was a strange summer to be out on the edge. Before it was over Jerry Garcia and Mickey Mantle would be dead, the President of the United States would be getting head from his 21 year-old intern, and the simple idea of climbing inside the collective psyche of hardworking musicians coursing their way through the main artery of the famed New Jersey club circuit had mutated into something akin to a wild catharsis. It was supposed to be a book, not some emotional spin cycle of Dante's imagination wrapped in a haze of alcohol and degradation. But one cannot deny the seduction of the endless night when defined by those who call it home. I spent nearly five months with those lunatic bastards, and although there is not a day that passes in which I fail to curse the very existence of DogVoices, I truly love them.

When the call came for an interview with DogVoices my first instinct was to hang up. No, that's incorrect, that was my second instinct. The first was to claim sudden mental paralysis—that's right—a rare disease which strikes those unwilling to review the horrible moments in your life which you laughably tell people you're glad to have endured. It's not like I haven't spoken to them since the publication of my first book, "Deep Tank Jersey." They are true friends, warriors all; it's just that somewhere out there they still prowl and feed on that double-edged candle which burns from both ends. To them the idea of excess and depravity is definable, where the meek get trampled in a ritual better left off the pages of this, or any other publication.

I agreed to talk to DogVoices simply because the story will not end. Since I escaped from its gnawing grip the band has gotten even bigger, and ever more unbridled. (a Budweiser sponsorship, the release of a compact disc, consistently packed clubs, and this cursed book I wrote which hounds us all) I use "unbridled" to let them off the hook. The naked truth is that the whole goddamn thing is out of bounds; wretched and maniacal, and a savage threat to all clear-thinking sorts who just want to spend their remaining days on this planet devoid of noise, senseless merriment, and sleep depravation.

Dogvoices is not merely a rock n' roll band. It is a New Jersey institution like swampland and traffic circles. There is not a soul in that godforsaken state who claims to know a thing about personal abuse and dementia without spending a night in their company. Rob Monte, Peter G. Stevens, Richie Moscola, Chris Sacchiero, and Rich Mattalion were once musicians. Now they are caretakers in this incredible phenomenon which survives on the fumes of its own momentum. It bends my mind to imagine what type of twisted constitution would continue to thrive in that mind-bending vortex between infinite adolescence and career drudgery, and still manage to stay out of hospitals and prison for any length of time.

****

The first rule of DogVoices is that rumors have the shelf life of canned yam. About six months ago I got a call from a mutual friend at about 2:00 am on a Thursday morning swearing on his grandmother's soul that Rob Monte was dead. "He's not dead," I managed to slur in a groggy stupor. "I have seen him die first hand." The man was apparently shocked at my cold admonishment. "Then he let out one of his infamous cackles," I continued. "Took a swig of beer, and ordered me to take that fucking stunned gape off my pallid face and grab my coat 'cause we're going to party."
Do you have any idea how many lives you've ruined?

Monte - (laughs) I don't have the scope of it, but people have told me. Most come straight from AA meetings and DWI court appearances. (laughs) And those are just the people who can actually make it back.

How much of the "Monte is insane" stuff is reality?

Look, I'm not as saintly as I say and it certainly isn't as bad as the stories make it out to be. There's some truth to it, but it's easy to say I'm a fucking maniac because that's all most people see. I take it in stride. I mean, the guys in the band get pissed, and then after their done yelling they'll pull me aside and say, "Hey man, it's because we're fucking worried. We really don't want you to die." I've promised to leave my autopsy report to them. They have a right to know what happens to me in the end. But, no bullshit; I'm in good shape. I'm up every morning, I exercise. Hey, I made the finals of a racquet ball tournament on two hours sleep.

Quick, what is the sickest thing you have presided over during a gig in the last three months?

I threw a man with no legs into the audience from a wheel chair. (laughs) The guy was born deformed, nothing below the torso. He wanted to come up and do a rap, and so I invited him up and asked him if he wanted to stage dive. I didn't force him or anything. The guy wanted to do it. Even I would draw the line at just doing it. So I picked him up and threw him into the crowd. The facial expressions of people ranged anywhere from horror to wide-eyed smiling, like it was the best and most courageous thing I've ever done.

What motivates a man who decides what he's going to do thirty seconds before he acts?

Adrenaline. Listen, when I leave the house I promise my wife a thousand things. But that's Rob promising, not Monte from DogVoices. On stage the moment takes over completely. By that point I'm not saying, "I promised my wife", it's more like, "How am I going to explain this to my wife?" (laughs) I guess its a survival instinct. Growing up in Paterson you have to keep your eyes open, expect anything. On any given night anything can be going on, especially at our shows. If I had a video camera on stage I probably would have won a thousand dollars by now.

What are you most proud of?

I finally have respect around the club scene. People no longer look at me as some Milli Vanilli character. I'm not a musician. I'm an entertainer, but there's some substance to it. I'm not just running along the bar and having a shot with some huge biker. People from other bands give me some credit. There's a method behind this madness.

****

The madness is best described by Richard Mattalion, who lives the life quite opposite to that of the obligatory crazed drummer. He does not drink or start min-riots. Once he stood staid, even incredulous in the eye of the DogVoices storm, musing that his band was simply a "Mac truck, down hill, no brakes."

About what point during the night do you want to stab someone with a drumstick?
Rich - Never. Well, once this summer. A particularly drunk fellow had direct access to me while I was playing. This guy would not leave me alone. Pushing me, making a nuisance of himself to the point that I had to ask security to escort him out. First time I ever did that.
You are the quiet observer of this outfit. Give me an overview of where you guys are now as a band?
The truth; I can't tell you. (laughs) We're at the point where an honest performance is paramount. If there is someone playing, any one of us, without honesty, it is a greater detriment to us today than ever before. People are more attune to personality than performance. I'm probably the most objective because I'm not under the influence of any substance and I don't talk at all, so I tend to just listen on and off stage. The feedback I used to get centered solely around the band 's performance, but now it's more about our interaction with the audience. Expression, body language, and verbal interaction is noticed more than ever.

****

When you're a rabid baseball fan, enjoy time with a good book, and prefer intellectual pursuits which involve solitude, it's hard to imagine a place in DogVoices. However, Peter G. Stevens is a consummate musician and veteran of the club scene who found himself in this circus before he was old enough to vote. He understands all of this, or claims to, and the humor of it never fails to escape him.

How good were the '98 Yankees?
Pete - Somewhere between the Beatles' Sgt. Pepper Album and the purchase of Manhattan for $26.
What is the appeal of DogVoices?
When you come see us you're allowed to act the way you're not normally allowed to.

Do you ever think that you should be doing something more productive with your life?
Yes.
Is there something while on stage you wish you never saw?
How about a really drunk girl on stage dancing for her birthday party wearing a skirt with no underwear, and in the middle of the song she unleashes the full potential of her bladder. Pissing full blast on stage. This woman was so drunk she had no idea. The best part was her friends took her home, changed her, and brought her back to the club. Apparently that wasn't enough of an embarrassment to keep her home.

****

Just last week I was confronted with the unenviable position to impart bad news to someone I care dearly for. It is one of those times when you wish you were the kind of person capable of putting a ridiculously happy spin on any situation. Someone who might be so cute, talented, and warm in that annoyingly innate, almost inhuman, way that the person may even smile when you tell them. I thought to call Richie Moscola for help.

Are you tired of all of this yet?
Richie - No. I still can't wait to go to the gigs. It sounds crazy, but when I was stuck in the Dominican Republic because of the hurricane, I could not wait to go to work. In the summer when we're playing all the time you lose that anticipation. But when there's a few days in between, and I'm not completely exhausted, I can't wait to play.
Do you ever take a moment and consider what you guys have accomplished?
I look at that both ways; what we've accomplished as a band, and what we haven't. I can't help thinking we could've been more successful, done more with our originals, pushed harder. When I look at us, it's "Hey, we're one of the biggest bands going," but I guess it bothers me that I'm not further along personally. I realize our impact though. Bad nights stick with me. If we're snapping at each other, or having one of those tough gigs, I'll remind everyone that people come to see us to forget their problems, not see ours.
What is the best part of this job?
I get to play my guitar for a living, which is my favorite thing to do in the world. Play guitar and perform. I wouldn't like the studio setting as much. To perform most of all.
The worst?

The constant partying gets to me. Not just me, but everyone around us, always partying. But how can you complain about doing what you love for a living? It's the nature of what we do. Constantly having to be on, no matter what the problem; sickness, exhaustion, just a bad day. You have to always find that smile.

Editor's Note:
DogVoices' bassist, Chris Sacchiero, is currently not speaking to James Campion. The author claims that Sacchiero tried to kill him in a nasty mattress-related "accident" during the writing of "Deep Tank Jersey" and Chris is pissed at being depicted as a self-obsessed perfectionist who thinks Nixon killed JFK. The last thing Campion remembers about their fractured relationship is an unprintable rambling dialogue centered around their collective hallucination of walking cheese blocks on television.

12/9/97

LOVE & HATE

"Hatreds do not ever cease in this world."
- Dhammapada I.5

So said the Buddha some 2,500 years ago somewhere in India where HATE was as strong a human emotion as it continues to be. The Buddha also spoke of LOVE. This emotion was not as prevalent. This is also the case in 1998 as we approach the end of the decade, century, millennium and tumble further from the truth of HATE. It is because HATE is easy, disguised in millions of faces and excuses. LOVE is far more difficult; attached to conditions and crying out for restitution. In the great battle of humanity HATE beats LOVE hands down.

Hitler called it pride. Ghandi called it oppression. Manson called it fear. Freud called it sex. Dylan called it order. Jesus called it devil. HATE has been structured, manufactured, bought and sold in a host of ways. It has seduced bigotry, war, murder, rape, and poverty. It has been run by politics, religion, and billion-dollar advertising campaigns. All the while it is disguised as LOVE: LOVE of country, LOVE of God, LOVE of family. It is the march of the damned.

HATE is an indomitable emotion because it can be recycled as revenge and equality. Centuries of repression have rendered African Americans, Native Americans, Homosexuals, and women reactionaries to HATE. To survive they must return HATE. This is the cycle of humanity. This is the bullshit we have been sold by HATE. It is silence and din all at once, running in the shadows of our best smiles and jokes. It is tossed aside as radical thought, or the babbling rhetoric of the silly street barker trying to struggle his/her way from under its weight.

HATE doesn't need a return emotion. This concept is left for LOVE. To HATE we only need difference: a different border, a different God, a different color skin, a different preference in lifestyle, different body parts. To LOVE we need beauty, warmth, a desire; a need to know that it will be returned with interest like a bond. LOVE has been shrunk into film, sex, jingles, or some petty greeting card sentiment mixed in a stew of pap.

LOVE is considered a given between parents and their children, husband and wife, or people shoved into the same nationality, race, and gender; by circumstance or generations of stupidity. LOVE is the sheltered emotion; beaten and tattered by ignorance and fear. To LOVE or speak so is to be buried beneath the pile of those who use its mask to separate us from the truth of existence. This truth is simple: Only LOVE can conquer HATE, not some attempt to fight fire with fire or stand in a corner and wait for a promised heaven if we're good boys and girls and eat our vegetables. Of course this is the type of thought which has put quite a few of the good people out of the life cycle. We know who they are and they are gone. We celebrate them. But we forget them. We are here. We should give it some thought now.

HATE is kicking LOVE's ass. Check the record.

12/16/97

ABOVE THE RIM - BEYOND THE LAW

In the wake of the Latrell Sprewell incident last month in which the feisty, and often maniacal, former guard of the Golden State Warriors attempted to choke his head coach during a practice session, there has been a growing discussion on how much professional sports mirrors today's societal problems. Television and radio talk shows, newspaper columnists, and the usual "chicken little" contingent have been flapping rhetoric about misbehavior and outright criminal acts by star athletes who care little for their game, fans, and otherwise lucrative existence.

Sure, most of the Dallas Cowboys have a rap sheet, and fun-loving jokesters like Albert Belle of the Chicago White Sox—infamous for assault and pouting—have left much to be desired in the land of self control. Of course, NBA blowhard, Charles Barkley has shoved a few guys through glass windows, and pro football players are seen regularly trying to maim one another on and off the field, (not to mention the occasional spitting in each other's faces.) And it really isn't fair to start going over the atrocity that is the hockey brawl or the whole boxing mess. But the idea that these people, and their sporting life, mirrors society is laughable.

Mindless thugs like Sprewell and his clan of macho freaks are hardly the norm. Only the smallest segment of any society has the type of cash these dolts find in their bank accounts every morning. Their celebrity, which buys them so much more than the money, is afforded to the very few. These two elements alone separate them from the rest of us who would not get through the all-to-prevalent speeding tickets, bar fights, drug and gun possession charges, and the rampant abuse of women practiced by these brutes without immediate and severe retribution.

The American star athlete lives in his own high and mighty society. It is a landscape of excuses and leniency, where young boys who are able to throw a ball 98 miles an hour, score a touchdown, or dunk a basketball, can run wild through infinite puberty. They are protected by coaches and parents who want to win and cash in on these talents so badly they are willing to turn their backs and slide them on through to an adult life of fantasy. This fantasy life includes the kind of sidestep of law which civilians can only imagine. Most of society could not gain the services of the bloodsucking media whores who pose as attorneys, and are far more interested in fat checks and getting on the tube, than anything approaching justice.

And for all those who might decry this Superstar Teflon theory one might be wise to remember there was a time when none of this stuff was even reported. We can thank society for at least taking the untouchable mayhem of a Babe Ruth and making some kind of example out of a Latrell Sprewell.

12/23/97

THE GREAT REAGAN HEAD SCHEME

Editor's Note:
     The following conversation took place just before the new year via a cellular phone in the flamingo lounge of a Ramada Inn just outside New Rochelle, New York. The man on the other end is an old college buddy of the author who is currently living in downtown Washington D.C.; and from the evidence presented here, has apparently lost grip of his better senses. His name will be Buddy for the protection of his rights and reputation among the attorney elite. What is most frightening about this ten minute ride through his damaged psyche, is that he's apparently not alone.

Buddy: Campion.
JC: I'm hanging up.
B: Don't be an asshole. I paid you that money for the Sixers game.
JC: How did you get this number?
B: I'm your attorney.
JC: I can't talk to you now. A tall, burly fellow named George is explaining to me how much he would like to kill his wife, and a dizzy blonde woman, who appears to know nothing about politics, is detailing a national health care plan on a cocktail napkin.
B: This is important.
JC: Does it have to do with betting on sporting events?
B: No.
JC: Then it can wait.

B: Look, I've joined up with a committee to put Ronald Reagan on Mount Rushmore.

JC: Great, good-bye.

B: No, I'm serious.

JC: I'm sure you are, gotta go.

B: I put your name on the heading for the North East petition.

JC: Sweetheart, this is no good, you forgot to carry the two ... WHAT?

B: Told you it was serious.

JC: Can I assume you're back on the crank.

B: Never touch the stuff.

JC: Then what's the motive for such an obvious act of mental insurrection?

B: C'mon, you love Ronnie.

JC: Yes, I like him better propped up on Nancy's couch in Southern California drooling on his bib and wondering why Doris Day doesn't make cute films anymore.

B: This is going to happen Campion, deal with it.

JC: Who's says?

B: The Reagan Legacy Project.

JC: Bar keep, set us up!

B: We at the Legacy have investigated the rock around the area and are convinced there is enough space for Mr. Reagan, the last great president of this, the American Century. (long pause while Mr. Campion downs a screwdriver) Hello, you still there?

JC: I'm still trying to figure out why the fuck Teddy Roosevelt's up there.

B: We have a goal before the end of 1998 to have at least one thing named for Reagan in all 50 states. Do you realize there is only one street named after him in New York? (now the sound of the phone being passed to someone is heard on the tape)

George: Ronald Reagan?! It's a miracle that fossil's not in prison after that Iran-Contra crap! And the goddamn waste of money on those Star Wars weapons! My wife is a goddamn Republican! Who the hell is this?

B: Who is this?

G: George.

B: Put Campion back on the phone.

G: I don't like your attitude.

B: Well, George, perhaps you don't appreciate the legacy of a great American. If you spent less time talking about killing your wife...

G: Listen you son of a... (a tussle ensues)

JC: I'm back.

B: Don't put that freak on the phone! I'm in the main office right now!

JC: You do realize you need an act of congress to start carving the likeness of 80s' icons on the side of a mountain in South Dakota.

B: Who do you suggest we put up there, Bill Clinton?

JC: Clinton? That worm's got his own problems. I'm engaged in a situation here, you've angered George and this chick isn't taking into consideration the congressional kickbacks needed for such a radical plan.

B: Are you aboard?

JC: Sure ... put him up there! You can stick his real head on the friggin' thing for all I care. Consider me the Eastern Chancellor of the Great Reagan Head! We shall overcome!

G: (more struggles) Give me the goddamn phone you little bastard!

B: Campion! Don't give that idiot the phone!

JC: Let the girl talk, you brute!

Woman: Hello?

B: Yes?

W: Hi.

B: Listen, if you'll be kind enough to put my friend back on I'd appreciate it.

W: You listen, Frenchy. If you think by mobbing together a bunch of Rush Limbaugh sycophants and screaming about Mr. Bitzberg is going to allow us to sit idly by and watch some two-bit sculptor put the likeness of a B-movie actor like Ronald Reagan next to Abraham Lincoln, you are sadly mistaken.

B: Is Campion still awake?

JC: Gotta go amigo. (hangs up)

12/30/97

LEISURE TIME DANGER

Politicians can't ski.

This much we know. But what of the rest of us? On the skidding heels of Michael Kennedy and Sonny Bono—both of whom died within a week of one another by careening downhill and smashing into a tree—there is speculation among the skiing elite that such fatalities, although uncommon, are far too ordinary for comfort.

Should affluent public figures be the exception or the rule? Can people without fame, cash, and a spotty personal record be able to ski competently without meeting an arboresque demise?

According to the National Ski Patrol, and the fact that this exists is proof enough that our chops are weak, there have been only 36 ski fatalities in the last two seasons. Consequently, if one takes the National Safety Council's numbers as creed you wind up with 716 boating deaths and 800 bicycle fatalities in the last calendar year alone. The rich and clumsy often use boats to unwind, and in most cases, as floating bars. Yet JFK Jr. has somehow managed to survive biking around Manhattan, so what is the answer here?

Most doctors and ski experts will tell you fatigue is a factor, but what in the name of bad 60s' icons and rich offspring has Sonny Bono and a Kennedy kid have to be tired about? As of press time both were cleared of any substance abuse—although with a Kennedy and a former flower child there is always the possibility—but this seems like more of a man and nature thing anyway.

So let's remove their public status and tax bracket, and if it pleases the court, their positions of public assistance, and concentrate on the skiers. Both were allegedly top notch.

Bono practically lived through countless Colorado winters and the Kennedy's move best in New England. These men were no novices. These were relatively good athletes, and by most accounts fairly coherent on the slopes.

What went wrong?

Maybe I am naive and ski illiterate, but what is the point of all these trees stuck on a five mile 3,500 foot drop of frozen water where humans speed brake-free at an average of 20 to 30 miles an hour? No one would survive a car accident with those numbers, even with Olympian skills. And how is it you have to wear a helmet to do everything in most of the 50 states, but not a consideration for skiers?

I, for one, do not wish to die in the snow. This is not my idea of laughs. But with this new controversy raging one key question remains:

How do we get Cher and Teddy up there?

1/6/98

THE DOWNTOWN DEAL

Fun, frolic, and the odd drug deal in Washington Square Park ain't what it used to be. Big Brother is not only watching, but well on his way to putting a stop to assorted frolic with aims at the fun. Now with Mayor Rudy Giuliani well ensconced in his four-more-years seat, it is crack down crime a-go-go, and those who run and gun will find themselves on camera or worse. This is the bust time, mama; and when the wings come off the sheen it won't be nothin' but the rent to pay.

"You want smoke?" The braided fellow with the wry smile and the long coat barked under a shade-of-gray last Friday in the wake of several busts on runners and sellers near Bleeker St. and across from the NYU Library. "What about these cameras the city's put up around here?" I asked him. "And what the fuck they gonna do?" he said. "Bust my ass? Done it five times last year alone, boy."

The word around Greenwich Village has been more of the same, but lately the heat is really on. Hanging in the cold with the steerers, bummers, and winos is the walk of folly if you're looking to war with Uncle Rudy and New York's Finest. Police Commissioner, Howard Safir, has come to play hardball with the movement of drugs around chemical play land and has boasted a string of arrests by summer.

And after summer?

"There'll be so much dope in this here park you'll be wise to check back later," my new friend pondered. "I don't want any dope," I told him. "Then what you doin' in the Square, boy?"

It was a good question, to which I had no answer save the opportunity to survey the surveillance. To what do I owe this penchant for seeking trouble well before the bell rings and my corner is ready? I've been practicing journalism for too long now not to realize that where the clouds form may be a good place to get wet. The Village has also been a second home to me, and around the West Side there are strolls over to Washington Square Park where the rush of drug cretins harangue the casual hipsters and funky customers moving through its heart.

Now with the subtlety of Kent State and Orwell's nightmare we have the overworked NYPD playing covert eye-spy with the underground merchants and vampires who choose tax-free income to the option of begging and wiping windshields for a buck. Sugar and vice, night sticks, bull horns, and everything nice. Uncle Rudy may have cleansed Times Square of smut, but he'll find the head-fix harder to exorcise. "I'll go to Sullivan if you want sniff," the gentleman caller said, as he stole back into the shadows. "I'll see you and the mayor on the other side."

There's a chill in the winter air, so I don't think I'll check on the gun runners on Canal Street anytime soon.

1/13/98

PAULA JONES: THE AMBIGUOUS VICTIM

Anita Hill was funny.

Paula Jones is funnier.

Loads of laughs. The Old Boy Network is filing up to the water cooler to whip the quips and break down the "dick" jokes for the less educated. This is, after all, the land of the boorish lout with his six-pack and shot gun scanning the roll call of fantasy triumphs in the bedroom of the mind. This is America; the free and sleazy home of the white man's burden and the women who love (strike that) tolerate them.

We, who cling to the notion that the work place is not a singles bar or the junior prom understand sexual harassment. There are those, however, who don't quite comprehend the severity of its existence, and, most importantly its consequences. Therefore they may need some definitive answers once again.

How is it that Paula Jones must prove to the clamoring mob at Voyeur Central that she isn't looking to cash in on Bill Clinton's alleged act of gubernatorial come on? What else is she going to get from Big Bill, an apology? Sorry, already denied by the White House. Is she going to see the President of the United States locked up? Not going to occur on this particular planet. So money it is. And for what reason do all of us have for placing the veracity of her story on a dollar amount her attorney may throw out to shine a larger spotlight on this possible crime?

Just because the president has released the hounds of spin—who incidentally have been punching overtime keeping Big Bill looking like Family Man Willie with his spanking new pooch, Buddy—this doesn't mean he ain't guilty of strongly suggesting that a woman please him sexually while serving as governor of Arkansas. Some of us in the male gender hardly occupied with the exploits of our imagined affairs and the odd peek at Pam & Tommy's Wedding Tape, would like some conformation on the conduct of our elected officials. Not to tar-and-feather, mind you, because Clinton can screw all the assistants and cocktail waitresses he wants as long as they're willing and able, and not on our time.

This little ditty with Ms. Jones is different. According to her—the real victim—she wasn't very willing

No dog-and-pony act could save Gary Hart, who was 100 times the man Bill Clinton claims to be. Gary never got a shot because he liked to bump and grind on the odd yacht. Sex is good business if you can get it in the 90s', but for the big players it's a flame not worth fucking with. God and country are hard images to sell when you squeeze in the occasional blow job request. Big Bill has survived every moral code the opposition could throw at him, and he'll survive this. But Paula Jones is the victim here, not the president. If he acted like a dime-store lecher in a place of business with a woman who was not the least bit receptive, and apparently did not find it amusing, he must pay the proverbial piper.

1/20/98

MONICA LEWINSKY: CRYING WOLF OR WEEPING LAMB?

Monica Lewinsky had better be telling the truth. All joking, snickering, and lewd, crude, tabloid mudslinging aside; this is as important a story in the history of this country as any, and may well have lasting ramifications for the next century. And all of this has nothing to do with politics, power, or the presidency. Bill Clinton is doomed to be remembered for his brainless libido now. He could lead the charge toward lasting world peace and discover hard evidence that there is, in fact, a God, and still be known as the guy who screwed himself into an embarrassing twist. No, this isn't at all about the most powerful office in the free world. It is about women.

If Monica Lewinsky, 24 year-old intern-groupie—who probably did not expect this kind of insanity as a result of her revelations—is not telling the truth about an alleged affair with the President of the United States, it will wound women's rights, and taint the battle to make men, married or otherwise, responsible for their actions. And what of women's responsibility for creeping around powerful men, who are weakened by a young, pretty face so alluringly available? It is ugly and dangerous, and if true, will breed deeper questions; but if false, will be society's tragedy.

This also proves that it is individuals, not agencies, governments, or organizations which change the course of human events. The National Organization for Women, once again nowhere to be found unless certain indiscretions jibe with their political affiliation, can close up shop if Lewinsky is spinning tales. Ask Al Sharpton about young women who make it all up. Visit Amy Fischer in her prison cell and ask her what kind of sympathy the world has for a naive girl suckered by a horny older man with the itch.

By the time this goes to press things could be radically different. This is a story that morphs by the minute, and the way Bill Clinton has fired back it looks like it will be decided by the type of lawyer circus which put a murdering thug like O.J. Simpson back on the golf course; even in the face of the relentless battering and abuse he heaped upon a myriad of women. But DNA and semen stains be damned, there is still a chance that this is another delusional child caught in the headlights of celebrity begging for her 15 minutes in its glare.

Let's hope this isn't so. Monica Lewinsky's fantasies could cost her gender dearly. This is society's most precious war. Whether any of us agree with it or not she is at its center. Before this is over this could be Rosa Parks and Roe vs. Wade all rolled up in a neat late 90s' package. If any of it is true then it becomes vital that it is not shoved into the Anita Hill/ Gennifer Flowers file and forgotten with a smirk. A president may have to take the hit, but, hey, what was all that Truman stuff about the buck stopping there for anyway?

CIGAR CHIC

When I was a boy I could smell the sweet waft of alienation coming from the back porch of my family's apartment in the Bronx. It was a fragrance like no other. Some called it rancid, others oppressive; my grandfather would call it necessary. So he was banished to the outside, alone with his thoughts, his tomato plants, and his cigar. But that was the 60s' and these are the 90s', and the world has spun a new coat. This is the age of alienation, where the jilted and ostracized run in herds. This is the generation of rogue chic; a time of change and true liberation. It is the outing of gays, the revenge of women, and a breath of strange religion. A time for expression of alien thought, and chest-thumping redemption. Redemption for the cigar smoker—but more importantly— redemption for the cigar.

Once thought of as the smoke of gangsters and ruffians, who roamed the hard city nights looking for trouble or a pub in which to cover in pulsing fog, the cigar has been wrested from the underground and splashed upon the spotlight of the beautiful people. Who could forget the sight of Demi Moore sporting a stogie, or perhaps Brad Pitt at a Hollywood premier biting down on a fat one? Is there more of an arresting sight than a big mogul, superstar basketball player, or fashion designer lighting up the once all-but-ignored leaves? Goddammit, if Cosmo Kramer can call it a trademark there could be something to this nasty habit.

But alas, when the art of rebellion is thrust into society's center it can lose its original zest. For instance, does the new order really have a grip on the essence of the cigar-smoking experience? Has it been diluted for the mainstream, ripped from its roots? Is the old man on the corner left to feel like those poor Beatnicks at the Haight when the middle-class goof-offs crashed their Hippie euphoria?

I first learned the pleasure of the cigar in the press box at Yankee Stadium, ironically, mere miles from my grandfather's porch. That smell; so familiar, so pungent, so enticing, would lead to a seven year love affair with the long-filler tubes of rolled tobacco. I can recall the romantic imagery of the grizzled sportswriter peering out at the action through the clouds of smoke rising around the brim of his hat. This was Americana to the core — I thought — and an exclusive portion of it at that. It was, after all, a rite of passage. A male bonding with the rough-and-tumble set. We were well-ensconced in our splendid isolation, years before what is now being dubbed in certain circles as "the cigar boom of '92." It was in that selective glow of sudden euphoria that I experienced the painful shun of the enlightened. Back then, a cigar smoker was not only berated by family, friends, and strangers — he was public enemy in most bars and night clubs.

Today the cigar is sold in malls, supermarkets, and convenient stores coast to coast. Cigars are now enjoyed by women, young adults, rock stars, and super models. There are an alarming amount of cigar bars popping up all around. Magazines and books on cigars, once limited to very few pages, are now thicker and more prevalent than ever. There is a burgeoning subculture riding the crest of the cigar frenzy, and, although no one knows just how it began, it continues unabated.

Forty miles north of New York City, where the cigar's popularity has been rivaled by only Chicago in the last 150 years, there sits an old cigar shop some 50 feet from a winding country road. Set against the backdrop of thick woods in the quaint town of Shrub Oak, its sign simply reads: "Doc James— Custom Blended Tobacco." Below is the obligatory cigar-store Indian staring out from the less politically-correct days of a hard rain and a good smoke.

On the afternoon of my visit, a friendly young man by the name of Adam DeSiena was standing behind a small counter donning a rather telling grin. Before I even finished introducing myself, DeSiena was boasting about the 25-year tradition of blending tobacco on the premises—something eminently obvious from the sweet odor permeating every corner of the tiny place. "Doctor Harold James blended tobacco here for years," he smiled. "Always been called Doc James as far as I know."

Adam, only 26 years-old, bought the store in 1994 and experienced a slow start which grew into a 150% increase in sales by 1996. "In '96 things just exploded around here," he smiled, wide-eyed and gregarious like a man who'd built a shack on an field of oil. "The target cigar smokers are usually between 25-40, male, mostly connoisseurs. But now I get 18 year-olds and more and more women."

When I pressed him on the reaction of some of his regular customers—those who've been lighting up long before Archie Bunker hit prime time— he did not hesitate to site the complaints. "Mostly the rise in cigar popularity has been pissing off the old-timers because of the subsequent rise in prices and," he laughed, "brands you could get anytime are selling out. Guys who've been smoking for 40 years blame it on the yuppies and women."

And just what brands are the yuppies and women smoking? "The most sought after cigar right now is the Arturo Fuente," Adam said, standing amongst the over 50 different brands placed eloquently in their boxes locked behind glass-enclosed temperatures provided by a sizable humidifier. "Mostly because of the fair price and quality. They go anywhere from $2 to $10, which is a far cry from David's White Labels which go for $25 if you can get them. They only sell to an exclusive clientele." When pressed on the best cigar he might sell, Adam was elusive. Although the Cubans getting the press for prime quality behind the curtain of Communism, it is what the Dominicans have been doing that seemed to entice his fancy.

Young Adam (like so few of his contemporaries) is far from the fast lane, tucked away in the nestle of bucolic splendor, likely raking in the profits of the millennium's closing fad. He is the missing link, that bridge to the next century so flippantly tossed around as campaign fodder only last year. He is a true frontiersman in a world of savage postulates clutching at the heels of the jet set. The private world of Doc James has been invaded, and only time will tell if those holding fast to the last vestige of the cigar as an image of precious individuality will fully welcome the clamor.

But, in the end, despite being shoved aside by the stampede of the hip, the cigar smoker can blend in with the chosen few. No longer will we be told to "put that stinky thing out" when the world shoulders our concern. The power of numbers rivals only the strength of perception. And now that the public at large eschews the image of Al Capone for the revised visage of Michael Jordan drawing a victory puff on the front page of USA Today there is progress.

1/27/98

THE LOYAL OPPOSITION

My friend from Georgetown called again the other day. He always calls when things get cloudy in Washington, and lately the fog is so thick it can cause the most nocturnal creature to reconsider the odds. He is a bit player in the Republican Party—but as a young buck conservative—well connected to the pipeline that reveals "the news." He wanted to kindly rebuff the First Lady's accusations that a covert Right Wing conspiracy has thrown enough dough around the Beltway to convince certain squealers to keep the president on the front pages for awhile. He says the Republicans, almost to a man (and woman), want Bill Clinton to finish his rollercoaster second term. My friend from Georgetown says the Republican Party has other plans.

Consequently, there seems to be growing concern among Democrats that a dullard like Al Gore, who, as vice president, will most definitely get the obligatory coattails nomination in 2,000, might not survive a summer on the campaign trail. Clinton may be notorious for a myriad of spicy reasons, but at the very least he gets notoriety. As he did back in '92 when he was a country bumpkin from Arkansas and George Bush was the most popular president since George Washington. Then he whupped Bush's ass. Back then Clinton lived, and apparently still lives, by the old adage: Don't worry about what they print as long as they correctly spell your name beneath the photo.

How in the world is Gore, a man capable of lowering the blood pressure of the most cranked among us, supposed to follow Clinton's high-wire act? The GOP feel it's impossible. If anything, an impeachment of Clinton may bring a benign personality like Gore a chance for the kind of national respite only coma patients endure. That will be harder to counter come next year. And according to my Georgetown friend Gore will never pardon Clinton, sparing himself from the political death reserved for one Gerald Ford after his pardon of Richard Nixon. Unlike Ford, who was barely convinced to accept the vice presidency after Spiro Agnew was sent packing, Gore wants to be president. If its on the gnarled bones of Big Bill, so be it.

But there will be no impeachment. And with apologies to the First Lady, there is no "Right Wing conspiracy." Even the most brain damaged among the Republicans know that anything less than murder wouldn't begin to equal Nixon's crimes. Big Bill is too media savvy to try anything as evil and stupid as the Watergate cover-up, and it doesn't take a politico to figure out that there isn't a lip in the present cabinet that wouldn't sink that ship before it left the dock.

"A doofus like Al Gore, attempting to ride the two-term fumes of this draft-dodging, pot-smoking, philandering, Baby Boomer celebrity will be like the Monkees trying to follow Jimi Hendrix," my friend from Georgetown concluded. "Gore is Bob Dole without even an eighth of the wit and guile, and Dole was the worst campaigner of the post-television era." The loyal opposition rests.

2/4/98

SONG OF THE BUZZMAN

"Fuck the Grammys," The Buzzman said. It was after hours in an Irish Pub on York Ave., north of New York Hospital on the Upper East Side, and the great underground voice was rising like a phoenix from the ashes of the Grunge pall. The Buzzman has spent too many evenings watching the parade of success pass over the flickering television screen above his head like the pops and whistles swimming inside of it. He would not be watching the "fascist elite" rob him of anymore hope. He's already paid at the office.

This was my second opportunity to see The Buzzman's unusual, some may say, groundbreaking act. It wasn't Springsteen stomping the Stony Pony at the turn of the 70s', decrying an aborted love-decade left stranded by its participants. Strangely, it wasn't anything resembling music at all.

Yet, an evening in The Buzzman's presence has that nostalgic ring to it. Given the chance he'll tell you all about the Beatles bouncing upon the rickety stage below in the Cavern. The Buzzman was nowhere near Liverpool in 1962, wasn't even born then. He doesn't quite recall Elvis, the Sex Pistols, or Nirvana. However, he'll remind you that none of them won a Grammy worth a damn.

The Buzzman is no one you haven't seen before. He runs to the bizarre like a nerdish kid whose been left out of the loop to discover the edge, where all the bleeding creeps go for their training in the land of scars across the floor boards. The Buzzman has been there and back, and refuses to recite history when he's busy making it. "What do those people know about the sound?" he hisses when asked about his pejorative take on the end-all music awards. "God is a satellite signal now," he continues. "Push the buttons and you'll see the end of time."

It is those type of statements which has set The Buzzman apart. That, and his work. This presently consists of a kazoo, a bass drum, and the clatter of mini-tambourines tapped between long, bony fingers. After nearly three hours of this "sound" God's satellite takes a back seat to a check of the fire exits.

It was no more than five, maybe six, years ago when I first heard of The Buzzman. He was working bars and strip joints in Woodstock with the half brother of Rosylin Carter. Ironically, it was during the week of the Grammys, perhaps the one Milli Vanilli swept. A few years later I heard he was warming up for Mazzy Star in Boston, but when I called ahead for tickets, he'd already canceled. He was always a man of little faith for schedules.

But on his slow crawl through the entertainment biz The Buzzman has built a strong hate for the Grammys. "Not only me," he said, after a monumental final set and three encores. "There is a change sweeping up the remnants of this crap passing for alternative music nowadays. Not going to vote on that!"

When Celine Dion is picking up her hardware I will be thinking of The Buzzman, and many more like him. God knows, I was there once. Sometimes I think I'm still there; me and the Buzzman throwing back a few and stuck in Lodi again.

2/11/98

MIA MADONNA

I miss Madonna.

Not the aging supreme diva, serious film actress, mysterious celebrity, 90s' mom, Madonna. You know, the one who's decided to inundate the masses with another tired public relations blitzkrieg after a couple of years of relative seclusion. That Madonna has kidnapped the one I fell in love with in the first place; bound and gagged in the back room of memory. Along with the 80s', my 20s', and any chance I had of seeing Ronald Reagan dragged from office in a muzzle; she is gone, and I miss her.

When exactly did Madonna become Diana Ross with a hint of Barbara Streisand and Olivia Newton-John thrown in for spice? This slipped by my usually sensitive pop-culture awareness. Somewhere between the turn of the decade and the last few weeks, a saucy, and mostly interesting talent, transformed a cute, quirky boy-toy into someone you might see on Larry King decrying the prudish traditions of Third World countries or mourning murdered designers in Time magazine.

Now there isn't an ounce of my resolve that I wouldn't trade in to wipe the entire decade of the 80s' from the history books, but Madonna was beyond all of that. Like Elvis, the alien of affluence for the 50s', she was someone you could count on for a laugh and a song. She was a New York punk with the kind of style one could best describe as "mistake"; at once a poster girl for the Salvation Army Surplus Store and the glamour of postwar chic. In her place now stands a mannequin for the allure of fashion snobs and Hollywood drivel.

I can remember her once exhibiting a sense of humor. When Madonna presented sex to a white collar America screaming for something a little less threatening than Prince, but a little more realistic than Michael Jackson, it was with the subtlety of a jackhammer and the wry innocence of a curious Catholic girl on her first date. I remember soft eyes with a hard stare, the belly button and the high pitched squeal, the dance grooves and cheesy ballads which stole their way into your heart. Since then there has been rumors of plastic surgery, muscle toning, the stupor of stardom, and a self-annointed figurehead for the invisible sexual revolution.

There was a time when Madonna shocked and provoked without fabrication. That Madonna would thumb her nose at a male-dominated business the same way she would at large cola corporations or church groups who would deny her access to her privates during stadium shows. She was the female David Bowie, Marylin Monroe with an edge. She was annoying, ruthless, and enticing; but she never once gave the impression she needed your love. She only craved it in a way a vampire must suck the blood from an innocent victim in the dead of night. That Madonna is lost. Now she is an award show/Oprah appearance away from show-biz has-been oblivion. Hey, everyone gets old. Only young mavericks become boring.

I miss Madonna.

She was good.

2/17/98

THE STARR CHAMBER

In the grand tradition of such inadequate notables as Joseph McCarthy, Earl Warren, and Marsha Clark, Independent Council dingbat, Kenneth Starr has taken the law and its intent to new and more despicable lows. No one with half the wit of a door stop has to ask what this man is investigating, trying to prove, or wasting taxpayers' money on. Merely because his lack of beef on matters presidential has left only one answer: NOTHING.

Starr is sucking up his 15 minutes of infamy with the gluttony of Marlon Brando on a chili binge. He leaks, freaks, and gives good press conference, but displays about as much ability to build a case against the President of the United States as the kid who takes your change for the newspaper every morning. If the tag team of Archibald Cox and Leon Jaworski were this incompetent Richard Nixon would not only have finished his second term, he could very well have won a suit against the government to keep him in office until his death.

Ostensibly, Kenneth Starr's original job was to dig up facts on illegal real estate deals. It has now become "Witness Bullying 101." Meanwhile, a 24 year-old former White House intern is slapping him silly. It is getting so out of hand that even if Bill Clinton is guilty of a third of what he's accused of in this interminable Whitewater case, its impact has long been buried in a pile of tabloid dirt. Ironically, the fingerprints on the shovel are Starr's own.

Let's just say Starr's job might have been to discredit the president, perhaps undo the popular vote and repaint the canvas of Bill Clinton's impossible popularity with felicitous innuendo. It has now effectively become hoarding incredible secrets from an insatiable press and a sympathetic nation which has resulted in jolting Big Bill's approval ratings to unprecedented heights while turning the 42nd president into the public's favorite martyr. Terms like "Executive Privilege" may excite those who believe Clinton has been nabbed on this Monica Lewinsky fiasco, but this is just one of many expected return volleys from Big Bill. Nixon ran that flag up the judicial pole with Jaworski and wound up on network television with a mountain of transcripts. Eventually Kenneth Starr will have the ball in his court and will be asked to lay the same loaf or get off the pot.

Starr has done all the stalling a man can do without having something, ANYTHING, tangible to back it up. As much a soap opera as this all seems to the layman, in a court of law, or for a grand jury, there has to be at least a shred of raw fact. So far Starr has been avoiding it like the plague. If he has something on Clinton, he should unveil it now or forever hold his peace. The longer this mess continues to build the more it starts to look like Geraldo peering into Al Capone's vault.

Senator Joseph McCarthy had his list of 205 names which never materialized, and before he was done they were naming a notorious era of unequaled fear and criminal stupidity after him. Earl Warren's commission had the "Single Bullet Theory" which turned a supposed assassination investigation into a magic show of government espionage spurning a flood of critical literature and wild documentaries. And lovely Marsha Clark had that friggin' glove which turned the "Trial of the Century" into an "I Love Lucy" episode. Kenneth Starr could very well add his name to these egregious mishaps of American history before the winter is out if he doesn't produce some serious grit.

The true humor in all this, of course, is that Bill Clinton appointed this boob, and if he had prior knowledge that Starr would be this ridiculously inept then maybe that is the independent council's best case against him.

2/24/98

A MATTER OF REASON

Sexual preference is not a civil right. Yet, by definition of one's sexual preference, basic civil rights cannot be denied. In other words, no one outside the willing recipient of your advances should care what the hell you do with your body as long as it doesn't interfere with the bodies of others around you. The Superior Court of New Jersey ruled last week that James Dale, proud scout leader, should not have been banished from the Boy Scouts of America on the basis of his being an admitted homosexual.

Hooray for the rare moments of sanity in the American court system.

In 1990 Dale was expelled by the Boy Scouts of America's Mommouth Council despite a 12-year pristine record including 30 merit badges. Two years later he sued. Three years later a Mommouth, New Jersey judge sided with the Boy Scouts, calling homosexuality "a serious moral wrong." Six years later Dale challenged and overturned the verdict. In turn, the law prevailed. The U.S. Constitution prevailed.

This case is not about gay rights. This is about human rights under the law of an oft advertised free country. However much homosexuality is perceived as a subculture lifestyle, deemed immoral by the great standards police among us, it is not illegal.

Hunting is immoral. It is legal. Drinking alcohol is immoral. It is legal. Gambling is immoral. It's legal everywhere. (see the state lottery). The fact is people are not nearly as afraid of those things as they are of sex. That kind of idiosyncratic dementia may fly at church meetings and red neck pubs, but it is garbage time under the law. You know how these things go; first its gays, then women, people with green hair, and finally anyone who breathes wrong.

Perhaps its Dale's fault for putting his trust in a group in the first place. The Boys Scouts is a group. Groups are the bane of individuality. Anytime you have a group, it inevitably must have rules to separate it from the rest of society. Then the group becomes its own society, like the military or organized religion. It is not so alarming that when someone leaves the military they call it becoming a civilian, or that the major religions enjoy tax exempt status. Groups are scary because the very essence of one inevitably turns into an "us and them" scenario which often ostracizes reason.

The Boy Scouts of America is a boys club. It is not an anti-gay boys club. There is an overabundance of those already. This time the group is wrong. It is illegal to discriminate against a perfectly fine member or employee on the grounds of their sexual orientation. Incidentally, that little tidbit has always been illegal. However, with apologies to the film, "Philadelphia", Mr. Dale's case is the first to expose it.

This will not be the end. The Supreme Court will have its say. Got some bad news for the Boy Scouts: the Supreme Court uses the same Constitution.

3/3/98

TUG OF MONOPOLY

The Federal Government, already embroiled in more court proceedings then the state of Texas, is presently investigating the monopoly known as Microsoft. Founder, and richest soul on the planet, Bill Gates, has become predictably vocal on the matter. Granted the sight of a dweeb like Gates attacking the system so he could bully competition and corner the P.C. market for gains beyond our imagination is nauseating, but what of the concept of a monopoly?

There are still some of us left who continue to decry the fall of Ma

Bell. Who wouldn't give back the store of free trade for a reprieve from long distance and collect call badgering? Just try and decipher your phone bill without six months training. There is anarchy in telephone land and we have the federal government to thank for it. Now it's the stronghold of Windows and the seemingly limitless landscape of the Internet. Communication and the almighty dollar is a cushy romance, and with billions of dollars floating through cyberspace, there is more than one man who knows the potential of its vast wilderness.

It is the $47 billion dollar man vs. Capitol Hill. Big Government honing in on uncharted lucrative territory. Right now the good people at Netscape see crime and call foul. Bill Gates sees good business from the guy who invented the wheel; namely himself. Presently Microsoft can offer an Internet browser for free while attached to the Windows 95 package. Windows is installed in 85% of the world's desktop computers. Netscape has little room for competitive nature there. "Free" may be the most popular word in the English language, but it is a death knell in the land of big business.

Gates, being one of the most ingenious and influential humans of the 20th century, is a tough nut to crack. Tall tales of strong arm tactics and backroom deals to squeeze out competitors have abounded for years. Yet Gates remains the nerdy intellect with the secret of a new universes dancing inside his bad haircut. He is no Jimmy Hoffa badass executive tiptoeing with the big stick. His image is protected by the visage of a shut-in who has cashed in on a life of bookworm heaven. Uncle Sam may see it differently.

Monopoly is a dirty word in the thorny landscape of capitalism. With the wounding of Grade-A Communism it is the last cancer of profit. Giants like McDonalds still has Burger King nipping at their heels. Pepsi and Coke tear at each other like rabid junkyard dogs. Microsoft is currently untouchable, ironically, the way the Internet itself is untouchable because the government cannot figure its parameters. Politicians and lawyers like parameters. Business moguls like soft lighting on their gray areas. Consumers like quality. If it comes in a package of dictatorship or democracy they don't care.

Bill Gates has been winning for the better part of a decade. Now there could be a chink in his considerable armor. If the phone companies are any indication, there could be a chink in the computer world the size of Jupiter. See the mirror for the answer to who pays the bill.

3/10/98

LEST WE FORGET

"He was our loyal captain and friend,
But now he is changed. He belongs to another nation,
The grim tribes underground.
We break their bones to hold them down.
We must not be destroyed by the dead or the living.
We have history ahead of us."
- Robinson Jeffers
"Ode to Hengist and Holsa"

Thirty years ago next month it all started. The most poignant civil unrest in America in almost 100 years. It was a time of real horror and tumult which finally culminated two years later with murdered children on a college campus in Ohio. It was a time of immoral police actions in Southeast Asia, street riots, assassinations, and a fractured government bleeding from every pore. A time of unparalleled confusion and violence, and a fear of the future that can bring down a civilized world with the slightest breeze. It began on April 4, 1968 with the abrupt end to a life. It was the day Martin Luther King was murdered.

The Civil War commenced with a single shot fired by a farm-paper editor by the name of Edmund Ruffin at Fort Sumter, South Carolina. The internal strife of the late 1960s' began its crescendo toward doom with one shot fired toward a balcony of the Lorraine Motel in Memphis Tennessee by an ex-con named James Earl Ray. Ruffin began the eventual dismantling of slavery. Ray put a lean on nearly a century of tenuous freedom.

Within 24 hours of King's death violence in black communities rose to frightening proportions. The foundation of race relations cracked like twigs under the rage of abuse. It was "us against them" forever. From the mania of Watts to the Rodney King riots, there appears to be little hope of slowing its sickening momentum.

Robert Kennedy, champion of civil rights for years, gave a speech that night to quell the charge for revenge. Two months later he would die the same way. Before the summer was done the Viet Nam War would escalate and every network would televise a full scale riot at the Democratic National Convention in Chicago. By fall a petrified voter population elected the voice of the "great silent majority", Richard Nixon president. His inept and paranoid domestic freak show would further alienate the vociferous minority and dig deeper roots in Viet Nam. Since that summer the word "protest" took on insidious measures which came to a head on May 4, 1970 when the National Guard descended on Kent State University, opening fire on students and killing four. Nixon had waged war on the country he was chosen to govern. It would be the beginning of the end for him, and a death knell for the age of blind trust in leaders.

Assassination threat is the chic of violence today. Race relations precariously balance on the brink of hysteria. Any mention of military action sends shivers down the spine of Americans. The blood of Martin Luther King inaugurated a time of near anarchy. America has not fully recovered. Lest we forget.

CHAOS IN MOTION II

Wear out the First Amendment.

Define normal.

It's better to be on the fence.

The view is much clearer up here.

America: The pot is melting.

Exact science is downtime until the exception arises.

The present just ended.

Complaining is good for the soul.

Phony smiles hurt your face.

Day and night.

Black and white.

East and West.

Left and right

Never shall we meet.

Lost is a state of mind.

Bob Dylan gave up.

The meek inherit the earth.

The aggressive take heaven.

Responsibility has become a non-factor.

Trust is folly.

A mirror always lies.

It's backwards.

Everyone should sleep one night on the beach.

The 3 R's of the American school system:

Reading.

Writing

Revolver.

It still rains.

People pay for water.

Insanity is realizing the truth.

Remove God from currency.

Make a congressman work for a living.

Whatever the question.

The answer is Arthur Koestler.

Never conform.

Sing often.

To Whomever it May Concern,
(and I use the term *concern* loosely)

"*The ways by which you get money almost without
exception lead downward. To have done anything by
which you earn money merely is to have been truly
idle or worse. If the laborer gets no more than his
employer pays him, he is cheated, he cheats himself* "
          - Henry David Thoreau
          "Life Without Principle 1854"

I am merely an exiting voice. So, before you begin
searching your computers for my name and position,
waste not another moment. It's just that I have a few
gripes about your current—at best misleading, and at
worst, spurious—policies with employees. It is my
ultimate hope that your company may prosper all the
more from my wisdom without lifting so much as a
digit of your conscience, because if what I've witnessed in the past months is any indication, the
following should ring your proverbial bell.

As an educated and thick-skinned American man I don't
expect anything less than the most heinous and repre-
hensible behavior from suits and management types
who put the bottom line above mere human existence. I
did not awake from a frozen scientific experiment,
nor arrive in a bate truck, so I am well versed in
business etiquette. It is shameful and insipid, and
only the most unholy among us can even fathom it
without a modicum of taint on our souls. However, it
strikes a rather rancorous cord in my better judgment
to allow the likes of you to relieve me of my job of
8+ years without so much as a day's warning. So, I am
not particularly surprised by this surreptitious manipulation of jobs which are obviously considered
fodder by management, but someone should have the
guts to answer for this vapid and unprofessional
behavior.

I have not seen, nor heard from a representative of
your company since you managed this takeover only a
few months ago. Let me guess: you don't treat your
clients with similar neglect. That might result in
the prevention of incoming cash. Even the Lord's of
the Industrial Revolution would cringe at such disregard for professional courtesy. Not that I don't
fully comprehend the dangerous concept of informing
the working masses that their time is short while
simultaneously working in a plan to replace them.
Some notorious moguls may even suggest to do otherwise is business suicide. But there are modes of
communication called tact and decorum to which I can
only assume muck-dwelling swine like you have little
working knowledge.

I won't waste time with quotes from the Bible or site
the conquest of Norma Rae in an attempt to make you
look like the disingenuous monsters you appear to be.
That would be too easy. I prefer the bloody verbal
joust to the massacre anyway. This isn't even about
me. It is about common decency and morals. It is
about understanding the plight of the people who
manage to keep your machine in motion. Replacing us
will save you money and make things more efficient,
and no one is denying that the element of personnel
is far more expensive and unpredictable than the
computer life. But as some great source of this
universe is my witness, there is a hell-rain of karma
reserved for those who do not place humanity as a
collective concept over a dollar bill.

And if there is nothing humans can do about the
prospect of love, at the very least, we need respect.
You have not only been inconsiderate, you have ignored the very truth of our fragile existence on this
planet by trampling over people with sickening apathy. This is why you will eventually fail. Somewhere
and sometime you will be the one dogged, and wonder

how and why. It's the great query of rationalization
to scream to the heavens about intangible foibles
like fate, but you will soon learn fate is the result
of actions.

Maybe you can live comfortably with your actions.
After it is all said and done we are judged ultimately by them, and not some omnipotent God scrolling
a ledger of our deeds to enact the great wrath. And
even if you haven't forfeited your spot in line for
the great payoff—whatever the hell that may be—you
have made a mockery of human relations and furthered
the notion that business is a cold and heartless
march toward the destruction of civilization. The
blathering Jewish historian Josephus told Rome the
very same thing. They laughed heartily before feeding him to the lions. But they were a doomed lot, and
so shall you be.

Finally, you have been nothing short of petty and
thoughtless. And although that may be gangbusters
for profits, it is rotten procedure and should not
lie without reflection. My colleagues and I could
have sabotaged your insidious plan to weed us out
with no warning, but we did not. Although we have
known about our intended departure for some time by
way of sources you may now guess upon, we find the
high road to be much smoother, and the dirt in which
you play a muddy prison. We can only leave you with
this age-tested thought: *Do unto others as you would
have them do unto you.* As a result of your dime-
store, low-rent gutless handling of our dismissal,
let that read...get ready for the boot.

Yours in grateful absentia,

jc

3/17/98

ASHES TO ASHES

"This is a valley of ashes—a fantastic farm where ashes grow like wheat into ridges and hills and grotesque gardens; where ashes take the forms of houses and chimneys and rising smoke and, finally, with a transcendent effort, of men who move dimly and already crumbling through the powdery air."
                                        - F. Scott Fitzgerald
                                        "The Great Gatsby"

Speeding through Wake County, North Carolina on 85 North, two lanes at nearly 90 mph; a dim afternoon of plucking grapes and fiddling with the radio. It is an eerie trip from the quake of the deep South to the blazing strip on I95. Winter gives way to Spring with the reluctance of slicing winds which carve up the vents and blade across my knees. The best woman I have ever known, by my side, frantically jamming towels onto the floor boards . America screaming by the windows.

First saw a sign for Stuckey's about 12 miles back, before the open fields and trailer parks. "Food, Gas, and Rest" it beckoned, like a lighthouse perched on invisible rocks. A second sign followed; two, maybe three miles later. Another, then another. One cannot grasp the anticipation of landmarks unless straddled with the eight to ten hour jaunt. Two souls, some fruit, and the music of a thousand channels and frequencies spread out over map towns and rest stops.

"Stuckey's: Over 50 Years of Service" read yet another sign after a few more miles. This one, the biggest of all. It was something out of Camelot; a search for the Holy Grail. Yet, Stuckey's is no legend. It has stood as a symbol of endurance and tradition for half a century. That is what the billboards promise, and I, in a state of paralyzing boredom, choose to believe them. Mom, apple pie, Old Glory, and the great game of baseball; spring eternal in a shack some 70 miles south of Richmond, Virginia. Been there for half of the American Century. Stood there before Elvis and television, before Korea and Viet Nam, before Nixon and the Amazin' Mets, before Aids and Scud Missiles, before James Cameron breathed new life into old disasters.

God wants Stuckey's there.

One more sign heralds the coming of the next exit. The Stuckey's exit. Time for emptying the bladder, stretching the legs, and enjoying a cola. But none of these happen. A final sign screams all too clearly that Stuckey's has been closed due to fire. And sure enough, as I pull along the gravel parking lot just off the exit and confront the bleak void inside my chest, it stands charred through the boarded-up windows. A bright red painted Stuckey's marquee looms like Poe's raven over the carnage ravaged with age. The highway markers were nothing more than warnings of time. This was not a time for rest, instead it was a rest for time.

Standing in the shadow of this ghost stop the echo of thousands of travelers on the American cruise bounce off the hills and penetrate the lonely valley. It is a roadhouse graveyard; the dying breed. It is a glimpse of Fitzgerald's nightmare, the last frontier; Stuckey's as a metaphor of the crumbling century.

The ride for Stuckey's had ended somewhere between the last 50 years and this moment. My ride continues.

3/24/98

UGLY TRUTH

My mother, not particularly known for her rousing patriotism, recently referred to the President of the United States as a "sleezebag." I cannot argue with her. This would be tantamount to arguing the color of the sky, or a bear's choice of surroundings while defecating. There is little elbow room when it comes to the art of defining the presidency. It is the home of bilge, a vast wasteland of honesty and integrity. Which is why it is a tad laughable when it comes as a surprise to those who once thought it the haven of the good and true. This is a dangerous fairy tale propagated by the silly and the disconnected, and should cease immediately, lest we continue to be appalled by Dan Rather's chilling referrals to copulation.

Come now fellow travelers, this is the waning century. Let us rise from slumber and count the coffee beans among us. Power corrupts, and absolute power is like an IV loaded with speed balls cruising the main vein. It is King Richard III wandering through the desert looking to trade the Third World for a goddamn horse. No human can survive it with a shred of their decency left intact. There are horrible places on this globe where you can go to see the fierce result of its wounds.

In order to so much as sniff the presidency one must abandon all hope for places like heaven, or even the local rotary club. Most leaders hardly get past the "Hi, howya doin'" stage without stomping a few of the innocents along the merry way. And who among us are truly innocent? Who can cast the proverbial stone whilst the best and brightest cop a feel in the oval office? Who can stand in judgment over the villainous when to lead the free world one must be devoid of solid character and personal morals?

I have young friends with political aspirations who've run scared with the prospect of even running for local office. The back-scratching, ego-smoothing, tape worm existence of smalltime politics pummels wishes. Some survive. But not them. One has rushed back to a private law practice and writing books, the other dabbles in sales and radio. Both agree there are some ways to sidestep the garbage heap at the homegrown level, but in order to land the truly big job there are compromises only the most heartless and morally corrupt may fathom without hesitation.

The campaign drivel tossed about in debates and the public minutiae which glows from the core of the presidency leave subjects such as humans anesthetized to real emotion. Check the records, the history, the long line of terror emanating from Pennsylvania Ave. and deny the ugly truth. Jefferson had his slaves, Lincoln had his fractured country, Hoover had his stock market crash, FDR had his manipulations, Truman had his bomb, Kennedy and Nixon had their terrible secrets. Bill Clinton has his penis. He is not an aberration. He is the proud sibling of this tarnished-crown legacy.

He is our boy. Salute his degradation and move on to the Cheetos.

3/31/98

GENERATION Z

No sooner had I put the finish touches on a book I was reviewing titled, *Kids Who Kill*, by a brave man named Charles Patrick Ewing, when I was confronted by the Jonesboro shootings. It was difficult enough to envision children committing the type of brutal slayings once reserved for the gnarled soul of adulthood as mere anomaly—but as the routine of the damned—it was near impossible. No amount of statistics and data could begin to explain such things, nor assuage the uncomfortable shudder of recognition that there could ever be a reason for it. Prepubescent maniacs clutching automatic weapons and lurking around the shadows of a twisted society waiting to enact a vengeance itch that will not wait another minute.

It took me only moments to locate my review, and this is what I'd written: *The idea that children could possess such intrinsic hatred and utter contempt for human life is more than enough proof of a real evil presence on this planet.* Then I took the damn thing and burned it. I curse, even now, writing such naive gibberish. I must have forgotten where I was for one murky moment. I must have lost my way. We often do nowadays.

Then I remembered listening to the good Dr. Hunter S. Thompson tell myself, and a congregation of burgeoning journalists, about the dangers of fearing the inevitable Generation Z. During the lengthy afternoon symposium at NYU almost four springs ago, Thompson, sucking on a hash pipe and sipping from his ever-present cocktail glass, decried the notion of a race of numb brains left without the guilt and morals of its straddled past. "Never mind these Generation X monsters," Thompson prophetically told us, "it's those Generation Z fuckers we must fear."

So our first taste of "Z" comes crawling from the melting Arkansas landscape loaded with Halden Caufiled's rage and fueled by hundreds of hours of MTV, computers, video games, gangsta rap, organized religion, and Pepsi nightmares spinning in their tiny heads. No one to tell them about the chasm between reality and fantasy. Two boys, 11, the other 13, straight from the local Soda Sip cranking the gearshift from baby teeth to body counts. The clergy and the doctors and the good people with their microphones can corral no real answers for this savagery. They told us to fear the blacks and the Russians and the hippies and the television and the movies and the cops and the parents and the rich and the leaders and the rock n' roll music. They didn't tell us to comb the preschools and day camps for killers.

Generation Z: armed and pissed.

4/7/98

GRAVITY SPEAKS

"Their children's children shall say, they have lied."
- W.B. Yeats

Peace in Ireland?

Hard to swallow, even more difficult to envision. Yet, two weeks ago an agreement between the North and the Republic of Ireland, the Protestants and the Catholics, Great Britain and a divided nation was ironed out in a final, Easter Sunday session which culminated 22 months of negotiations. The reaction from the press and the political world is guarded optimism, with the operative word being "guarded." Hand shakes and papers are notions often ignored by the passion of the heart.

Those who compare this monumental event to the fall of the Berlin Wall, the Middle East Peace Accord, or the dismantling of apartheid in South Africa can chill their collective heels. The Almighty Dollar destroyed communism, the Middle East has, once again, lost its way, and sometimes dissident numbers outweigh the color of one's skin; but what has transpired in Ireland for centuries—most notably the last 30 years—has run as deep as the blood lines it has cut. The war in Ireland is, and has always been, less about revolution and politics than pride and religion. And for generations it has thrived on the heat from both.

The history of Ireland is fractured. Thanks for that has to go to England. The wounded spirit of a people unable to run their own country has led to finger-pointing agenda which has sunk into the mire of violence. The word "traitor" has been echoed through families and neighbors for as long as any of them can remember. It is passed down with the subtlety and adhesion of the language. Spend some time in cities like Belfast and Ulster and a friend of a friend might tell you that there was no potato famine, but a form of political genocide designed to break the will of a nation. The type of violence familiar to Ireland, terrorist or overt, is the result of the kind of lies and manipulation reserved for an apathetic ruling class.

But most of all, the soul of God's country is pierced by its faith. Religion has claimed more lives throughout the history of civilization than money and sex combined. Great Britain's political control of Northern Ireland through the backing of the majority Protestants—and consequently the agitated response of the Catholic rebels fueled by the bloody existence of the Irish Republican Army—has gleefully perpetrated this fact. In the grand tradition of the Crusades and the Holocaust, Ireland is marred by a hatred justified by the abuse of organized faith. Christianity has imploded on the unyielding bloat of its own frightening convictions. The roots of this is what makes paper-thin hopes like peace agreements seem like a whistler's stroll past the graveyard.

It is the graveyards in Ireland that may well voice the best tale of freedom and peace. Filled with the bodies of revolutionaries and their innocent victims, they are instead, merely silent. Their loved ones can only recall the horror and futility in which they lost their lives, and as a result, the ability to see a unified nation devoid of sectarian madness and foreign control. On May 22 the survivors will vote on the ratification of this agreement. Then maybe documents can become reality, and the dead finally heard.

4/14/98

SEINFELD EULOGY

To what do we owe the author of popular culture? Mark Twain might answer, "everything." Twain, a biting satirist and all around funny guy, put quite a signature on his time; an age of literature. This is a far different age. It is the television age; a time for the fast, hard, and cold who have become increasingly disinterested in the romance of passing time. To the television age, time and emotion are the weight of the slow and distracted whose finest payoff—love and friendship—is an excruciating lumber. Rationalization is the speed of the 90s; the healthy bouncing baby of excuse. It is within the hub of this landscape that *Seinfeld*, arguably the greatest and most enigmatic of the sitcom genre, has thrived as if it were a running commentary of its time.

Seinfeld has managed this because it reflects as well as connects. It has taken the difficult road from imagining America to becoming a part of its lexicon. We share in *Seinfeld's* quick-fix definition of our worst side because deep down we know that life is not only funny and tragic, but often both, simultaneously. *Seinfeld* has taken the masks of drama and comedy and jammed them together; blurring the lines, and gleefully ignoring its impact. It is indeed, as many have called it, including its creators, a show about nothing. Yet, we know it is simultaneously a show about everything. It is the Zen of a caustic and apathetic age. It is great art, moreover, it is funny. Damn funny. And soon it will be finished.

Seinfeld, born and flourished in the 90s', has really been the story of a city; the story of New York. All that is concrete about comedy swells from it's bowels. New York City is funny because, like *Seinfeld*, it is simultaneously drastic and miserable, sarcastic and ambiguous. For eight seasons *Seinfeld*, raging from the core of its four main characters, has been a case study in all of NYC's misgivings and more. They mirror the dark side of us. Elaine; pushy and conniving, struggles to find the right someone who will gladly accept that she must eventually hate them. George; the world's victim, shoved around reality by the force of his own imagination to become history's most insecure narcissist. Kramer; a creature of innocuous dementia, perpetually ignores society at large in order to better carve up its fringe. And finally Jerry himself; a helpless walking commentary, who juggles all the idiosyncrasies and quirks of our id crammed into a world he cannot decipher without the assistance of a one liner.

These characters live and breathe inside each one of us. They are the demons we hide in order to live in relative harmony with each other, but secretly wish could prosper.

Seinfeld must be remembered as less a television show then the type of living theater that transformed its medium for just one half-hour a week. There will never be another like it. After all, true genius is not about transforming, or starting trends, it is to carve a slice from inanimate rock and break the mold. The mold is dead. Long live the reruns!

Excelsior! I mean, who cares.

4/28/98

IF THEY BUILD IT, YOU WILL PAY

Uncle Rudy has taken a holiday from ridding the Big Apple of smut to crawl up New York Yankees owner, George Steinbrenner's rectum. It is the mayor's opinion that not only should the Yankees be afforded a new stadium, but that it should reside on the West Side of Manhattan. An avid fan and polished public relations monster, Mr. Giuliani continues to champion this cause fueled with the fear that he will be the man in charge of the store that lost one of its greatest treasures. Meanwhile, Mr. Steinbrenner leaks rumors of a New Jersey defection in the grand National Football League tradition of the Giants and Jets. As these chummy fat cats play their hissing game neither has any idea who or what will pay for this laughable endeavor.

Meanwhile, New York Mets CO-owner, Fred Wilpon is busy heading press conferences on his new retractable dome stadium to be built in 2002. Two weeks ago Wilpon regaled the gaped mouths with a neat model of the proposed establishment like an excited kid on science project day. Freddie doesn't know where this money will come from either, and quite frankly, this is not a concern for anyone around the Mets right now. As the mayor slums around in the Yankees pocket, and the team thrives on the field, Freddie draws flies to Shea Stadium to watch his mediocre club.

Egos and politics aside, the idea of building two new ball parks within a boro's radius in a few calendar years is fantasy-land squared. At least Wilpon has offered some funding. Steinbrenner, with coffers laced with more television and merchandise revenue than any owner of any sports team on the globe, has offered nada. This blowhard—whom I must admit I possess a soft spot for signing my hero Reggie Jackson and bringing the Yanks back to prominence in the 70s'—chooses instead to ride the crest of his team's popularity and success while holding New York City up at threat point. Hence, Uncle Rudy is a more than willing pigeon if King George promises to go for the West Side theory.

Let's get this one straight. The city, incapable of fixing a bridge or a roadway in less than two decades, will build a massive sports complex on the West Side Highway—already known as the black hole of traffic Hades—by the time the Yankees lease is up in 2002? This is the yammer of the desperate and insane, and it will not fly. Uncle Rudy has already bilked Disney into cleaning up Times Square, but whom shall he turn to for funding a monstrosity in the most heavily populated areas in this country? This is a billion dollar venture schemed by ten cent foresight.

King George does not care. He wants luxury boxes and back-page headlines. He will milk Uncle Rudy's city like a bloated Guernsey by hanging New Jersey over the mayor's beleaguered head. But many polls conducted around parts of N.J. reveal that the populace is less than thrilled at the prospect of ponying up tax dollars to bring another New York sports institution to the Garden State so it can still be called Bronx Bombers. The time is ticking and the alternatives for King George and his mayor lackey would be to refurbish the original stadium or shift a tad north of Yonkers Raceway.

Anyway the cake is cut it will be Johnny Lunch Pale who pays the freight. Uncle Rudy will not be denied here. When he speaks of losing the beloved Yanks he looks like Captain Bligh at the climax of his mutiny denial. Unfortunately, for us, this is one bounty that won't soon disappear.

5/5/98

JERRY SPRINGER'S BEEN FRAMED

Appealing to the lowest common denominator is the golden rule of flash entertainment. The Romans knew a good Christian lion feeding meant big numbers, but the advent of television put to shame anything those monsters could've ever dreamed up. But, alas, this type of romp has a limited shelf-life, and the purveyors of it are often left to point fingers like naughty children caught red-handed. It happens to game shows and pro wrestling, and now it happens to Jerry Springer. He is TV's latest and greatest flavor of the month, and with the belated revelations that his daily panel brawls are staged, abandoned by the very people who gave him the rope with which to tie around his own miserable neck.

The Jerry Springer Show is now the dean of daytime television. It has been whupping Queen Oprah for months, and smack dab in the middle of May ratings sweeps, it is planning on setting records. Studios USA, its production company, has been defending the mounting accusations by releasing several rebuts intimating that Springer has presided over a sham, when all they ordered was a spicy talk show with real-life confrontations. Instead of fessing up to P.T. Barnum's greatest adage, those in charge now choose to let the show's namesake twist in the wind and suffer the arrows. Springer, nothing more than the ring master for this freak show—whose true talent consists of acting as though it is all some kind of shock—has been left to play scapegoat.

Springer finds himself the subject of countless articles and investigative reports screaming fraud and misrepresentation. All the while he claims to have been given the license to kill, but when the inevitable backlash hit, was asked to play nice. As a result Studios USA is threatening to pull the kick-and-shove plug and force Springer to carry a far more calmer show home. No more chairs and bodies will fly say the "innocent" folks at Studios USA. It is quite curious that they have waited until now to locate decency in programming, and are so way off the reality scale here it is almost impossible to get a reading.

Those who push the buttons must land hard when the tower crumbles. Making Springer the bad guy is gutless and cowardly. It was the same deal when Jenny Jones found herself dragged into court for some ugly mess involving a madman killing a homosexual who admitted to having a crush on him during her show. Now the disingenuous cretins who put this junk machine in motion promise whoever wants to listen that by next month Springer will not get to keep his thug-fest. When the populace turn to his daily skid mark of a show it will no longer be what they want, which is garbage, and plenty of it. This may seem like a P.R. gem for the big boys at Studios USA, but what are they really saying about their audience? *We will drag you into the muck with us until it starts to make us look bad, and then we'll take it away like some East Side drug dealer.*

Jerry Springer is an exploitation punk who took a few cheap actors and regurgitated subplots and built a ratings blockbuster, but he only followed the lead of his production company that hired him to do just that. Now they run like rats from the sinking ship. To his credit Springer welcomes the negative press and has managed to turn it into more attention. If Studios USA wanted anything different they should have baled from the gravy train long ago. Now they find a conscience and expect to wipe the slate clean with Springer's carcass. But the Piper always comes for his check, and the one who dances must pay.

WHAT THE FUCK IS WRONG WITH BASEBALL?

Spring is earth's way of reminding us that life is cyclical. With every turn of the season, there is death and birth anew. America is the land of the second chance—the rehabilitation, the divorce, and the almighty receipt kept for things we purchase but decide we no longer want.

America and spring have a game. It has been called a game for scores of generations, but has thrived and faltered as a business. It begins with a pitch and ends with an out; except for the times it ends in ways we cannot know. It is not a game bottled by time, but an institution which marks it. It is baseball; the nation's pastime in the nation's century. However, as the 20th century comes to close, baseball has become feeble to defend itself against those who run it and play it at its most brilliant level.

Professional baseball has been in existence since the decades following this country's darkest time—the Civil War. It was born in the camps where the soldiers killed time before killing each other, and it barely survived the first nineteen years of this century before the mighty Babe, George Herman Ruth lifted it upon his broad shoulders and carried it through the Great Depression.

There was the Second War To End All Wars, another one cold, jukeboxes and hippies, Watergate and break-dancing, and the advent of other-things-sporting pounding at its doors. Yet, Major League Baseball (MLB) still stands, similar, perhaps, to the Roman Empire until even it could no longer stand. It is currently a monopoly of madness struggling against its own will and fortune, maniacally gnawing on its trapped leg like a rabid animal encased in steel. It is at once tragedy and comedy; Oedipus and Othello, the irony of a hundred "Twilight Zones." And those who love its timeless beauty have begun to locate its greatest enemy; itself.

THE DIAGNOSIS

MLB is hanging by a thread in the arena of the sports entertainment dollar. The choice of gamblers, the National Football League, kicks its ratings/advertising dollar ass. And the popularity of the grand urban leisure, the National Basketball Association, stomps it into the ground. These are leagues full of violence and posturing with speed and thunder riding on the waves of public relations normally saved for presidential elections.

Perhaps the pastoral splendor of baseball's cerebral eloquence has been lost on this "sound byte" generation, or perhaps the well of good sense has come up dry on the game's authors after years of a threatening drought. But, anyway you break it down—the paltry television ratings, the drop in attendance, and the scramble for quick fix window-dressings like "wild card" playoffs and inter-league play—all speak of a desperation throbbing.

As MLB enters its 1998 season, the question has to be, "What in the name of the Mighty Casey has gone wrong here?" Glad you asked.

MISPLACED GREED

No one living outside of Alice's looking glass needs a lecture on this subject, nor does anyone have to deny that where there is cash to be made, so go the hounds. But even the grubbiest of street scum must admit that the Lords of Baseball (owners) and its tobacco spitting brethren (players) have taken this sin to new sub-levels of greed.

Before the dawn of free-agency, on which most baseball fans blame just about everything this side of the Kennedy assassination, the owners of MLB teams took hoarding their considerable profits while hiding behind some atavistic Anti-Trust Exemption. Up until the early 1970s' it was quite common that any player, other than the game's elite, would be forced to work an off-season job. That is until the U.S. government decided to step in and present the legal monkey wrench known as free trade to the owners, launching the type of landslide player payback that has now taken the concept of revenge to Biblical proportions.

Most players today, including the ones who otherwise stink up the joint, want to be treated with the immunity of dignitaries while taking nearly the entire store home. This has caused ownership and its working class to inflict all sorts of ugly things upon one another. It has stretched from walkouts to collusion—culminating in the ill-fated coup that shut the game down in the black Summer of 1994—leaving the irritated and, in some cases, irreconcilably scarred fans with no World Series for the first time since 1904.

THE TWISTED WORLD
OF '90S MACHISMO

Baseball suffers from what all sports must endure, the asshole athlete who believes because he has a talent and gets buckets of cash for it, he must be allowed to run amok through society with no repercussions. However, a game as wounded as baseball cannot withstand this type of pariah.

What was once considered a "boys will be boys" mentality has turned into a cottage industry for slick-talking lawyers and rehab centers. Where once it was manly to drink, carouse, and cause the mayhem of the infantile, it is now front page news, juicy gossip, and social disease.

Public relations nightmares and pouting millionaires may be taking the fun out of the other professional sports, but it is killing baseball. It is a game of recognizable figures; the man on the mound against the man at the plate. It is a six-month marathon of long breaks and simple delights, a subtle exhibition of patience and grace. This is the least likely place to hide a thug, drug addict, or social deviant. In other words, if a firecracker goes off in a cathedral, someone will notice.

DILUTION OF TALENT

"Where have you gone Joe DiMaggio?" Indeed. At this point we'd take Mickey Rivers.

Expansion is the owners way of recouping player salaries by adding a revolting amount of new franchises. It is also the players' way of opening up more jobs. As a result the lack of true young talent choosing a dying game has made the quality of play drop considerably over the past 20 seasons.

In prior years players who would have mired in some level of minor leagues or bagged groceries at the local supermarket are now grabbing six-figure salaries and performing for our hard-earned dollars. And, quite frankly, they are failing miserably.

By the middle of this century, MLB was the only pro game in town worth a damn. Every stud kid from Midwest farms to urban plight dreamed of playing baseball. Today that dream is reserved for football and basketball. Even High School kids cash in quickly in those arenas.

In order to compete, MLB franchises are drafting kids younger and rushing them to the big leagues to compete with insane expediency. But baseball is a game of time and experience. The nuances demand more seasoning. Today the big leagues are littered with mediocre lifers and neophytes with attitudes. The product is far short of pristine and consequently tedious. This has caused complaints of lagging games and softball scores, but any self-respecting baseball fan will tell you that a crisply played nine innings, with the occasional thrill of extras, is a fine thing to behold no matter if it goes on all week.

DEATH OF THE ROMANTIC NOTION

For over 100 years the game of baseball has defined the very nature of America. No matter what transpired outside its lines, the game moved along the shifting pulse of a country embattled inside and out.

There was once a great romantic notion to all things, as naive as that might have been—film, music, art, marriage, graduation, and the lazy Sunday afternoon had a certain Norman Rockwell flair that has been abandoned for many reasons, both good and bad. For the first time in its span baseball has not adjusted. It is, after all, a game of mystique. It has preserved its heroes and heritage more than most institutions, but has, at crucial times, become a slave to it. The image of the game endures while the reality slips away with the ticking minutes.

Cole Porter and the trolley have given way to Marylin Manson and the Internet, but the charm of baseball is still its warmth. This has been a blessed hindrance that no modern convenience can wipe away.

CRACKS IN THE DAM

Baseball's allure has waned because it has ignored the beauty while enhancing the glitz. Sure the game needed to update its play-off format and try scheduling tweaks, but these changes are tantamount to placing a Band-Aid on a gaping wound.

There are more post-season games now, but due to the late-night starting times people are expected to stay awake until well after midnight to witness the conclusions. Last season's exciting final game of the World Series was pushing 1:00 am by the time it was decided. Most viewers were likely long asleep by then.

That is just one of the many examples of how MLB has ignored its fan base and the future of it. This is especially true of the children. Baseball was built on imagination and hero worship. Two generations removed from the day when kids brought their radios into classrooms to catch Don Larson's perfect game, baseball has lost its hold on the youth of America.

Today players charge for autographs—if they even give them at all. The crowds are more boisterous and crude than ever—busy throwing expletives and bottles, and beating the hell out of each other.

THE CURE

The pro game should police its public relations and image, perhaps reach down to the little leagues and instructional outlets the way basketball and the growing soccer contingent do.

Those who run "The Show" should also spend more time concerning themselves with the quality of play and not the quantity of players and teams. More product does not necessarily translate into a better one. Fundamentals, developed skills, and a respect for the game should be stressed among the players, and a respect for the fan should be remembered by ownership.

Hustle and pride are things to be displayed without debate, and the occasional double-header and an increase in day games couldn't hurt.

Those who see the holes in the ship should be more dedicated to filling them. They can start by electing a real commissioner and send "conflict of interest boy" Bud Selig back to Beertown. Perhaps go as far as cleaning up the umpire and player unions. Remind the power-mad warring factions that the great gravy train has only a few more stops before reaching the graveyard, and now is the time for some solidarity and reason.

The owners should share the wealth on television revenue and the many perks only found in media capitals like New York, Los Angeles, and Chicago. However, places that cannot support a team should not bring the rest of the game to its knees like they did in '94. Sometimes the corner hamburger shop can't duke it out with the big chain boys, so they've simply got to go. MLB is a business, no matter what the government chooses to deem it.

The players should thank their blessings that they have a place to display their wares. It is a privilege, not a right, to play the grand game for the big bucks. No one pays the most talented entertainer for performing in their basement. It is true that the big leaguer is both employee and product, but their audience must be given the respect and notice it deserves or it could easily find somewhere else to turn for its sports entertainment.

The game of baseball is still the ballet and the tussle all at once. It is a place to go, not an event to attend. It possesses an elegance and nobility not found in the instant thrill of other sports. The game is about tension and rivalry, thunder and silence, rapture and devastation. It is a buildup of varying plot-lines like a grand novel. Currently, it is being trampled on by the obstinate myopia and apathetic arrogance of its authors.

As long as the memory of Bobby Thompson's "Shot Heard 'Round the World" and Lou Gehrig's "Luckiest Man Alive" speech echoes, there is room for baseball. As long as there is dirt and grass and the beauty of spring eternal, there is a place for the glorious game.

It is all too true there are ominous clouds setting in for the duration, and unless the games' weathermen shift the wind, it will bring a hard rain they will not be able to assuage.

The following letter was written on the day baseball died. Wednesday, September 14, 1994, at 3:30 p.m.—as acting commissioner, Bud Selig addressed a nation a baseball fans with a smoking gun in his hand. It was subsequently faxed to his offices in Milwaukee every hour on the hour until Friday evening, Sept. 16 at 5:00 p.m.

Dear Bud,

Congratulations.
    It is certainly an impressive feat for an insignificant peon such as yourself to spearhead a

crusade which has brought the 125-year treasure, the
national pastime, and a multi-billion dollar industry to its knees. To think that four short years ago
no baseball fan could pick your face out of a police
lineup, and now you join the ranks of America's most
notorious.

You have gone from owning a cheap third-rate sports
franchise in a city whose biggest contribution to mankind
is brewing cheap beer and slaughtering the tribes of Native Americans who bare its name, to joining the role call
of evil names that will forever be cursed for marring the
20th century.

You have succeeded in committing economic suicide on a healthy patient, Bud. The same way Al
Capone soiled the pride of a city, Richard Nixon
stained the presidency, Charles Manson warped the
vision of the underground movement. The same way
Robert Oppenheimer darkened the bright future of
science, you have wounded the American spirit.

Notice how I chose the word "wounded" over
"killed", or "destroyed." The reason is quite simple—
much meaner, greedier, and certainly tougher men
than you have tried to destroy this great game, so
you don't even make the repulsive cut. No, Major
League Baseball has been run by an endless parade of
human debris which rivals the ledger of German politics since the turn of the century. You, and your
minions, are a mutation Bud, nothing but an amalgam-
ation of bloated greed heads, racists, foul-mouthed
drunkards, diseased gamblers, and back-stabbing li-
ars who have sold men against their will to make a
buck under some atavistic antitrust exemption law
which reduces the Bill of Rights to a bastardized
punch line in American history.

You know about history don't you, Bud? Or has
it been that long since you emerged from the hollowed
halls of the University of Wisconsin-Madison as a
history-political science major. That's what boggles
those of us in the know, Bud. The fact that you would
be so witless as to attempt to dirty your hands with
this nasty business of union-busting by pulling the

strings of that fathead, Richard Ravitch. Even you must have tossed and turned some nights wondering if that brute would try something violent and stupid, landing you in the east end of Giants Stadium buried next to Jimmy Hoffa.

Those of us who've been paying attention came to the realization years ago that this "lockout" of yours has been a coup d'etat in the truest sense of the word. First you colluded with the other morons who own teams in cities where baseball sits behind Monster Truck Rallies for the recreational dollar. Then you perpetrated that little act of illegal she-nanigans which kept the San Francisco Giants from moving to Tampa, Florida so big shot Peter O'Malley would keep his Giants/Dodgers rivalry, and more importantly, his big mouth shut. Followed closely by the systematic booting of commissioner, Fay Vincent, who did everything but finger this charade in the press before he was sent packing. (And I won't even mention the deal which had to be struck with George Steinbrenner for his silence in return for an early escape from his messy suspension. Because, let's face it; Big George would sooner swallow a tripwire explosive devise that share his hard-earned Yankees television revenue with the owners of the Seattle Mariners.)

Don't think anyone's forgotten that this in-sipid SALARY CAP idea has been sitting on some mouthpiece's desk for close to two years now. Not all of us are anesthetized by award shows, Oprah, O.J., and infomercials. And not all of us take Rush Limbaugh seriously. We've been paying attention, Bud. And I promise you that we'll pass this information on to future generations, so one day the very name Selig will conjure up insult somewhere.

When the majority of the populace realizes what it is you and your band of cronies are trying to pull, when they realize how corrupt it is to try and set a limit to what an American worker has a right to make in the open market; when they start to peruse their baseball history and see that this is just another ridiculous attempt for the owners to horde the loot taken from their pockets, your place will be duly noted.

If you've been trying to drive your Studebaker in the fast lane, if you've been selling burgers next to McDonald's, if you're stuck with a hunting knife in the war of big business, then take your tail, place it between your crooked legs, and get out.

In conclusion Bud, I just want to tell you that this is nothing personal. "Get what you can," I always say. I'm 32 years old. I've had a childhood with baseball. My team won. My heroes came through. My relationship with my Dad was built in the upper deck of Yankee Stadium a long time ago. I write this because of the kids, my kid someday. I blame you for robbing them of this Summer, this October, this lost World Series.

I could not care less about millionaire ball players, or sanctimonious owners who've been granted a legal monopoly and still manage to close the store. But every now and then freedom is threatened for the sake of a buck, and that rabid dog must be leashed.

I blame you, Bud. And if there is any justice at all, I hope when your number comes up and there's an impasse on your destiny, the deciding factor is the Summer of '94.

It's time to dust off that college degree of yours, Bud. Time to find that history book from freshman year. Time for you and the other 27 owners to locate a copy of the Constitution of the United States. The original is in a case in Washington resting on the bones of your past brethren who tried to ignore it, but eventually found it had longer shelf life than any of them; longer even than any game. You sold your soul to rock n' roll, Bud. I hope for your sake, it was worth it.

jc

5/12/98

WILD DAYS IN A VIAGRA HAZE

We arrived at Denny's at around 4:00 p.m.. Willie had started drinking long before then. I met him around dusk and he already had that unusual glow about him. "God, what the hell are you on, Ecstasy?" I queried. "Nah, that's for pussies," he hissed, waving his hand around like a magician trying to distract from his next move. "Three hundred milligrams of Viagra man! I gotta hard-on that could slice diamonds." His pupils widened as his speech heightened. It was like watching Lon Chaney Jr. attempting to hold back the pulsing black hairs from his face. Although it was hard to believe even a werewolf could claw a hole in table cloth so completely.

"Where the hell is the waitress in this racist joint?!" he bellowed.

"Three hundred milligrams?" I asked him politely, not wanting to aggravate him further.

"Yeah, want some?"

"Are you impotent?"

"Fuck you."

"I'm getting an ambulance."

"Goin' to a party baby!" he screamed. I could tell immediately he had little use for minor details like doctor's orders, and what can you really say to a frothing psycho who starts experimenting with prescription drugs that have been on the market less than a month?

Then the poor innocent waitress made the crucial mistake of interrupting to take our order.

"Where are all the black folk in here?" Willie asked her.

"Excuse me?"

"African Americans, bitch!"

"I don't have to take this abuse," she snapped, storming off mumbling something about managers.

"Get a grip, she looks pissed," I said with some urgency.

"We gotta Viagra party thing goin' down off forty-sixth, you in?" he continued, hardly noticing the expedient approach of the skinny gentleman dressed shoddily in a white coffee-stained dress shirt and a ravaged blue tie dangling loosely from his neck.

"I think you had better leave," the gentleman began innocently enough. Then Willie started climbing on top of the table and cleared his throat as if he were going to address the masses. "What is wrong with this man?" the gentleman asked me.

"He's out of his mind with erection," I explained.

"What?" he responded without taking his eyes off Willie.

"I wouldn't agitate him any further, don't you read the papers?" I said. "Viagra is potent at one hundred milligrams, but this lunatic has swallowed the mother load, and right after he starts seeing blue he will find it necessary to trash this place. So if I were you I'd diversify the races in here before we're all sorry."

The gentleman adjusted his tie and backed away from the developing incident, his stare fixed on Willie, who was now using his cupped hands as a makeshift bullhorn to get his twisted racial protest across. To the relief of everyone within earshot, the police arrived around 5:00 p.m..

Before Willie was dragged away, he'd sufficiently demonstrated that any drug which would get Bob Dole hot would drive a young man into the kind of bloodcurdling frenzy no waitress would say was worth seeing when all you wanted was the goddamn order and a two dollar tip. But most importantly, Willie proved that a man half out of his mind on Viagra, sweating profusely with a raging hard-on and jabbering on about the lack of color in a major restaurant chain—in the company of a desperate journalist with a relentless deadline—constitutes a current event.

5/19/98

FROM REVOLUTION TO RESURRECTION

F. Scott Fitzgerald once mused that their are no second acts in America. Of course Scottie was quite the scribe and could hold his liquor like no man roaring through the 20s', but he knew nothing of politics. Threats be damned, some 70+ years later the comeback rate for civil servants is booming. No better example is one Newt Gingrich, lord of Capitol Hill, and the nation's golden boy only four short years ago, whose *revolution* halted a half century of democratic rule in Congress and had the President of the United States scrambling like a pickpocket at an NRA convention. Lean years followed with a downward spiral toward the discount bin, while Big Bill rode the crest of a

booming economy with the smirk of a martyr. The wave had all but buried him.
Not so fast.

The dead speak in Washington. It happens everyday. Anyone who
has been there for even five minutes knows it. Inside the Beltway Lazarus
would have to take a ticket and slink to the back of the line. Newt Gingrich,
shoved into the rear just two summers ago while the GOP was dulling its edges
and lifting the collective face in order to ramrod Bob Dole into autumn, now
rises like the legendary phoenix. Narrowly avoiding the boot, and writhing in
the stench of inevitable backlash from nasty allegations and incredibly bad
press, he is not only hankering for a scrap, but warming up for the big prize.

Word out of New Hampshire is that Gingrich was sharpening his fangs
for a dog fight to remain the Grand Pooba of Congress with his full frontal
assault on the present administration. His diatribe sounded more like a rabid
snarl for meat than a nostalgic skip down memory lane. The right people will
tell you that only a man with his eyes on the White House has such a bark.

Not even a fear pimp like Gingrich could hope to equal his fanfare of
'94, ripe with steep promises and some flaccid "Contract With America" which
has been broken into pieces on the flimsy facade of image. No, the Newt Boy
has other plans for his comeback. Most of the returning record freshman —
the backbone for the takeover — will survive Clinton's popularity following
this rambling bungle of an investigation being conducted by that lightweight
Ken Starr. So when the dust settles this November Gingrich will still keep his
old gig, but by that time the seat will seem like a cramped spot in coach compared to the first class ride along the campaign trail. This is, after all, Elvis in
'68, Ali at the Garden, and Nixon off the carpet; a hell-fest of strong language
and brash statements flung from the deep grudge. Mark your calendars and
strike up the band: Newt Gingrich has begun running for president.

It's a done deal. The Republicans need a new pit bull. Pat Buchanan
will dust off his rumble-act soon, but with the snub in San Diego at the convention in August of '96 serving as the "last straw", he will likely abandon the
party ship for an independent run. Gingrich was also bumped from a prime
time network spot, but at least he got in the building. He is presently the GOP's
answer to Buchanan-Lite, and whether the silent right-wing softies like it or
not, the recycled Newt Gingrich is growing in Pat's horrible wake.

Let the gallery be forewarned; the Speaker of the House has slammed
on the retreat brakes and cranked the engines into overdrive. His days at the
gavel are numbered now that the president is bleeding from every pore. They
said it couldn't be done. Houdini scoffed at such nonsense. Newt laughs out
loud. At dusk, if you are quiet, you can hear him.

NUKE JUNCTION

For the first time since Harry Truman decided to test the parameters of Oppenheimer's great experiment by ending "the war to end all wars" there is a threat of real nuclear damage beyond even the most doom-sayer, granola-addled, peace-pusher's worst Kumbaya nightmare. What has been escalating between India and Pakistan for the past few months can only be described as "bad" by any chicken-little standards, and if the might of the 20th century's most heinous mistake can rest in the hands of the desperate and hate-fueled mere yards away from brutal hand-to-hand killing, then the whole thing makes the infamous Cuban Missile Crisis look like a debutante slap fight.

It is difficult for those who swim in the luxuries of freedom and relative safety to fully comprehend the immeasurable depths of hatred that exists between cultures, faiths, and politics on the other side of the globe. It has been two years since I spent some time in the Middle East and left with paradoxical memories of tense beauty that is still disturbingly vivid. To compare the evening news video with the fear reflected in the eyes of a young girl trapped in Bethlehem on the border of Palestine mere weeks after clay bombs rendered a Jerusalem city bus to melted char, and days after rankled IDF soldiers secured the barbed wire fences outside her backyard, is futile. But an attempt at studying the motives behind India and Pakistan's long running blood feud is far more ludicrous, and wholly dangerous.

My brother, a hardworking, God-fearing American capitalist non parallel, having just returned from India ten months ago, was so appalled at the level of poverty and deranged behavior of the region's inhabitants that he could not sufficiently forward the details of his stay without the proper medication. He is no dummy: a first class engineer, well-versed in current events, and yet, he was truly frightened. This raised my awareness of the area and the potential for the unlikely occasion that such a people, unable to feed the bloated numbers of starving, would spend money and time flexing their muscle so close to the 450 warheads buried in the Chinese landscape. The minute India began overtly testing their nuclear arsenal in May the red flag had to be up in all-points-reason, not to mention the raised ire of the already seething Pakistani government which ignored the threat of world sanctions to start testing the parameters of the carnage age as a knee-jerk return lob to their despised neighbor's display of machismo.

Iran and Iraq is a tea party now; a second-rate, five & dime whiz bang of a blip on the ass of this horrible development. Not even Hussein's babbling psycho-rhetoric can rival the impoverished and enraged populace due East. When angry Muslims, sitting on billions in crude oil, start pouting, there is still common ground in God and cash. But it is bush league rage in comparison to a savage religious brawl between nations on the brink of giving in to the "what do we have to lose" sweepstakes. It is cultural suicide of the first order and a periscope to the apocalypse for the big daddy Jehovah Witness who will be knocking on your door with more than a pamphlet and a bemused smile when the glow starts seeping across the African plains and dances on the blue Atlantic.

6/3/98

SELECTIVE PATRIOTISM

"Thomas Jefferson said, and I think rather eloquently, that 'every American should have a gun.'"
- Charlton Heston

So puffed the newly appointed president of the Nation Rifle Association in the midst of making the talk show circuit a couple of weeks ago, which coincidentally paralleled the organization's big convention in the city of brotherly love. The man best known for Biblical bombast and taking the limits of overacting to toxic levels has been pulled from mothballs in order to bring a new face to the NRA's otherwise controversial public image. The crusaders of the Constitution's second amendment have decided that they have been going about this weapons love-in all wrong. Instead of hammering away at the sensibilities of the American people with hard-ass old Southern guys attempting to wax poetic about hunting and self-defense, they have gone the route of shmaltz.

The state of its wounded public relations is important to the boys at the NRA. Last year they elected a woman by the name of Marion Hammer and watched their female ranks swell. A joint organization, the National Shooting Sports Foundation, is run entirely by and for women. It's coordinator, Jodi DeCamillo hopes through a newly created outreach program called *Step Outside* that the numbers will continue to rise. Having attacked the notion that they are just a "good old boys" network, the NRA now turns its sights to the Hollywood elite with an ancient right-wing mouth like Charlton Heston.

It has not been a good year for the NRA. What with the increase in teens and toddlers loading daddy's piece and opening fire during first period, whirlwind promotion sweeps by wildlife kill-freaks like Ted Nugent, the endless parade of racist mutants running around the back wash of Texas and Alabama, and the Phil Hartman murder, in which his wife—wired on cocaine and boozed to the gills—shot him in the face and took her own life with a pistol Hartman bought her for an anniversary gift.

Changing the NRA's image is now left up to Heston. But as evidenced by the opening quote, and most of the inane babble Chuck regurgitated again and again for whomever would listen, the plan could transform from the dangerous to the bizarre. Heston is fried. His atavistic, almost sickeningly pretentious, delivery and morbid rants are eerie. The more he implores the uneducated that it's the lack of prisons and executions and not guns that has the crime rate soaring, the more he sounds and looks like a methedone-soaked Bela Lagosi trying to legitimize a pathetic Ed Wood 50s' flick. When Heston starts quoting one of this country's finest minds he is conveniently ignoring the fact that Thomas Jefferson was busy reminding everyone that they should also have two or three good slaves to go along with those guns.

Everyone hates to be unprotected, most of us like the Constitution, and although militias have been out of vogue for nearly two centuries, it is the right of the people to protect itself from itself and its government. But these were the sentiments of a long-gone age of fractured rebels still leery about any official language that would have them hightailing it further westward. Some would have us believe we live in a similar era, with the same insatiable cry for fractured freedoms and less government. But that is a bargain-basement sale on fear the rest of us are not buying.

Of course, most paradoxical twist to the NRA's choice of Heston is that Chuck, although a reigning authority on the unwavering might of the Constitution's 2nd Amendment, spent the last few years threatening, and then pulling his considerable stock concerns from Warner Bros. to protest the release of Ice T records, completely ignoring the document's 1st Amendment along his merry way.

6/10/98

BIG BILL TO CHINA: A QUESTION OF DIPLOMACY OR PROFIT?

> *"The present policy subjugates human rights*
> *and national security for trade interests."*
>   - Senator Tim Hutchinson of Arkansas

> *"No shit."*
>   - An Unnamed Source at the White House

The President of the United States' visit to China in the shadow of allegations on whether his current administration sold out to an American company which provided the Chinese with more toys to escalate their already bloating nuclear arsenal has the pundits and riled talking heads emerging from their coves for a magnification of that country's considerable crime record. Not to mention the recent wig-out of the Pakistani government backed with muscle from the Red Menace and the annual furor over the rape of Tibet. This has stirred the pot on the age-old question of what to do about an abusive power and its place in the heart of our government.

Due to attend a welcoming ceremony in Tiananmen Square, where the massacre of pro-democracy demonstrators nine years ago was spread to the world through news footage of young people being run down by government tanks, Bill Clinton is getting the expected backlash once reserved for Ronald Reagan when he attended a funeral ceremony mere yards from the burial place of Nazis in Bitzberg, Germany. Reagan, whose penchant for song-and-dance showmanship puts even a master like Big Bill in the second class, ran a story of "peace through healing" up the PR flagpole. And while addressing this issue of having political brunch with monsters, so has the current President.

Isolationism is a nasty word that was shoved back into the bleary world of history books with such blockbusters as *Manifest Destiny* and *Passive Aggressiveness*. As long as the United States is the leading power on the side of democracy then it is on the side of free enterprise and the almighty dollar. The fall of Communism in Russia had less to do with missiles and Ronnie Reagan's shoot-from-the hip John Wayne rhetoric than it did with a shrinking marketplace. Communism failed, as most political ideologies do, because there was no money in it. Unlike the former Soviet Union, China's present human rights horror show is relegated to within its borders. In other words there has been no attempt by the Chinese to expand their power beyond its immediate borders. So China's forced abortions and suppression of basic freedoms appears fine and dandy with us.

What is presently going on in China is comparable to most atrocities being committed around the world by oppressive governments with less geopolitical swagger. With 22% of the world's population, a devaluation of its currency, its reuniting with tourist hot-spot Hong Kong, and the load of American companies interested in exploiting its starving market and cheap production, Big Bill has no choice but to get off Air Force One, skip into Tianannmen Square, and start up his mutual admiration spiel before he is swallowed by the machine which bore him.

The reality of Clinton's trip is simple, and has been regurgitated by nearly every president this century, from FDR's lean on Japan to get this country into a World War and out of a Great Depression, to the assassination of Jack Kennedy to allow the Pentagon to play footsies with helicopter manufacturers, to George Bush's prostration to petroleum concerns with his silly "Desert Storm." When diplomacy suits our fiscal landscape then it's smiles and handshakes. When all-out war can grease the cash engine, then its wave Old Glory and send in the dupes. Richard Nixon sipped tea with Mao Tse Tung while he engineered the massacre of thousands of innocent people by "bombing Cambodia back to the dark ages." He sat by and listened to the numbers of young Americans being shipped back in canisters while opening the Far East to recover from a Recession.

Twenty-six years later Big Bill follows those footsteps. He will not be the last.

6/17/98

ANYWHERE BUT HERE

Steve Jorgensen is missing. This may not mean a thing to you, but he was my friend. Not really a friend, more like an acquaintance, a contemporary of sorts; someone who you may look at from across a candlelit table and whisper, "there for the grace of God go I." And when he doesn't quite hear you over the din of the jukebox and the giggling women at the next table, you say, "Nothing, I was thinking aloud." A few months later you get a phone call from another friend who tells you that Steve quit his 70 grand-a-year advertising gig, hopped in his economy roadster, and headed for Fahnestock Park somewhere up the Taconic Parkway. It is there he exited and never returned. He didn't bother shutting the door; ending a determined trip to "anywhere but here" in the grand style of Henry David Thoreau, or perhaps, Jim Morrison.

Strange memories of three men; Mr. Jorgensen, a stoic, but humored Asian fellow named Phil, and myself, closing every bar in Putnam County New York on a mission to blot out the mental demons. Phil, the CO-producer of an independent film I'd been asked by another friend to help pen, and Steve had just wrapped a 3-second scene that had taken two hours to complete. A lifetime in a mosquito-infested swamp beneath the oppressive heat of a June night. We had come for revelry. There was no mistaking it from the look on Steve's face when he slammed his open hand on the table and demanded a pitcher of something. For the rest of the excursion he threw around cash like a dying man having just realized he'd hit the lotto by default; a magnanimous Elvis-after-dark rampage which had half the place toasting him like the denouement of some Viking flick. It was the last time I saw him.

When the detective assigned to his case asked me to describe the evening I had no definitive answer. Sure Steve was lost, but aren't we all? His story was all-too ordinary. One day you're a struggling actor with an indefinable cause and a cute young girlfriend who thinks she might have bagged the young DeNiro, and next you're a 41 year-old "loser" with nothing to provide but stale routines and a paltry check. I can remember even now Phil expounding on the Steve's "loser" comment with sad-sack stories of women he'd met who thought it better to ask his current salary than his penis size. Very troubling news at 2:30 am.

Phil was goofy — and maybe half-right in the foggy twilight of revisionist thought — but that night, when Steve reminisced, he seemed to be flirting with doom. You were left wondering why a man might worm his way into a higher tax bracket in order to ignore a fleeting dream and allay his fears of impoverished loneliness. As the drinks flowed Steve had serious, almost disturbing, questions about the purpose of survival, love, and keeping the home-fires burning. This, he'd decided, was not the plan. He was standing in the shoes of some other poor sucker who he'd passed on the way up some invisible ladder. He'd chosen a place on the couch next to his beloved in the warm light of convenience, lying somewhere between the Baby-Boomer thrust and the Gen X squeeze, where the fractured few struggle to hide the scars of circumstance.

It is the first sign of secession from society when a singular voice tells you it's time to check out—not some attention-starved suicide binge—but something far more permanent in this wandering trip we call life. Steve Jorgensen heard that voice. I have heard that voice; comes and goes like an annoying jingle when the uncomfortable silence becomes an unbearable symphony. The only difference is Steve Jorgensen heeded its message and quit what he'd eventually deemed "the charade." He became a stranger to himself and needed a vacation. The thing about humans is we're far more fragile then we let on. Six years from now I might take my Suzuki for a ride up the parkway for a vacation from myself.

It has been three weeks, and no one who's paid to know has any idea where Steve Jorgensen might be. Anywhere but here.

6/24/98

DAMNED GOOD YANKEES

Having spent some time in baseball clubhouses for the past nine years it was still a pleasant surprise to enter the domain of the best team in baseball a few hours before it would take the field against the New York Mets in the Major League's second foray into Subway Series baseball. That evening the New York Yankees were not only a mind-bending 53-19 and sitting atop the Eastern Division of the American league by 10 games, but to date there had only been two teams this century with a better run through their first 72 games. The 1998 version of the once legendary Murderers Row has not only run rough shod over the entire landscape of the game, but in doing so has not boasted a single ego-inflated, overpriced superstar in the bunch.

The minute one comes in contact with the Yankees it is easy to see in its collective demeanor how the rest of baseball has found it close to impossible to topple. Patience at the plate, awareness in the field, and an uncanny ability to find the weakness in a foe and exploit it, has turned a mortal baseball team into a machine; the hardball equivalent of Sherman's Army plowing down the coast line and leaving burning cities in its wake.

The manager, a soft spoken Brooklynite named Joe Torre, has a penchant for answering the odd second guess with a crooked smile straight from central casting. He has owned the Big Apple since his '96 edition took the World Series and returned the fabled franchise to the pinnacle of the game. Torre returned my query on the assumption the Yanks will win every time he sits on the bench by stating that it is not the so much assumption than expectation. "We always expect to win," he smirked. "Luckily this year it has happened more than not."

Of course, a baseball lifer like Torre even raises his eyebrows when the outlandish numbers his team has compiled is read back to him. By the last week in June the Yanks were in the top ten in every offensive and pitching category imaginable. Yet a week later the American League would announce that none of its players would start on the All-Star team, although six would eventually be selected as reserves.

The lineup, pitching staff, and the game's most stacked bench—assembled in the rarefied air of owner, George Steinberenner's wallet—exudes the same *Terminator* philosophy as their skipper. To watch them in the field is to watch the smooth, equal parts of a fantastic whole. The first baseman, Tino Martinez starts most conversations with a simple, "Sure." The catcher, Joe Girardi has spend the first half of this historical season by training the very man who will take his job, Jorge Posada. The left fielder is a three-headed monster made up of one part fallen young-stud jock, Darryl Strawberry, one part, player with the third most steals in league history, Tim Raines, and a dab of scrappy journeyman, Chad Curtis, who on this night was filling in for the team's best player, a reserved intellectual jazz guitarist called Bernie Williams, whom I had the pleasure of meeting the day he stepped off the minor league bus and has not changed a bit.

When the game was over the Yanks had number 54 in the books on right fielder, Paul O'Neill's three run homer in the seventh. Less than an hour later he slipped on his jeans and answered every question politely before making sure everybody was ready for the departing bus to the Bronx. Derek Jeter, having just turned 24 that night, is the new young darling of New York sporting life, and the prime example of this club's cool confidence. Fresh from his breakup with diva deluxe, Mariah Carey, Jeter sat at his locker amid a cluster of balloons, flowers and stuffed animals and smiled. "I don't get it."

"All this attention on your birthday? Or 53 wins in 73 tries?" I asked.

"Oh, the 53 wins I get," he answered, looking up. Then a million dollar smile creased his face. And with tongue firmly jammed into cheek, he hummed, "We gooood."

Fear No Art

7/1/98

THE SELLING OF DOOMSDAY

"To what shall we compare our miscalculations about divine providence?"
- Soren Kierkegaard

It is the immutable right of every generation to believe that it will be the last. This is especially prevalent so close to the change in millenniums. One thousand years ago people were so silly with apocalyptic visions of a world so blatantly screwed up and irrevocably evil that the idea of an all-out slate-cleaning was not only expected, but welcomed. Now that we've evolved from the dark ages and have some basic understanding of the tangible universe to which we precariously cling, it has suddenly become fashionable again to postulate scenarios in which we are inadvertently headed for ultimate disaster. And there seems to be a veracious need to dole them out in neatly wrapped packages of doom.

A solid hour scouring the Internet for signs of the final days here on planet panic could have you quitting that otherwise innocuous job of yours, unloading all your meaningless wares, and swan diving off the nearest bridge extension. Those enamored with weather signals will be glad to tell you that one sniff of El Nino, volcano activity in the Virgin Islands, and the recent glut of tropical squalls is tantamount to the two-minute warning. Hollywood has taken the dollar sign bell and rung it to the tune of endless tales of irate aliens, careening super-meteors, and freaks of nature stomping through major cities. And this is all just scratching the surface of deep-rooted cries for repentance available daily from spiritual crackpots, fear-sucking television preachers, and the district manufacturers of the final hour; organized religion.

These are the salesman of guilt who peddle the silent mass suicide dream of those afraid of the final score: Earth: (having its ass kicked for centuries by human apathy) Y2K - Humanity: (busy with video games and pornography) 0. It is the Super Bowl of retribution which peaks our interests. The Final Judgment set to music and special effects.

Have we become so completely sick of ourselves that we must scrape the bottom of psychology's barrel for the answer to questions better left dormant by minds best used wrestling with tonight's dinner menu? Are we afraid to admit that we are nothing better than our minuscule eight percent of brain matter can comprehend? Maybe we're just steering our minds from the real truth: We are jealous.

We will never get to see peace and harmony in our time. We will never live in Nirvana or Heaven here on this miserable rock which spins lonely around an indifferent sun. So we invent the obvious solution; end the charade that is us. That is the raging human ego solution. Because, after all, what could be better than what we have built? After all, haven't we scaled the heights? What could our collective genius have missed? We must be failures; wounded boxers hanging onto consciousness and painfully waiting for the final blow to put us out of the misery of mediocre rational thought, confusing art, pompous science, inadequate medicine, and evil computer quirks. Nothing but supernatural omnipotence or the vengeful backslap of karma could save us from the pain of existence.

Of course, nothing could be further from the truth. The idea of incessantly mulling over the violent culmination of a life ignored is asinine and petty. We should be better than that. Everyday is upon us. Life is happening. We should rely on our ability to grasp the moments which prove we are all here in the same life raft and stop trying to invent cruise liners that will swoop in and rescue us, or fear the impending tidal waves poised to wipe us out.

Certainly, it is entertaining, even comforting, to put the final onus on someone or something else; but the track record points to you and me exiting stage left with no idea what, if any, the next act will be. This obsession with piecing together a plot that fits our fears is lunacy. And those who profit from, or perpetuate, it should spend more time living than waiting to become fossil elements.

In the meantime, put down your last will and testament, eat some broccoli, take a long breath of fresh air, hug a friend, be nice to children and those less fortunate than yourself, crank up some Beethoven, have a fucking beer, and chill out.

7/8/98

MEDIA ON TRIAL - CHECKS, BALANCES, & RELIABLE SOURCES VS. SPEED & SENSATIONALISM

A few weeks ago CNN and Time magazine ran what turned out to be a bogus story that US troops used sarin nerve gas to kill defectors in the Secret Operation Tailwind in Laos, Viet Nam in 1970. Time repudiated the report, but this was a CNN gig from jump street. Consequently, producers were sacked and heads rolled behind the scenes of the Ted Turner run cable network, except, predictably, for high profile Pulitzer Prize-winning Peter Arnett, who claimed everything from "coming in at the end" to "not contributing one comma to the story." Arnett comes off like a pompous drone who is happy when lifted above vacuous talking-head status, but when his credibility is questioned hides behind some lame "I'm just the guy who reads this shit" excuse. And yet he is only one symptom of a growing problem in hard-facts reporting.

This whole thing is sad for many reasons, not the least of which is that it scored one for the Pentagon, which has been bullwhipped by the media for three decades far more egregious crimes against humanity in the jungles of South East Asia. Another, more pressing reason, is that this type of half-assed reporting has become more prevalent today than ever, making it harder for genuine investigative reports to receive serious consideration. Could the exemplary job Woodward and Bernstein did in uncovering the Watergate scandal be repeated in the wake of today's media mishaps?

According to a recent Newsweek poll 53% of Americans don't believe a damn thing they see on nightly news programs. This is the result of more than a wrong signal, or a quick slip of the TelePrompTer like Harry Truman holding up a headline stating he would lose the presidential race 24 hours after locking it up or Dan Rather telling the world that Ronald Reagan was dead after he had survived an assassination attempt. Lately the art of reporting has fully devolved from exposure of pertinent events to quick-fix entertainment.

The landscape of news reporting has changed drastically in the past 20 years with the advent of cable networks running 24 hour updates, the rise in Internet information, the decline in ratings for the network evening news, and plummeting newspaper sales. The time it takes for a responsible journalistic approach to a breaking story has tightened considerably, and as a result, the veracity of the reporting has suffered. The competition to rush the latest word in breaking stories has turned the profession into a quagmire of guess work formally left on the speculation cutting floor. Now the 'round-the-clock blitz-krieg of sound bites and over-analysis has taken the place of tough, honest reporting.

Enter the O.J. Simpson trial, which forever heightened our appetite for immediate info gratification. When it was over hundreds of media jobs were left idle and hordes of insatiable viewers feeling empty. A cottage industry from Geraldo to these insipid "expert" gabfests peppered throughout Cableland needed something to spotlight, whether there was fire behind all that smoke or not. It is ironic that CNN, the genesis of this *need to know immediately and anywhere on the planet it happens* frenzy, is now the focal point of the public's derision. But who will be next? The entire industry took a hit over the botched coverage of the Olympic Village bomb explosion in Atlanta two years ago when the public hanging of the innocent Richard Jewel had more than one news source apologizing, and in some cases, defending itself in court.

Alarming reports of fabricated stories by The New Republic, manufactured quotes by a Boston Globe columnist, and this latest CNN/Time fiasco have further lowered the wounded competence curve. The lines have always been blurred between hard news and entertainment. Television, radio, and the print medium is in the business of making a profit, but should truth be a casualty in the battle for our fickle attention?

7/15/98

SWING TOWN

The cab pulls up to the curb spraying water onto the carpet leading into the club. The rain has come and gone and it is one of those Manhattan evenings that make you wonder why any human would want to be too far from this island. The echoes up 8th avenue bounce off the awnings and the windows steam with the tepid breeze. Saturday night burns in the Village, and on the Upper East side the pubs are jacked with vampires. But in Mid Town the heels never touch pavement, floating into the Supper Club around 1:00 am. Boogie time.

The lobby breathes with swarming youth; baggy pants, suspenders, and loud hats with feathers. Fourth generation flappers and droopy-eyed bugle boys cueing up behind skinny ties and rising skirts. The groove seeps through the curtains past the high desk out front. I slap down my 12 dollars, another 12 for the beautiful woman who dared to tread the tight rope with me, and before long the hall opens like parting clouds in the wake of an airplane's ascent. And the music; it rips, cuts, hammers the floorboards where the kids stomp and sweat — spinning and flipping and devouring the night with dance. It is a passion lost on troubled days of staring at the walls waiting for the disco rhythms to save the biz.

Somewhere between the frost of late February and the stifling heat of the summer of '98 the clocks have been yanked back to the Big Band boom of the war years when the US of A was riding several simultaneous crests and the sound of brass and double bass raised the blood of Times Square. Swing is back. The Bebop cools slinking through the shadows of the past, tan deep in the sunlight of resurgence. Where do they come from? How do they move like that? The band is barely in their twenties. Most of the people flirt with three generations. They are all on common ground here. They can feel something in the air.

I grab her hand and wind through the crowd of bopping heads and snapping fingers like a faded Harlem Club film. We hit the dance floor. The lights don't move unless your eyes swing with the tremble in your step. You've got to hope your partner snags the jive and pulls back from the bodies swinging around the floor, for the tempo does not cease its relentless assault on your legs and arms, and the fire breath fights to keep in time with the music. It is not loud, but it booms. All good dance bands boom. There is no sidestep, slow dance, bullshit at the Supper Club before the dawn finish line. Resting is for the tables and the long bar out back. This space is for the long-distance trot with the pros and the hopefuls.

Not long after 2:00 a.m. the circle forms, and the real talent rises from the wood beneath our toes. A black couple pierces the cylinder. Shaking shoulders and wet arms entangle; a spin, a dive, and the slender woman is being pulled through his quivering legs. A mere precursor to things less believed. A Spanish couple follows with wide spirals and flying leaps. Great faith in the man who catches a woman twirling like a top toward the ceiling. A younger couple takes a turn and gets a hand. Finally, two tall white kids start on their knees and plunge into sexual rage, so righteous and free. The rest of us join for one last song before the band gives way to more rhythms from speakers raised on high.

"My father played here in the 50s'," my good friend Al, comedian and lover of ancient Jazz and forgotten tunes, once told me. "Couldn't get a fuckin' gig anywhere else when rock n' roll took over." Now that the jumpin' jive has made one more splash he is no longer with us. "These kids," he asks. "You think they know a goddamn thing about this music?"

Moves 'em.

7/29/98

WAR IMITATING ART - "SAVING PRIVATE RYAN" & TRUTH IN CINEMA

Once in a great while I am confronted with an art form that moves me in some way. Mostly it is short spurts of emotion from sharp kicks to my nerve endings like a note in a piece of music, a line in a poem, or some minuscule part of a grand painting, drawing, photograph, or sculpture. Very rarely does a film hit me with that kind of gut level reaction anymore. However, a strange thing happened to me on the night of July, 24 when I settled into my aisle seat to witness the new Steven Spielberg World War II epic, "Saving Private Ryan." Two hours and forty-some minutes later I had visited places of thought and provocation I'd previously disbelieved existed. A trip to the core of our worst reality; the raw fear that humanity is ripe with evil, suffering, survival, and the inevitable sting of death, all played out in mere seconds for young men on the battle field. The war which split the American Century and effected the future of civilization forever reduced to precious seconds of terror. For this alone the film is at once a triumph and a standing mockery of all that has come before it.

There have been more films made about war then any other subject. They can now be thrown into a pile and set on fire. After 10 minutes of "Saving Private Ryan" all of the rest seem like some ridiculous theories about the sun revolving around a flat earth. Spielberg, and screenwriter, Stephen Ambrose, have taken the bloody, disturbing, completely insane core of such cinematic hints as "The Deer Hunter" and "Platoon" and driven the point over the edge. War, even one necessary for the survival of humanity, is an agonizing peek into the blackest corner of hell. Truly great art will do that, can do that; and this film does it in spades.

Death and violence are as prevalent in the history of film as the obligatory close-up of the star or the happy ending. Bodies pile up in science fiction, gangster, and police movies, and none of it seems to mean a damn thing. The clean break with a character who must go is mandatory for advancing the plot and adding a little theater to the proceedings. But in the wake of "Saving Private Ryan" this must also change. After seeing any part of "Saving Private Ryan" who will take the slightest casualty for granted? When a soldier dies in this film there is no drama; just pitiful, horrifying destruction. He does not grab his chest and moan at the sky. He either falls to the ground like a lifeless rag doll or screams in shocked pain trying desperately to return parts of his massacred body to their rightful place. This senseless waste of life hits hard because the realism of each death and its murderous vengeance is not hidden by swelling music and teary-eyed buddies singing patriotic praises.

Finally, and most importantly, "Saving Private Ryan", will forever make the industry get the story right. There is no more room for embellishing fiction and silly sidelights to the already incredible realm of true history. The D-Day Invasion, for which the film takes it's dramatic lead, forever known as the single greatest sea invasion, was truly a human slaughterhouse. Tired and petrified American kids, who were sent as sacrificial lambs to lead a bold and historically altering raid, hoped to speed the conclusion of the last war to end all wars. The heroic deeds of these men were not in their fearless march up a beach to crush a faceless evil, but to succumb to or endure a chaotic crossfire of machine and hatred in a mortal combat with the apocalypse in order to ensure a way of life for people they would never know.

"Saving Private Ryan" is a brilliant film for so many other reasons, but to change the blueprint, to break the mold, to open doors, to wipe the slate clean and forge uncharted territory; this is what art aspires to. Once in a great while it can make everything different.

Y2K: RECIPE FOR DISASTER OR FAST FOOD PARANOIA

"Woe to the inhabiters of the earth and the sea for the devil is come unto you, having great wrath, because he knoweth that he hath but a short time."
- Revelation 12:12

"We walk in the trail of the dinosaur."
- Arthur Koestler

The politics of doom have been alive and well within the human spirit since such a concept was discovered even possible. For thousands of years the fragile bond of societies have been warned of the slightest crack in their facade. Ours has been the whispers of dehumanization in the wake of technological evolution. Have we lived like kings on earth by creating machines to speed us through life and free us from the mundane? Or has this been a blissful decent into automated slavery?

The answer may come when the clock strikes midnight, signifying a new century—when the modern doomsayers say the mighty microchip will self-destruct and leave us literally in the dark.

Subscribing to the theory that, "it is always the smallest rock in the forest that trips you up, not the largest," the core of the impending problem with the omnipotent cyber world is a simple number. The stress-addled believe two lousy digits may send a generation plugged into life support skidding toward a fateful crash. The ironic twist of its origin is that the nasty glitch was placed into action to save money, time, and manpower—the very reasons the microchip and its computer children rose to such all-consuming prominence in the first place.

When computers were assembled into the everyday plan some 30 plus years ago, the programmers had to stare down astronomical costs in hardware. Space was at a premium, so in order to reduce the amount of keystrokes necessary to enter the proper year, the final two numbers had to suffice.

Say you were programming the data for a bank in 1969, to inform the computer what year it is, will be, and to give it direction to move back in time, you would type "69". This was sufficient, even genius, in its simplicity, but apparently practiced the foresight of General Custer at Little Big Horn. By the end of the millennium '99 will become '00 for the year 2,000. Any computer, no matter how complex and diverse or brilliant in its speed and efficiency, only knows what it is told. Most computers don't know a damn thing about two zeros unless they're told to shut down from some failure. Thus, when those two simple digits flip over that bank of yours may have no records of any cash being anywhere near it.

As far as the computer will be concerned it is Armageddon baby, and even some computers which do not self-destruct by reading zeros will only recognize them in context with the 20th century. Suddenly your cash, so plentiful and ripe in 1999 will magically disappear. Obviously, there was no way you could have done any banking in the year 1900, when baseball was a baby and the telephone was a luxury item for the elite. So you and your money will cease to exist.

A modern prophet by the name of Peter de Jager, for an article written in the 9/6/93 edition of *Computer World* magazine, provided this disturbing preview. "We are going to suffer a credibility crisis. We and our computers were supposed to make life easier, this was our promise. What we have delivered is a catastrophe."

Five years ago Peter was a voice in the wilderness, decrying the evils of the brave new world completely unaware of the impending screech of steel wheels grinding on the tracks. Two years later the voices numbered among the majority. Today there is no question that an alarming number of the world's computer technology will suffer a breakdown of Biblical proportions.

The U.S. Government's Accounting Office is predicting that 700 US banks may close their doors on 1/1/00 due to what those in the know have dubbed the Y2K problem. Yet, as late as last year *Business Week* magazine predicted that 20% of the banks in the world will fail to prepare for the inevitable.

The Gartner Group, the self-proclaimed world's leading authority on Information Technology, recently released the results of a poll spanning 49 countries stating that a scary 33% of 33,000 personal clients very well might close their bank accounts by the end of '99. It does not take an economic professor to conservatively pro rate those numbers and come up with a state of monumental fiscal panic.

So why aren't more of us sweating? Those shuddering on the edge of disaster describe the relatively reserved reaction thus far as a failure of the person on the street to relate to the computer world. Many people are still leery of banks handling their money despite its alluring convenience. And removing your money from a bank is a simple hop and a skip, but what of the inescapable props to modern living? A report in *CIO* Magazine claims that nearly 70% of those informed of the millennium bug are not confident that it will be fixed by the 12/99 deadline, 60% plan on investigating their banks' Y2K compliance, 50% will not fly a commercial airline on the first day of the new year, and 30% believe their jobs are in jeopardy if they are unable to prevent this automated disaster.

Many Americans still suffer from techno-phobia and could not care less how their junk works, but it is not just the disassociated computer egg-heads who will feel the savage brunt the Y2K problem. According to Dr. Leon Kippleman in a January article for *Wired News* only 10% of the 4 billion microchips manufactured in 1996 actually went into devices we think of as computers. Standards such as gas pumps, automated tellers, badge and keyboard readers, buses, ships, airplanes (including the all-important air traffic control), alarm clocks, and cable television are all included. The Chairman of the Special Committee on the Year 2,000 Problems, a government funded group, defines utilities and telecommunications as the nation's top priorities in the Y2K problem. Dozens of consumer electronic products including microwave ovens, stereo systems, televisions and VCRs are equipped with embedded microchips, most of which are expected to fall prey when the clock strikes midnight on evening of December 31, 1999.

In the grand tradition of widespread panic resulting from Orson Welles' infamous broadcast of "War of the Worlds" many dime-store geniuses have been running around their homes testing the Y2K merit of their appliances by turning the clock forward to that fateful date and time. However, many manufacturers have warned against this practice for reports of screwing with products like alarm devices have shut them down completely, and tampering with the ever-complicated VCR clocks have caused them to refuse or reject tapes and function any further. In other words, if you might have been stuck with a terminally ill microchip product you might as well live it up while you can or take the damn thing into a shop and have them yank the friggin' clock out of it.

Good luck trying to track down the right source of whatever ails you.

Thousands of software houses, network integrators, telecommunication pro-
viders, and power companies which allow you to stick that piece of plastic in
the slot for banking purposes, are spread out like a desert of red tape and black
holes. It is nearly impossible to pinpoint where the innards for the clock in your
microwave oven might have come from, even if it does tick unceasingly toward
the bitter end.

The business world, from the lofty global connection to the depths of
Wall Street, is where the real first-rate grade-A panic has set in. A study by
Real Time Engineering in the September 27, 1997 issue of *Computerweekly*
reports that "One in five embedded systems responsible for running critical
processes in power and aviation manufacturing firms will fail in the year 2,000."
The Federal Communications Commission, taking precious time away from
monitoring saucy morning disc jockeys, have stressed major concern for the
carnage that the simple loss of the dial tone will do. Chairman, William Kennard
has intimated on several occasions that many businesses will have to close
shop as a result of phone companies not ready for the calendar change. "If we
have major network outages due to the year 2,000 {and we are likely to have
them}, many small and medium-sized businesses could find themselves in dire
economic straits," Kennard warns. "Many must rely on one telecommunications carrier. So if their phone network or their data network goes out, they
have to close down. And many small businesses don't have large reserves, so
if the problem persists for a few days {and it could}, they could be out of
business."

In the dim light of all this gloom most companies have begun, if not
already finished, their pursuit of prevention. The trick is finding them. For
instance the Big 3 American automobile manufacturers; GM, Ford, and Chrysler
have assured their customers, both future and past, that none of their cars in-
corporate the date in its processes — although Chrysler is still figuring out if
this statement covers their complicated Travel System or Trip Computers.
AT&T is happy to inform you that things have reached hunky dory status in
their neck of the woods, but who is vouching for your local telephone or long
distance server?

Ask yourself the following questions: What company which serves your
needs has offered some assurance that by January of 2,000 you won't be scrambling? Did the person that sold you that slick, expensive PC inform you that it
will be worth the price of five day-old lettuce before too long? And what's the
deal with traffic lights, air traffic control, tolling, billing, e-mail, faxing, and
most importantly, hospital and medical equipment? What will these phone
jockey types do now without that monotone voice offering a myriad of numbers to connect them with a human, or at the very least, the human's answering

service? There may be no one on the line to save the day, as in the case of 911. The probable inability for that system to send out a patrol car or fire truck is down right worth the price of distrust.

Of course, prophets have been making a good buck on predicting the end long before the microchip, and let's face it, we do have months to erect some semblance of a technological ark. But if growing popular opinion is to be taken to heart, the next century may begin like some cheesy science fiction matinee from the 50s' where the machines revolt and leave us all at the mercy of nature, scrambling to remember how the hell we can get from point A to point B without them.

8/5/98

RUMBLE IN THE ARENA OR BIG BILL'S RABID DEFENSE OF HIS GNARLED LEGACY BEGINS

> *"Some have the speed and the right combinations*
> *If you can't take the punches, it don't mean a thing."*
> -Warren Zevon

Bill Clinton is fucked. Just as he was fucked in New Hampshire in the winter of '92—facing sure defeat at the hands of the grossly popular George Bush—fucked by allegations of pot smoking and draft dodging, fucked by Gennifer Flowers, Whitewater, corruptible campaign contributions, and fucked by the selling of the Lincoln bedroom like a low-grade flop house. The President of the United States has proven that he is at his best when fucked.

At the time of this writing Big Bill is still contemplating the silly notion of chucking his decade-long streak of bullshitting everyone within earshot by somehow turning the Oval Office into his own private confessional. Those close to the boss have continually denied this as being a sane option. Why would the man drag himself and the country through seven months of bad tabloid TV? And those who wish to see Bill Clinton take that Nixon helicopter off the White House lawn into ignominious oblivion forever argue that it is the way of the snake to slither at every opportunity. But outside of the rising sale of news magazines and daily papers, the glut of talk shows, and a plethora of material for comedy routines, the polls show that America wants the gravy train to roll on regardless of who's the conductor. So, assuming there ever was one beyond political vengeance, exactly what is the point of this endless charade?

Regardless of whatever fanciful jive Bill Clinton has laid on the American public in response to being yanked into court like Pee Wee Herman fresh from the porno theater circuit, the majority of us no longer give two donkey pies what sort of heinous garbage public officials are dumping as long as we are swimming in clear economic waters. And there hasn't been such clear sailing without the benefit of a major war since George Washington reluctantly agreed to give this president thing a whirl. Any poll in which you choose to subscribe will be a steady opposition to removing this president under any criminal circumstances short of murder. It stands at a healthy 62% approval rating despite 60% of Americans believing that the Commander and Chief is a cheating, sneaky, lying scumbag.

People hear semen-stained dresses, 21 year-old interns, back room meetings, and blow jobs, they will turn an ear and snicker. But people love their cars, pools, and stock options much more than some half-assed political morality play. Big Bill is sitting on fun times, and whatever percentage he claims to that party he knows that in an election year stretch drive no one in Congress, Republican or Democrat, will have the balls to impeach him if he can either deny with extreme prejudice or weep like Jimmy Swaggart.

You see Bill Clinton grew up with the same abuse of the presidency as we all did. He treats the office like a sham because it was reduced to a sham long before he took over. No one who lived through the Kennedy assassination, Watergate, the pardoning of Richard Nixon, or Reagan's Iran-Contra fiasco believes a saint can lead this nation. Jimmy Carter was as close to that as we're going to get, but with a gas crisis, nasty recession, and hostages nipping at his heels, he was ushered out of town as nothing more than a silly footnote.

After four plus years of searching for Elvis and Bigfoot in convenience stores and burger barns, Ken Starr has finally handed the brass ring to the groupie and her mom. And he will use them, and that attention-starved leach Linda Tripp, to drag down Mister Popularity with one bold stroke. Problem is that Big Bill is comfortable in the cornered animal role. Has Starr, the Supreme Court, or the 104th Congress of the United States have what it takes to meet him in that dark alley with rusty knives and broken bottles?

8/12/98

THE BALLAD OF BIG BILL

Days to go before Bill Clinton becomes the first President of the United States to testify in front of a Grand Jury. I ffind myself, once again, at the doorstep of my friend from Georgetown, who currently enjoys a better than 90% winning percentage in the landscape of political prognostication. Leaks and rumor coming from all ends has Big Bill claiming anything from covert alien attacks to a monumental bout of amnesia. I have stood by my theory that the president will continue to run the large lie up the flagpole and dare Congress to push him out the door in the face of overwhelming public support. The following is a transcript of the discussion with my Washington friend, Georgetown about other options the president may still possess short of blatant perjury.

JC - What do you think he'll do?

Georgetown - He won't lie. He won't tell the truth. He's been doing this since Gennifer Flowers, when he first denied any relations with the woman. Then he said one liaison does not make an affair. You know, the old, "Oh, that's what you're asking? Well, yeah, of course. Sorry about that." You know, he smoked pot, but not really.

JC- But how will he do it?

GT - He can go two ways here. Let's say he takes the "I didn't have sexual relations with that woman, but there was some kissy-kissy." He can pull out of perjury charges by defining his terms differently, which I expect he and David Kendall (Clinton's lawyer) will calculate. However, a back-up plan may be to refuse to answer direct questions dealing with Lewinsky, just address the main reason he's there; obstruction of justice.

JC - See that would work in the cloudy world of law, but the American people will feel cheated.

GT- The man is banking on high approval ratings and a strong economy. And let's not forget that the deposition in question was during a case (Paula Jones sexual harassment suit) which was thrown out of court.

JC - It still holds weight.

GT - Yes, but how much? Clinton's lawyers have been studying the tape for almost a week. Why? Because there is a loop hole, you betcha.

JC - Where does that leave Starr's case?

GT - After almost five years Lewinsky is Starr's only case. Whitewater is bupkus, Travelgate was a joke, Filegate, nothing. Many people either want to believe Clinton or feel he's a victim. And the majority of them don't care. This is wholly different than Nixon, who misinterpreted the public's love for him.

JC - Yes, but Nixon had the tapes. Clinton has the dress.

GT - Of course that changes the rules. If the president's semen is on that woman's dress he will have to go with plan A.

JC - The lie/truth plan.

GT - Sure. If it ain't broke don't fix it. No one has been able to crack this guy. His ability to address a group, large or small, is legendary.

JC - So lying would be best.

GT - No, not lying. Not telling the truth.

JC - You mean like O.J. not being innocent...

GT - ...but not guilty.

JC - What if he looses his mind and comes clean?

GT - Bill Clinton? Well, (long pause) if that unlikely scenario does come about he can go on the offensive and attack Starr for leaking Grand Jury information. You know, nail him on surreptitious maleficence, espionage, bullying witnesses, threatening the office of president. Then he can come clean on what this has cost the American people and assuage the shock of his lies with higher crimes against the public and its elected government like treason.

JC - That's craziness.

GT - You ain't seen nothing yet.

8/19/98

BILL CLINTON - AN APPRECIATION

By my count Bill Clinton has now surpassed Ronald Reagan for most speeches filled with monumental dog crap. His address to the nation on August 17 was, although not quite as pathetic as Ronnie's "I didn't know anything about any Irna-Contra thing" babble or certainly no match for the all-time disingenuous pap of then vice president, Richard Nixon's pathetic Checker's Speech, it is nonetheless an historical moment in the presidency.

Officially, after 220 years this country has not produced a better liar than William Jefferson Clinton. For your dancing and listening pleasure here is that speech with defining comments parenthetically inserted.

Good evening. **(hello suckers)** This afternoon in this room, from this chair, I testified before the Office of Independent Counsel and the grand jury. **(I'm shoveling the crap from here for three minutes so you won't be needing to hear the nearly five hours of embarrassing and incriminating testimony I spewed under the guise of federal law)** I answered their questions truthfully, **(sort of)** about my private life, **(blow jobs from government employees)** questions no American citizen would ever want to answer. **(Of course no American citizen has a rent-free airplane, limos, and hundreds of armed guards)**

Still, I must take full responsibility for all my actions, **(7 months and $40 million of your dollars later)** both public and private. **(blow jobs in the rent-free White House)** And that's why I'm speaking to you tonight. **(ran out of legal options)**

As you know, in a deposition in January **(when I thought I could beat this rap)** I was asked questions about my relationship with Monica Lewinsky. While my answers were legally accurate. **(legally O.J. Simpson is innocent)** I did not volunteer information. **(pretty much the definition of perjury)**

Indeed I did have a relationship with Ms. Lewinsky that was inappropriate. **(inappropriate is an ambiguous term for kinky shit)** In fact, it was wrong. **(it was fine until I heard the word DNA)** It constituted a critical lapse in judgment **(fucked up)** and a personal failure on my part **(key words are "personal" and "my" - tell you why later)** for which I am solely **(key word)** and completely **(another key word)** responsible.

But I told the grand jury today, and I say to you now, that at no time did I ask anyone to lie, to hide or destroy evidence or to take any other unlawful action. **(I'm using the words "personal", "my", "solely", and "completely responsible" so you'll buy this new and improved lie about obstruction of justice)**

I know that my public comments **("Listen to me, I did not have sexual relations with that woman")** and my silence about this matter gave a false impression **(more fancy verbiage for lied)** I misled people, **(politically correct way to say lied)** including my wife **(you know, what's her name)** I deeply regret that. **(I'm pissed she found out)**

I can only tell you **(because you buy most of my bullshit)** I was motivated by many factors. First my desire to protect myself from embarrassment of my own conduct. **(I'm out of control)** I was also very concerned about protecting my family. **(the sympathy props)** The fact that these questions were being asked in a politically inspired lawsuit **(those bastards want to bring your beloved president down)** which has been dismissed, **(if it wasn't for my damn penis I'd be scott free)** was a consideration, too.

In addition, I had real and serious concerns about an independent counsel investigation that began with private business dealing **(illegal land scams)** 20 years ago **(I was young and stupid give me some slack)**, dealings **(crimes)** I might add, about which an independent federal agency **(this Ken Starr guy you'll be seeing trying to impeach your beloved president)** found no evidence of any wrongdoing **(guy couldn't find Godzilla in a corn field)** by me or my wife over two years ago. **(its been awhile, give it up)**

The independent counsel investigation **(I'm off the blow job/lie thing and on the attack - follow me now)** moved on to my staff and friends **(more suckers I bilked)** then into my private life **(you know, the kinky in the rent-free federal office)** And now the investigation itself is under investigation **(they're bad too - two wrongs equal innocence, use your imagination, like, my father beat me so I have to rape you stuff - you're catching on!)**

This has gone on too long **(if it weren't for cum stains it would still be rolling)** cost too much **(my fault)** and hurt too many people. **(my fault again)**

Now, this matter is between me, the two people I love most - my wife and our daughter - and our God. **(those two can't impeach me and I've got to throw God in here somewhere, don't I?)** I must put it right, and I am prepared to do whatever it takes to do so. **(I'll be redefining that hyperbole later)**

Nothing is more important to me personally **(are you getting my third grade attempt at telling you that I can handle this thing - there is no use in putting me on trial, I'll handle this - me, the guy who lied)** But it is private **(get it?)**; and I intend to reclaim my family life for my family **(redundant but slick)** It's nobody's business but ours. **(something I borrowed from Al Capone)**

Even presidents have private lives. **(and cats have whiskers boys and girls)** It is time to stop the pursuit of personal destruction and prying into private lives and get on with our national life. **(national life? Made that up - like it?)**

Our country has been distracted by this matter for too long. **(driving it home, baby)** and I take responsibility for my part in all this **(that's what this charade is about)** This is all I can do. **(didn't I just spew some garbage about doing whatever it takes, guess this three minute thing is "whatever it takes")**

Now it is time - in fact, it is past time - **(driving it home mamma)** to move on.

(I admitted stealing the eraser, so no one should have to stay after class) We have important work to do **(more chicks)** real opportunities to seize **(IRS investigations of all my enemies)** real problems to solve **(Paula Jones will be making a comeback after this)**

And so tonight, I ask you to turn away from the spectacle of the past seven months **(I say its past and you will ignore it - damn it - you love me!)** to repair the fabric of our national discourse **(made that up too, dig my cryptic jive - yeah!)** and return our attention to all the challenges and all the promise of the next American century. **(how do I sleep at night?)**

Thanking you for watching. And good night. **(The brainwashing is done, go back to Jerry Springer and professional wrestling and leave me alone)**

8/25/98

THE NEW WAR

Terrorism is the New War. This is not a particularly original, or spanking new statement; but in light of recent unconscionably violent events in East Africa—and this country's air-raid response—it bares blatant repeating. There are no more flags to wave, songs to sing, or Nazi's to fight. There are no more beaches to storm, or jungles to raid. No Star Wars nuclear five alarm missiles can assuage it. No CIA covert underground Pentagon dealings can stamp it out. No walls, fences, barbed wire, and fancy airport detection systems can bare it out. It is no longer just a military problem. We are all in danger.

Allowing American embassies to exist in this arena of hidden blood lust is Russian roulette of the most pathetically stupid kind. It may make political sense, but it makes no humane sense. Anyone finding themselves inside one of these places should not expect to live for too long. More than 250 people are dead in Kenya and Tanzania after targeted embassies went kablooey.

What chance does the most powerful nation in the world have against that kind of insidious cowardly act?

Answer - Bombing someone and something quick. That is the only political answer to this barbarism. Any protest outside the targeted countries, in this case Afghanistan and Sudan, is first-rate naive blathering or partisan-politic whining.

A host of nations' underground diplomacy are being carried out by invisible religious wackos with a suicide kick and chemistry sets. A putrescent maggot by the name of Ramzi Yousef sits in front of FBI agents and tells them that his only regret to the carnage at the World Trade Center five years ago was the failure of both buildings to topple upon one another. The United States of America is being held up by two-bit hate-jockies festering in the United Nations shadow. That is the New War in a nut shell. Finally, unfortunately, only one language speaks to it: FORCE.

Of course, unloading high weaponry on possible Pharmaceutical Industries is deplorable, but chances are they were terrorist camps filled with a whole new arsenal of madness just itching to be unleashed on the next unsuspecting American outpost. It's a tough call. Either way it has to be done.

Before you finish reading this the structure that houses you right now could be history, making you, in turn, history. This is always a possibility in the New War. I spent weeks in the Middle East, and trust me when I tell you, those people are more frightened of what will happen in New York City than in Jerusalem.

Another foul gutter snake by the name of Osama Bin Laden, Saudi millionaire and hate monger nonpareil, has recently been fingered by a federal grand jury as the prime source for most Islamic Radical attacks. This maniac has been allowed to throw his oil money around to fundamentalist murderers for too long. Five US servicemen die in Saudi Arabia in 1995, six US planes are shot down over the Pacific in 1996, German tourists are gunned down in Egypt in 1997, weapons continue to pour into the Hamas; and they all have Bin Laden's fingerprints all over it. This is no sand-dune weeping peasant being stomped by imperialist America. This is a multi-million dollar guerrilla operation aimed to terrorize the free world. Bin Laden is not doing it on an evil island like some James Bond flick. Some country is giving this lunatic asylum.

The New War is raging. There are examples yearly, monthly, sometimes weekly, and soon there may be far too many of them daily. The United States has two options—and one is not feasible—reeling in the embassies and booting the goddamn UN out of NY, followed closely by a closing of our borders. The workable one is an all-out defense of human rights, and a bitter fight for the eradication of real fear all over the globe. In political foreign affairs speak : Bomb someone or something quick.

9/2/98

FREAK SHOW BASEBALL

As of the second day of September, Mark McGwire, 34 year-old first baseman for the St. Louis Cardinals, has hit 57 home runs. No player at this level of baseball has ever reached such heights of power this quickly; not Babe Ruth, not Hank Aaron, not even Roger Maris, whose 61 round-trip season record is about to crumble. None of McGwire's blasts have been of the cheap variety. If anything, he has taken the feat of hitting a baseball to literally new lengths.

Miraculously, a 29 year-old right fielder for the Chicago Cubs named Sammy Sosa has whacked 55 home runs to date. A record that has stood for 37 years is about to go down twice.

The most intriguing aspect of these historic runs is that McGwire and Sosa are not totally alone atop the home run circus. This has been the year of the dinger, the goner, the goodbye-Mister-Spawlding. Since Maris broke Babe Ruth's record of 60 homers, which stood for 34 years, only a few men have eclipsed 50 in a season. Now six players have a legitimate shot at 50, which until this season usually meant breaking through in the final week. The two big boys have 22 games to knock Maris out of the books. Possible? McGwire has cranked 10 in the last fourteen days.

There is something about the home run which overshadows most sporting accomplishments. For the better part of the American century only the Heavy Weight Championship of the World holds a loftier position than home run king. It is a well known fact among baseball people that there would be no McGwire/Sosa race or even professional baseball without the immortal Babe Ruth's explosion of power in the early 20s'. The Bambino's feats followed the Black Sox gambling controversy of 1919, and the question of whether the game was on the level lingered. The birth of the home run with its immediate thunder and triumphant trot was the rebirth of the game. In 1998 there is a similar resurrection. The home run chase has brought Major League Baseball, marred by a ridiculous lockout which shut the game down four years ago, back into the realm of good times and wonderment.

The last waning weeks of the McGwire/Sosa two-step will bring the type of media crush that would make the Lewinsky/Clinton waltz seem like a piker convention. Every newspaper in the free world will be sending someone to cover whoever reaches 58 first. According to Gannett newspaper sports columnist, Ian O'Connor, whom I spoke to the night McGwire ripped two baseballs into the deepest reaches of Pro Player Park in South Florida, "I will be sent to follow him for the duration. If it takes two weeks, so be it. And I won't be alone." The real story will be if half the sporting press is sequestered in St. Louis waiting for a Big Mac attack the same night Sammy Sosa decides to go ballistic and rip four homers in Chi-town to break the Maris mark. In this season of the homer anything has become possible.

It is also not completely far-fetched that Ken Griffey Jr. from Seattle and Greg Vaughn from San Diego, both with 47, could go on a tear and join the 60+ fun. This is what the new age of baseball has wrought: Bad pitching from a dilution of talent due to four new teams in six years, juiced baseballs, tiny parks, and players living in weight rooms with special diets and questionable forms of "natural" supplements.

Yet, neither Sosa, a Dominican born bundle of enthusiasm and histrionics, or McGwire, a mountainous brick wall of a man, should be given an asterisk for their collective achievement. Maris had to endure one for the remainder of his life for taking eight more games to break the beloved Bambino's 60. It was eventually lifted more than a decade after his death.

It will not take McGwire or Sosa nearly that long to knock both legends from the record book. They have made a freak show of this magical '98 baseball season. It is the story of the year; sports or otherwise. America loves freaks.

9/9/98

FAMILY OF HATE

Fear is the offspring of *Ignorance* and a father to *Hatred*. All three claim the symptom called *Violence* as a sibling. The appropriation of *Violence* results from a lurid instigation wrought from the savage combination of *Fear* and *Hatred*. No humans beyond the realm of blind faith have been able to juggle these elements and come out using a words like *Order* and *Peace*. So the city of New York, and the good people who trumpeted the Million Youth March on September 5, which devolved into a near riot, can take their mojo rhetoric and save it for the dullards who buy that kind of rancid tripe. It will be needed to survive in the land that redefines *Ignorance, Fear, Hatred,* and *Violence.* A land called *Rationalization.*

The NYPD, who stormed the circumference of the alleged 15,000 young black men gathered for a rally in Harlem, were dealing with their own brand of special *Fear.* Born from hundreds of years of *Ignorance* and a pay check that can never equal the damage done to a psyche faced with having to negotiate an angry mob with a helmet and night stick. In the center of this emotional hybrid was rally organizer, Khalid Muhammad, fueled with ultra high octane *Hatred,* peddling *Fear* and *Ignorance* in a five-and-dime carnival barker style all too familiar in the annals of imperious hype. In a six block radius filled with 6,000 frightened and contentious armed policemen, a rabid *Fear/Hate* specialist like Muhammad barking at a load of riled up citizens, there is bound to be nothing good. Sixteen injured, 13 of which were cops, is a jackpot of luck considering the odds and elements involved.

Mayor Rudy Giuliani, czar of civility, has done all he can for the Big Apple's revival with hard-nosed tactics that were desperately needed in the innocuous wake of David Dinkins. But similar to Dinkins' crucial miscalculations in moments of potential *Fear* and *Hatred* explosions, Uncle Rudy screwed this one up. Uncle Rudy's barrage of public criticism and legal actions, attempting to halt a perfectly legal, albeit dubious, gathering laid the dangerous groundwork for this explosive farce. Giuliani, acting on the *Fear* quotient, provided the needed sulfur for a blaze of "Watts Riot" proportions by giving Muhammad all the ammo he needed to lay down the torch of his own bloated *Hate* agenda.

However disdained by city hierarchy, Muhammad did obtain the necessary permit to stage his rally. Guiliani, like an angered parent who has to capitulate with their child's seemingly meaningless activity with the understanding that it will be over exactly when he deemed it so, decided to flex his muscle by turning the place into a demilitarized zone less than one minute after the demonstration permit had expired. This act of intimidation/instigation played right along with Muhammad's *Hate* style. His reaction was typical. Its effect was a call to *Violence.* Before long Muhammad was a madman demanding kids to take up chairs, pipes, and anything else the throng could get their hands on to oppose the tyranny of King Rudy.

One thing that needs to be said about Giuliani is that he stands for something tangible; law and order. No matter how he may occasionally warp these concepts, he kneels at their alter daily. Muhammad is a far different public creature. He stands by nothing. His anti-Semitic, police-bashing speeches fall somewhere in the misty fog of defense against racism. So when kids who just want to march for racial pride fall in with him there is no category being filled. If the grand pooba of the Klu Klux Klan decides to hold a peaceful rally in Mississippi next week, and says it has nothing to do with racism, you can bet anyone showing up will be deemed a fucking pin head, red neck, dumb-ass hate monger. You know where the grand pooba stands on the issue of *Hate*. Muhammad has been able to work out that little glitch.

Now the public, media, and other local politicians, playing to what-ever crowd welcomes their two cents, have set forth the rabid animal known as *Blame*. *Blame* knows no logic and cannot begin to fathom the depths to which *Ignorance*, *Fear*, and *Hate* have gone to provoke its ambiguous presence. *Blame* leads the torch-carrying ilk who chase down monsters in black and white hor-ror flicks. It sniffs out the innocent and the guilty without prejudice, because when *Fear* gives birth to a healthy bouncing baby called *Hate*, there is every-one to *Blame*.

9/16/98

ALL OR NOTHING: THE STARR REPORT AND ITS EFFECT

So here we are, over five years and millions of our tax dollars, and what do we have? The dreaded Starr Report has yielded little more than juicy plot ideas for Melrose Place, a seemingly endless stream of talking heads, pundits, and sensationalized pap passing for news shows commenting on blow jobs, abuse of power, and denials. What is truth? and What is perjury? and What the hell is anyone going to do about it all?

Kenneth Starr certainly has made a name for himself finally corner-ing a President of the United States on the misguided use of his pecker. But is this enough to complete the job he so obviously set out to do; remove Bill Clinton from office, or has he added legal masturbation to the haughty list of civil misconduct.

Moreover, as cited time and again in this space, does Congress, whose job it is now to decipher this tome of pathetic conduct and come to impeachable conclusions, have the collective balls it will take to boot a hugely popular president within six weeks of election day. And if those with the power to speed this mess to any, God help us all, any definite decision, let this thing conveniently drag on through the new year, will anyone, outside of political fanaticism and moral hypocrisy, care enough to drag the country through impeachment proceedings? Although a dubious request, considering the gutless swine who occupy these positions; SOMEBODY BETTER DO SOMETHING!!

Having just made my healthy quarterly tax payment to Uncle Sam I can only say that I want blood. Anything short of putting Al Gore in charge—a thought so vile and degrading it is hardly worth contemplating without sedatives and whiskey —I would love to see Bill Clinton, decked in prison orange and being lead into a paddy wagon with hands shackled and ankles in chains. For this much effort Starr should demand execution by firing squad at halftime of this year's Rose Bowl. For my money, everyone occupying the president's cabinet, and all White House officials, should be beaten by teamsters and fed to Dobermans on Capitol Hill.

However, Kenneth Starr's tedious dirge down Grand Jury Lane has produced 11 crimes in which he presents as grounds for impeachment. Six counts of perjury, three counts of obstructing justice, one count of witness tampering, and one count of constitutional abuse. All of it stemming from the president's ejaculating onto an intern's dress. Where is the good stuff? Where is the illegal land deals, missing documents, misuse of funds, selling weapons to China for campaign cash, even murders, we've been salivating for? If some chubby girl hadn't agreed to immunity two months ago, Starr has taken money out of my pocket to nail the president, in the tradition of nearly every other president, on fucking around in the oval office.

The saddest part of all is that Big Bill is most likely guilty of all those crimes, (I'm a little fuzzy on the murder thing, but it has been brought up), and then some. But, instead of having to hit the hard-biting slider down and in, the president will get a chance to win the pennant looking at a hanging curve ball in his wheel house. As a fiscal investor in this atrocity, I feel like George Steinbrenner dolling out millions to watch some stiff pitcher get tattooed by an expansion team. It is starting to bring up the same bile processed by the sickening revelation that O.J. Simspon walked on cheap technicalities brought on by shoddy prosecutors, a vapid judge, and a jury of knee-jerk reactionaries.

It is the contention of this space, as it has continually been, that Bill Clinton will walk—perhaps the worst being a fine—on these charges. If this is all Ken Starr has wrought then he has failed the government, the people, and whatever sucker hoped he'd impale that fucker Clinton. Doesn't anyone remotely recall what it took to yank Richard Nixon out of this gig? Good luck cutting down an oak tree with a butter knife. I'm preparing a lawsuit to retrieve my tax money from Mr. Starr.

9/31/98

THE POLITICS OF LAW

*"It is my belief that nearly any invented quotation,
played with confidence, stands a good chance to deceive."*
-Mark Twain

"What is truth?"
- John 18:38

The release of the president's grand jury appearance has yielded very little in the way of true impeachment grit. The independent council has no case under the law of the land. Bill Clinton was evasive, vacillating, and for those kneeling at the alter of common sense, frustrating as hell. However, according to the law, not the "spirit of" but "the letter of", Bill Clinton did not technically lie under oath. It is tough enough to nail a citizen on perjury, but for a politician; especially one as shrewd and morally bankrupt as Bill Clinton, it is an impossibility. This is what semantics in the era of lawyer-speak has gotten us: a lie is no longer a lie if based on the use, tense, and vague ambiguity of the language.

For four hours under oath in the first ever grand jury appearance by a sitting president, Bill Clinton said that receiving oral sex is not sex.

This may come as a surprise to those of you reading this who have been tossed into the street by a significant other for having been caught in the same act. But in the eyes of the judge presiding over the Paula Jones case, Susan Webber Wright, in which Mr. Clinton was to have perjured himself, sex is gratification or stimulation on breasts and genitals performed by the deposed, not the other way around. Although it sounds eerily like an Abbott and Costello routine, you ain't heard nothin' yet.

Mr. Clinton says, let's face it, rightfully so, that lips and mouth are not genitals. This officially makes oral sex, to which the word "sex" is ironically a part, not sex. In other words, sex is not sex when it's not sex. Stay the course, you're doing fine.

Mr. Clinton expounds by saying that "normal" Americans also understand sex to mean sexual intercourse. All puns aside, this is a slippery road to travel. If you have never engaged in sexual intercourse you are still a virgin, but if you are married and getting hummers on the side you will have a hard time convincing anyone you're being monogamous.

The law apparently needs the "intercourse" word to define sex, but does this constitute sex? Many "normal" Americans who suffer from sexually transmitted diseases contracted from the act of oral sex may argue, but under "the Clinton definition", they would be wrong.

Moreover, during the Jones' case the president's lawyer, Robert Bennett, stood in court and boldly claimed that "Mr. Clinton is not engaged in sexual relations of any kind with Monica Lewinsky." Is this a lie? Bill Clinton says it is not, because by that time he was good and done with Monica Lewinsky's lips and mouth, which, by the by, are not genitals, mind you. Mr. Clinton, within the boundaries of the law, and well within the boundaries of politico-speak, says that tense is a factor. "He (Bennett) used the word 'is' and so he was technically telling the truth," Mr. Clinton said. He also made the distinction that a lawyer can speak for the client, but the client does not necessarily have to concur with his lawyer's opinion.

Mr. Clinton almost went as far as separating his dingle from his brain.

Are you technically puking yet?

Finally, what exactly does "alone" mean? Mr. Clinton went wild in the oval office and his private study with Ms. Lewinsky. Clinton's secretary, Betty Currie said under oath the president suggested that he and Ms. Lewinsky weren't alone because she was in the vicinity. What he was most likely suggesting was for her to lie, but Mr. Clinton contends he was just making sure she understood that she was always there by saying, "We were never alone, right?" or "You were always there, right?" With this type of specious deduction, who really is ever alone? As long as someone is inhabiting the planet you are not alone. If you were sucking air sometime over the last few years, then Mr. Clinton was never alone with Monica Lewinsky.

The most frightening prospect of all is that this dump truck of colossal bullshit is what passes for law these days. Technicalities and semantics stomp on common sense, overwhelming evidence, and witness accounts. The law is a minefield of veracity and inaccuracy played out over a war of words with the truth as its most precious casualty.

10/7/98

NEW YORK'S GREAT POLITICAL DIVIDE OR HOW THE MUD SLINGS

Senator Alphonse D'Amato is a marked man. Less than one month before he is either validated as the incumbent or sent packing by a rabid campaign junkie named Charles Shumer, he finds himself in a cat fight. Shumer, a Democrat who had little problem dispensing with Geraldine Ferraro in a primary she lead going in by 25 points, is known in circles that count as a "dismantler" of the first degree. Shumer plays the every man attacking political celebrities like a wounded ferret lashes out at its would-be predators. "Dismantlers" take the pedestal apart brick by brick. D'Amato is no easy mark. He is a bulldog,, and his campaign is being run by human machetes sharpened for back-alley rumbles. This is a fight card which makes for a wicked cage match, and an even more interesting campaign for the U.S. Senate.

Ferraro, once a vice presidential candidate, and sometime CO-host of CNN's "Crossfire", is considered a political celebrity. She could not fend off Shumer. D'Amato is a celebrity, well known on the talk show circuit, even calls Howard Stern a friend. He currently stumbles in his attempt to rid himself of the Chuckster. D'Amato is showing blood in the water. This is obvious by the way his campaign has now turned from talk of tax hikes and wars against crime, and sets its gun sites at Shumer himself. "The best offense is a defense in the case of Shumer," a D'Amato aid whispered to me at a recent news conference up in my neck of the woods. "We don't like that bastard, and he don't like us."

My home base is smack dab in George Pataki country. The Governor of New York is a folk hero up here. Having served as mayor of a dying economic town called Peekskill, Pataki is defending his position this fall against Democratic candidate, City Council Speaker, Peter Vallone. Four years ago Pataki, everyone's favorite country-bumpkin candidate, beat Mario Cuomo by accusing him of sucking up to the black hole of NY tax hell called New York City. Even Uncle Rudy, Mayor of the Big Apple, stood by the Democratic incumbent, crossing over party lines in what amounted to a vain attempt at saving the city from state oppression.

Ironically, now D'Amato, well known for his city ties, is being harassed in constant Shumer-funded television, radio, and print ads as a man so mired in Big Apple funk he is unable to serve the state. D'Amato has swung back with vicious ads decrying Shumer's party as "New York City liberals swimming upstate like sharks from NYC to gorge on state tax dollars." Democratic Committee Assembly Speaker, Sheldon Silver, carrying a NYC agenda five boroughs wide, has barked back, calling the attacks on Shumer's smears "smut-like" with "nastiness oozing from the Republican camp."

Shumer's people refuse to comment further. A call into their headquarters reveals less than my D'Amato pal who seemed to have no trouble confiding in me how much Shumer disliked his opponent. "We know all about him," the gentleman said, pointing forcefully at a notebook filled with scribbled chicken scratch interrupted only by a random date and ballroom address. "Shumer hates Al's guts," he said calmly. "This thing will get uglier, and it won't be our fault. We know where our bread is buttered."

D'Amato's butter had apparently been rationed during the summer. Shumer has gained significant ground. But no one in the Republican camp has any allusions about Pataki losing Albany. Vallone is spitting into the wind right now, and part of his vote is sliding to an Independent Party candidate named Tom Golisano, who is spewing much of the same education, tax, and state debt reform rhetoric. Golisano is on my dung-list for blowing off a local television news show I work for in late September mere minutes before it was to go. I drove well out of my way and ended up holding the bag with the entire crew. I will revel in his dismissal as a cheap fraud of a mouth piece that will usher Pataki back into power with minimum effort.

As usual NYC is the mud-sling magnet for the rush for Senate and Governor, one that will benefit the GOP because of a crippled Democratic president and a weakened voter pool. Both the D'Amato and Shumer campaigns disagree, but the inside word is that sickened by political smut overkill people do not want to vote right now. The odds makers that I can reach by phone list those already in charge as 5-2 favorites. This space will not argue.

CHAOS IN MOTION III

Convince your brain of its surroundings. Then change it.

Children suffer.

Advertising is legal brainwashing.

Love is a four letter word.

Woman is a five letter word.

4+5=9

There are nine letters in salvation.

Memories are cheap.

Iniquity is not sin until it fits the crime.

Days are so much longer when you're a kid.

Achieve heaven.

There is no such thing as a new cliché.

Dr. Kervorkian was paid up front.

BANNING GUNS IS LIKE BANNING SUNBURN.

Turn on. Tune in.

No gain. No sin.

Fact is what you make of it.

Make room for the Gay-Irish-Lefthanded-Red Haired-Marchers.

Stand by yourself.

It's time for Saddam Hussein to meet Jimmy Hoffa.

Hate is a stimulant.

Steal the dawn.

Nothing comes from crying.

Crying comes from something.

We do what we want.

Comedy need not apologize.

The good hands of Allstate:
One hand takes your money.
The other jerks you off.

Pay college athletes.

Read the Constitution.

Pro-life protesters killing doctors is confusing.

Avoid affiliation.

Never leave "why" out of your conversation.

TV evangelists are lying with the truth.

10/21/98

IMMORTALITY AT THE CROSSROADS - OBSERVATIONS FROM THE MEDIA WAVE AT THE WORLD SERIES

Yankee Stadium - October 18, 1998

Traveling through the bowels of Yankee Stadium hours before the first pitch of game 2 of this year's fall classic, it is easy to be caught up in the crush of numbers. This place and its team were built for the past. That's the way legends go in sport. The Stadium was not yet a year old when the New York Yankees won its first of 23 titles. That was 75 seasons ago. Now the team goes for number 24.

There have been 94 of these Series, and 35 of them have taken place just above me. A left at the home team's clubhouse, and a short, but breathtaking, stroll down the path of the Bambino, the Iron Horse, Joe D, the Mick, and Mr. October, is met by the bustling media hordes outside the dugout. Fifty-six thousand seats are empty now, but the vacuous ambiance creates the inevitable aura of "an event." Before the Super Bowl and the Academy Awards, before MTV, and super models, the World Series was the Mecca of hype. The scene before me—hundreds of photographers and television cameras, scribbling pads and tape recorders—was born here.

Surviving the Great Depression and four wars the World Series is the mother of all American spectacles. Four short years ago the sport closed its doors on a night like this and almost buried the memories of this perpetual autumn rite. There is no way to tell how close it all came to oblivion when one is faced with the mob before me. Even their clamoring crawl is dwarfed by the backdrop of deep blue and pristine white, broken by red, white, and blue bunting draped about the decks of this magnificent shrine to the game. Yankee Stadium stands as a metaphor for baseball's resounding resuscitation. "This is the House that Ruth built," a Japanese reporter says to me with a knowing smile. "Yep, the Babe saved the sport so they built him a park to play its biggest games," I answer.

Milling about amongst the growing crowd representing every media affiliation, sports or otherwise, I recall first stepping foot in this place. Holding onto to my Dad's hand for dear life as we came up out of the darkness and into the incredible light of day awash in green and blue; the sky gripping the peak of the famed facade. It was a different Yankee Stadium then; the old beast with girders and wooden chairs which squeaked with the echoes of summer. I worked here as a member of the media for the first time in 1989. The team was awful, probably its worst period. I remember my first trip on this hallowed ground, feeling the grass bend and the dirt crackle beneath my steps, and how the echoes were still there. So was my Dad, and his Dad, and all those who'd come before. I stopped coming around when baseball closed its doors in 1994, and the echoes were silenced.

"One thing about the World Series," Boston Globe baseball guru Peter Gammons tells me, "is that it makes history tangible." Gammons does most of his work on television these days, but he is a writer first and foremost. His book, "Beyond the 6th Game" is a masterpiece worthy of this moment. He thanks me for the compliment. Most of the reporters here are members of a select group of crazies cooped up in Never-Never Land waiting for the kind of nights when they can push and shove and ask questions with words like "pressure" and clutch." The World Series creates those nights and the people who are connected somehow through a love for this game. These souls are the underbelly of the journalism trade; the toy department, and the World Series is their FAO Shwartz.

Before long I'm in the press room surrounded by the clicking and clacking of computer keyboards. Once they were typewriters and smoke wafted aloft from pungent cigars. But there is no smoking here now. A sign of the times maybe, but there is still no talking; just sighs and coughs, and the odd story. "I remember being terrified to talk to those old Yankee teams with Billy and Reggie and Thurman during the late 70s'," Daily News baseball columnist, Bill Madden tells NY Times columnist, Dave Anderson—two deans of this subterranean world of covering the game—"Those guys were maniacs, yelling and screaming at each other all the time," Madden smiles. Anderson agrees.

These men and women of the sporting press, some old and most younger, know the difference between the '98 version of these Yankees and the past glory of this place. The team sequestered in the clubhouse a few feet away has won more games than any previous baseball juggernaut with less fanfare than a Tom's River Little League team. Quite a feat in New York. This is, after all, Yankee Stadium in October.

After a 9-3 drubbing of the San Diego Padres I venture into the Yankees clubhouse. It has been a few years for me. Here is the domain of the million dollar athlete, donning towels and flip-flops, cursing and laughing and forgetting the long strange trip from Little League to the world stage. After 123 wins the Yankees need two more victories for their own history to begin to echo. "We haven't done anything yet," says first baseman Tino Martinez. "This is the World Series, and anything can happen." It sounds familiar. It is the answer every other soul in here will say before boarding the buses steaming up outside the press gate. On my way out I see the players, their wives, and the traveling media board for the airport and championship destiny on the coast. "The old girl is dark," says broadcaster, John Sterling. A good place for echoes.

11/4/98

MANDATE FOR DEMOCRACY

Exit polls, pundits, expert analysts drooling on their power ties at CNN headquarters, and withered mug shots of Dick Army and Newt Gingrich spinning lovely in the face of ugly political foreshadowing continue to spew reasons for the surge of Democratic victories on November 3. This is the Pollyanna rant trying like hell to ignore a story and its harboring issue which has been crammed down the throats of the American people for what seems like forever.

The 42nd President of the United States stands at the precipice of being yanked out of office, and the voting public wants no part of it. Those caught up in the rhetoric of impeachment proceedings and those dancing on the grave of the political Houdini known as William Jefferson Clinton now lick the wounds of the big hurt, and they have only to blame the choice of party ideology over personal survival.

The American people have spoken once again on their moral apathy. As stated over and over in this space, until the bile drives up the esophagus, any member of Congress with balls enough to take on a popular president in the shadow of an election will be whistling past the emergency room. The results are in, and the GOP isn't flat lining, but division on a plan of attack and what to do with a reeling president has landed them in intensive care.

White House leeches were talking about being ecstatic with loosing four to eight seats in the House of Representatives when Clinton wrapped up his hilarious, but apparently effective, mia culpa speech on August 17. Three months later the Democrats *gain* eight. The Republicans were all but banking on upping their legislative stranglehold to 60 Senate seats, but settle with a 55 to 45 majority.

Along with CNN's Bill Shneider, who saw "not much evidence" to voters being fed up with the attack on poor old Big Bill, majority leader Trent Lott cited Social Security, Health Care, education, taxes, blah. blah, blah.... Lott joined Army and Gingrich during the televised election-result bloodletting by stating emphatically that "politics is local" and that in no way did the Monica Lewinsky public feeding determine the outcome. Meanwhile, Gingrich is on ABC telling Peter Jennings these issues are helping the Republicans kick significant ass in the gubernatorial races. But the scroll on the bottom of his chin tells me the Democrats are winning in South Carolina and Alabama, two former Republican strongholds with booming economies. Consequently, Shneider does a 180— rear wheels spinning, neck wrenching—U-turn an hour later, stating that "pursuing impeachment by this Congress had an enormous unintended consequence for the Republicans. It nationalized this election just like the 'Contract For America' did in '94."

Back on ABC George Will noted, "The Republicans wanted to focus on Clinton's behavior, and it backfired."

Locally Chuck Shumer turned a close race into a whitewash by parading Hillary, Bill, and Al Gore around New York no less than twice each the last six weeks of his expensive campaign to drive home Al D'Amato's attacks on the Clintons during the senator's ill-fated Whitewater investigation a few years back. A mad-dog slime of a race by two previously undefeated lunatics eventually turned into a national martyr response by New York voters who claimed neither taxes or abortion was much of a factor. It was simply time for Crazy Al to go. George Pataki, attempting to will D'Amato to victory—as the 18-year senator had effectively done for him four years earlier—received no resistance in his race. He now listens to whispers of a millennium run for the White House which will be eventually derailed by a second resounding victory for George Bush Jr. in Texas. With Gingrich's boys taking one for the team, Dan Quayle's sad showing on last year's book tour, and Pat Buchanan laying low for an independent run, Little Boy Bush, and possibly his now victorious brother, will lead a GOP 2,000 ticket.

As far as this silly notion of impeachment, the House may have enough partisan votes to pin Clinton to the wall, but the squeeze in the Senate will all but squash a solid conviction. It would have been a savage battle to wrest Big Bill from his playpen on Pennsylvania Ave. without these results. Now it becomes the Indianapolis Colts winning the Super Bowl. A preponderance of lame duck congressmen swimming around the Beltway pond the next two months could prove crucial for not only the future of Bill Clinton, but the leadership of the Republican Party. Does the majority power in congress slow the rolling impeachment ball and start smoothing things for a run at the White House in two years? Or do they go the spite route and serve the chilly revenge dish for what could end up being a closing act?

Clinton played possum four years ago when it looked like the GOP would stomp him back to Arkansas. Maybe his enemies can learn a lesson on timing and public salesmanship from the master and let him walk for the survival of the team.

11/11/98

DEMAGOGUE FOOTNOTE - THE RISE AND FALL OF NEWT GINGRICH

"Out, out brief candle! Life's but a walking shadow, a poor player
That struts and frets his hour upon the stage
And then is heard no more: it is a tale
Told by an idiot, full of sound and fury,
Signifying nothing."

- William Shakespeare
"Macbeth"

Newt Gingrich was an egomaniacal lout who rode the crest of fear mongering like a bad ass revival of Joseph McCarthy meets Jimmy Hoffa. But I, for one, am sad to see him go. And not because he was a source of constant derision from political cynics such as myself, but because he was finally railroaded by the naive notion that all type-A personalities with a snake-oil salesman smile and PT Barnum's wit will infinitely have a place in the heart of America. I feel sorry for Newt Gingrich because these attributes lifted him to the status of Speaker of the House, although not king as he originally thought, on the wings of outrage and fear. But these are the very concepts that felled him. It is the ultimate political tragedy: The sword cuts both ways.

Now that Bill Clinton is on his seventh life it is hard to remember a time four years ago when no one would have spent subway fare to impeach his sorry ass. After two years in office Clinton's approval ratings were so miserably low that he lost both houses of Congress in a political fallout that will be dissected by historians one hundred years from now with the same quizzical fervor as the fall of Rome. Newt Gingrich was the figurehead of the *Republican Revolution* which danced heartily on the president's bones. Sold as a self-annointed czar of change with the subtlety of Attilla the Hun suffering from formally uncharted delusions of grandeur, Newt Gingrich was a willing Brutus to Big Bill's stumbling Ceasar.

Newt was the Anti-Bush. The GOP was so pissed at Old George's impotent defense of the White House they went full-bore nasty at his successor. Clinton was reeling with the initial whispers of Whitewater, gays in the military, midnight basketball, tax hikes, and Hillary making mince meat of Healthcare reform. Gingrich lead the first Republican majority in three generations into action, waving his "Contract With America" as a battle flag. He was a brash, bold, and a mean son of a bitch, and he stomped into Washington like Patton entering Italy, throwing around the old Al Haig line, "I'm in charge now!" And for awhile he sure was; this curmudgeon of bombast, pounding his gavel and quipping lustily about finally getting things done. He had the President of the United States on the run, becoming the first Speaker of the House in this country's history to wrest the mantle of public conscience away from the White House. He even pulled the dutifully middle-of-the-road Clinton to the right. It was sweet victory.

Then Gingrich made his fatal mistake. He believed in the power. He became the ideology rather than letting it glide his momentum. In sports terms he became bigger than the game. First he led the shutdown of the government less than a year after his triumph. Then his originally misunderstood ideas of cutting government programs started making their way out to the hinterland, and all those clamoring for tax cuts realized their free rides were being trampled on. Gingrich did not hear them, nor fear their wining polls about cold, calculating Republicans ruling with iron fists and spitting on the poor and feeble. Instead he acted like the spoiled brat with the mouthful of spoon, sounding more and more like a tyrant. This was followed by misappropriations, strange book deals, and increasingly bizarre quotes.

Perception or reality: Newt Gingrich became Herod the Great slaughtering the innocents.

Consequently, Bill Clinton's comeback was Newt Gingrich's downfall. Like the painting of Dorian Gray rotting in the attic, Gingrich's popularity withered while Clinton became Big Bill again. It declined so badly for Newt that by the summer of '96, while his beloved rigidly-conservative-religious-right party paraded sweet, kind Bob Dole around the country with socially liberal Jack Kemp by his side, the GOP threw their once golden boy a bone. By giving his speech at the pulpit hours before the network cameras were turned on during the Republican National Convention, Newt Gingrich, the once prime time player, was a CSPAN reject now.

To his credit Gingrich knew his days were numbered earlier this year when he set New Hampshire ablaze with savage rhetoric aimed at the immoral president and his waltz with perjury. Many, including this space, translated the tirade as an early declaration for presidential candidacy in 2,000. But after his ill-fated rally against the morals of the White House, which resulted in a devastating blow to his party this past election, he is left only to quit like a spurned schoolboy cut from the varsity.

Newt Gingrich is the best example of how this world of politics spins, how fickle the public can be about their celebrities, and how the glare of the footlights blind. Make no mistake, Newt Gingrich traded public servant for superstar long ago. Four years earlier you heard the cry that Gingrich will go down as one of the most influential people of this, the American century; but although the wave upon which he rode to prominence will be discussed for some time to come, his decent from legislative lion to raging demagogue has rendered him nothing but a footnote.

11/17/98

MISSION IRAQ: EIGHT YEARS OF BUNGLED FOREIGN POLICY, UN SUBJUGATION, AND GRANDIOSE STUPIDITY

Saddam Hussein has been fucking with the United States of America for eight years, one Gulf War, and two administrations; all the while surviving countless international threats and savage bombings. During that time he's stashed nuclear and biological weapons around the desert like Easter eggs, invaded and threatened neighboring countries, played the United Nations like a well-oiled accordion, and lied to anyone within earshot and beyond with monumental consistency. On the second weekend of November, Hussein acquiesced with UN policy within minutes of the second American air raid in seven years. No one with half the capacity for brain function believes this latest foray into bullshit. Yet, miraculously, he is allowed to stick around. He has become this generation's Fidel Castro, and no matter what rhetoric his latest ruse produces—or another brash speech by an American president—the main fact remains: He will have to be assassinated.

What has happened to the United States since Hussein marched his troops into Kuwait in August of 1990 is nothing less than a pathetic embarrassment. The last remaining world power since World War II has been playing footsies with a truck stop in the sand for nearly a decade with no real plan of attack. Bill Clinton's latest foreign policy mistake was his predecessor's last. George Bush, using the U.S. military as muscle for the United Nations, found his hands tied by a divided Arab state surrounding Iraq before and after the Gulf War, but let's face it, the reason Hussein still annoys the shit out of this administration was Bush's subjugation of U.S. foreign policy to UN wishes.

As late as March of this year the former president told Time magazine that the job of the United States during the war was to boot Hussein out of Kuwait, even though his advisors strongly suggested that infamous "left turn into Baghdad" to finish the job. The Bush administration cured the symptoms, but left the disease right where it started.

The UN is now dictating U.S. foreign policy. Secretary General, Kofi Annan has wooed both sides of the issue. He laughably negotiations with this maniac using American troops as a threat, while repeatedly redrawing the proverbial line in the sand. Hussein plays Annan like Hitler played Chamberlain, meanwhile U.S. threats are reduced to pissing into a stiff wind.

What has eluded the UN's peacekeeping sensibilities is that Saddam Hussein is nothing more than a glorified camel salesman with fancy medals and a cute beret without these weapons and his "mother of all crappolla" anti-American propaganda. He will give them up when his buddy Big Bill gives up the White House.

The President of the United States may be a wild man in the oval office with interns, but he has been rendered impotent in this latest fiasco.

Halting the last planned raid on Iraq buys Hussein more stalling time. Weapons inspectors, sent packing by the Iraqi government more than once since the Gulf War, have hinted that it would take no less than six months to fully inform the UN of Hussein's alleged potent arsenal. With the usual delays and red tape he could drag this out until another administration inherits this mess. Meanwhile, Israel, Syria, Iran, ect. live in constant fear that he might get goofy — not to mention the thousands of U.S. military personnel standing around waiting for apparently nothing.

Clinton has met his match in the rotating bull dung arena. At this crawling rate Hussein will outlast him like Castro has outlasted nine presidents.

Long gone are the days when the CIA drugged, poisoned, and coup de tated their way to U.S. victory abroad. Repeated failures to whack Castro, fuck-ups in Viet Nam, the conveniently ignored Iran/Contra thing, and all that nasty bad press since the Cold War ended has obviously removed it from being a factor in Hussein's timely demise. Clinton's hint that someone on the inside start to erect a new government in Saddam's stead is naive. Iraqis hate America and fear Hussein; a dangerous combination which in the history of world politics never ends neatly. Removing Saddam Hussein from the human race always has been, and still remains, the only solution.

12/23/98

THE TRUTH ABOUT IMPEACHMENT AND THE SLOW DEATH OF PARTY POLITICS

The following is a public service for those still mired in the belief that the two party system works in a democratic republic after witnessing the farcical events of the last month. Since the assassination of Abraham Lincoln, and the ugly impeachment of his successor, Andrew Johnson, the Republican Party and its loyal opposition, the Democrats, have been waging a private war completely devoid of voter will. This week a trial before the Senate will decide the fate of the 42nd President of the United States. In addition to its growing entertainment value to political junkies such as myself, Bill Clinton's continued pathetic grandstanding, the subsequent timely bombardment of Iraq, and the embarrassing show of pure hatred the majority party in Congress has for him, it will successfully pound another nail in the coffin of 120 years of obligatory colossal partisan bullshit.

1. Impeachment? Or Let's Scare the Shit Out of that Horny Bastard - This space stands firm on its summer prediction that William Jefferson Clinton will survive. The House will send their little obsession into the Senate where the need for 67 of 100 votes after months of dramatic trials and CNN overkill will most certainly fail. Clinton will be humiliated further, the stock market will bounce around like a five year-old at the airport, and the economy will take a minor to annoying hit; but the president will finish this mess of a second term and turn the quagmire over to that doofus Al Gore for a run against George Bush Jr. at the turn of the century. All the rest is a song and a dance and a shot and a beer. Nothing will be cleansed. No one will be saved.

2. Moderate Congressmen, Unicorns, and Other Myths - Regardless of what they claim, all Republicans are enemies of the president and every Democrat will back him no matter what level of embarrassment he reaches. If Clinton is caught in the oval office gorging on the intestines of a dead secretary, Democrats will say, "Man's gotta eat." If Clinton trips and leans on a woman for support the Republicans will cry rape. For the GOP, impeachment is revenge for 50 years of Democratic control in the legislative branch, Iran/Contra, Clarence Thomas, and the mother of all Republican martyrs, Richard Milhous Nixon. For the Democrats, keeping Clinton in power is vengeance for the assassinations of two Kennedys, the humiliation of Jimmy Carter, and the pummeling of Mondale and Dukakais. The idea that either party gives a rat's ass about any constitution or protecting the integrity of the presidency is crazy talk.

3. Less Government more Harassment - The next time some Republican asshole tells you he's for less government to allow the populace to take full advantage of the free-market system, punch him hard. The same mongrels who were calling Oliver North an American hero, and whining about welfare and social security, could not give a flying copulation about the economy and the net worth of a buck as they drag an impeachment trial into the Senate this month.

4. Special Interest Slaves - And all those hypocrite Democrats who suck up to special interest groups espousing the evils of the angry white man like the National Organization of Women and the ACLU can kindly shut the fuck up now. The same cretins who jumped all over the Anita Hill thing are ignoring the blatant fact that the president has acted like a rich, powerful, womanizer who doesn't give a stool about anything but his own busy cock and self-preservation.

5. Change the Playing Field - Republicans say this is not a matter of morals, it is a matter of *law*. In response, the president's lawyers have proven within the confines of *law* that their client did not legally commit perjury. Detractors smirk and say, "Come on, he was misleading, dishonest, and stomped all over national trust." But these are moral gripes. Consequently, Democrats say that it's no big deal, it was a lie about a liaison. When members of the judiciary committee rightfully point out that when a man schooled in law goes out of his way to stretch the boundaries of credibility — TWICE — under oath and toes the line of federal crime, it constitutes a big deal.

5. All's Fair in War - Remember when Dick Gephardt's clan was busy ripping George Bush a new corn hole for bombing Iraq seven years ago? They're so juiced about this round they may stain their draws. And all those right-wing sycophants like Dick Armey and Trent Lott, who horsewhipped the bleeding-heart liberals in Congress for castigating "Desert Storm", seem to be pissing national security and pride out the window by stumbling over each other to be the first to oppose any military action which may interrupt their witch hunt.

6. The Death of the Gray Area - If you are Republican, you will vote against anything that has to do with keeping Bill Clinton in office. If you are a Democrat, you will do anything possible to fight it. Personal conscience, constituent outcry, polls, history, law, and the best interest of this elected government to serve its people be damned.

7. Citizen Solution - Don't listen to these dime store snake-oil salesman tell you we are doomed if a Senate trial drags on. We've survived depressions, world wars, assassinations, and Gerald Ford. And don't buy any talk of a reversal of election results. If Big Bill goes, Bob Dole ain't president; it will be Al Gore, which is a break for the Democrats anyway. Finally, if you want to feel better about all this, seek out that wretched gnome Ross Perot for dropping out of the presidential race in August of 1992 and beat him into a gory stump with chains and a tire iron. It's time for an independent presidential candidate who's not a nut, although, at this point, an independent lamp post would do better than the zombies on Capital Hill. Otherwise, ready your muskets.

12/30/98

WASHINGTON IN WINTER: LOWDOWN AND COMEDOWNS IN SEXTOWN

An airport somewhere between Dulles and Raleigh-Duram during holiday rush. My Republican insider friend, and champion of all who religiously read this space, is stoked on three cups of high-grade java and loaded with rumor and venom. At first he makes me nervous, wiping the beads of sweat from his brow and jerking his head left and right as if unseen assailants are about to pounce at any moment. As usual, I tape the proceedings for personal and legal safety, bringing the highlights to readers in its edited-for-space-constraints form.

JC: Is this Senate trial political suicide for you guys if Clinton survives or not?
Georgetown: Election's over. Two years from now no one will remember this bullshit. A few historians and James Carville, maybe. The public has a short attention span. I recall when George Bush couldn't get beat in the summer of '92.
JC: So what you're saying is this is not politically motivated?
GT: No way. That's just what these greasers like (Bob) Livingston and (Trent) Lott and that pain in the ass, (J. Dennis) Hastert want you to think. Yeah, "we're bucking the system and putting our political lives on the line to save the fucking Constitution." The dirty little secret's finally coming to light. It's what I've been telling you for ten months now, you hack. Haven't you written anything about it yet? The GOP wants no part of booting Clinton.
JC: Been there, done that.
GT: This is about dragging him through the slime like the goddamn Democrats did with Reagan when he was riding high; a few nasty allegations, a few impish denials. "Make the bastard deny it!" Isn't that what LBJ used to scream? This is a public shakedown of the first order. You want to live through two terms you damn well better be prepared to endure it. I talk to guys who work for the party, money guys, who tell me straight out that all that shit when Clinton got elected, that "don't stop thinking about tomorrow" garbage, that "yesterday's gone" song. That burned their ass man. That was the Baby Boomers flipping the bird to the people who gave them the money to afford to tune in, drop out, and fly off to Oxford and dump the draft. This trial is payback for gays in the military and all that Hillary crap. She watched Nixon drown, stood over his

corpse with a goddamn sickle.

JC: Revenge. I called that. Cost you guys a few bodies in the House though.

GT: Small onions to pay to put the fear in that bastard. Give him the old one two and then cut a deal. There is no way that giving Gore a chance to right this mess and prove he can surf this economy into 2,000 is flying with the big boys at the GOP. Clinton is going to have to stand and take it, or resign.

JC: Which he most certainly will not, sans gun point.

GT: It's the Democrats who really want him out. They're shaking with this trial.

JC: They already have the votes to block this thing.

GT: Don't be so sure. There's always a chance.

JC: A chance?

GT: There's always a chance that when this thing goes into second or third gear...

JC: The Senate trial, you mean.

GT: Yup, when you start parading witness after witness and the ugly rumor and innuendo starts getting some television time people may be so repulsed by Clinton the Democratic Senators may have to run for cover. Remember, people never heard of Watergate until the cameras started rolling. Some of these guys are no fans of Bill Clinton. This ain't a lap dog operation like the House. If (Daniel Patrick) Moynihan smells blood he'll will whip these guys into a rabid frenzy for Clinton's head, you can be sure of that. Congressmen are hookers compared to the Senate. Before you start writing that "they need 67 votes, no way" bullshit again you better remember that most of these Senators have been around a whole lot longer than Bill Clinton. And they plan for it to stay that way.

JC: Where were you when the Democrats hit the rose garden ten minutes after their boy was the first elected president in the history of this republic to be impeached? Those crazy fuckers were whooping it up like he'd just won the Publishers Clearing House Sweepstakes.

GT: Pikers. That's party survival. Just like our guys going against the election results and plowing ahead. You did see that parade of GOP congressmen holding press conferences, did you not? One after the other, painting themselves as agents of judicial mercy. The Republicans don't want Clinton gone when there is so much more damage he can do, and two years of economic fluctuation before the next fight. But they had to run the party course. Democrats did the same thing, but they are far more scared of Clinton than the GOP. He could cripple the future of his party.

JC: But what does he care? He's gone. They laughed at him in '92. Sent him to be shredded by wolves. He was the Democrat sacrifice. Why should he take one for the team like Nixon.

GT: Clinton ain't going anywhere.
JC: A deal.
GT: By Valentine's Day.

Next week a new and improved Democratic insider waiting to anonymously harass my pal Georgetown in print. This is beyond my control now. Stay tuned.

e-mail mania

Date: 12/23/98 10:19 PM

Campion,

Please delete whatever I might have said to you this afternoon. I was tired and irritated. My fucking airplane was three hours delayed, and whatever passes for the an airport bar these days refused to serve me Chivas "in the state I was in." Those fuckers booked me on the last available plane west, and then you corralled me for God knows how long. I'm sorry, but everything you taped is far too incriminating. I'll be weeded out. And that'll be the end of your contact here. I'm fucking serious. It's bad enough you printed that crazy shit about the lie/truth plan. You know I think Clinton is one of the great presidents if not for his lustiness. We need to step back and analyze the underlying behavior of it all. This is a sick, sick man. What are you going to write when our beloved flawed president stumbles to the rose garden podium and starts masturbating like a sleazy subway lecher inside his tattered rain coat. I cannot be party to this irresponsible tripe you've forced out of me, and will no doubt print to my ultimate consternation. I have better, more useful information for you.

It's just like Nixon. No one believed they would send that broken-down schizophrenic to prison. He may have been deranged and evil, but he was the President of the United States. He wanted to crush the Left, saw their shadows on his four-poster bed like Ebaneezer Scrooge on lithium, but he weeped like a child when they came for him. No amount of pills and therapy could save Nixon those last few months. No, the vociferous calls for impeachment came not when the burglary first occurred, and the subsequent cover-up slowly became public, but rather when the sordid details became apparent and his behavior was fully unmasked. He tacitly commissioned a crime, and then used the machinations of the Oval Office to conceal it, for sheer political advantage. His sole motivation was a brutal game of partisan one-upmanship - a game he ultimately lost. To even staunch Republicans, this type of behavior was patently unacceptable, and the president had no choice but to resign. Even you can see it's less political and more behavioral. Nixon was a frightened dupe, God's mistake. But he was president, and we couldn't see him rot in prison. Clinton has merely half of Nixon's potential for guts and glory. He cannot fight!

Print that. Because if you plan on going through with printing that excruciatingly long line of bullshit I rendered in that fuck-awful state I was in last week, I will have to act, and act swiftly. It's a fucking election year. I'll sue you and that rag of yours. Try me.

georgetown

Date: 12/24/98 1:52 PM

Mr. Phony,

You don't believe any of this tripe. You're busy trying to land in the middle to procure your own writing gig. Who the hell do you think you're fooling with that pap about Clinton being one of the great presidents if not for his prick? Behavioral? Get a grip, man. You're a conservative! Mommy can't fix the president. He's a criminal now, like his hero Jack Kennedy; who fixed an election with daddy's mob money and put poor Dick Nixon on a mental bell curve found only in the deepest reaches of hysteria. This man's foreign policy is nonexistent. And just like that fucking fraud Reagan, he's been riding this economy thing (which he has little to nothing to do with) in order to fog our true vision of him as a failed liberal white elephant. Big Bill should weed out Allen Greenspan and offer him oral sex. And where the hell is health care reform? Bill Clinton is a joke, and this whole Lewinsky crap validates it.

Also, stop giving me a history lesson and dredging up Nixon. You sound like those tired hacks on MSNBC. You're better than that.

Your points on the lie/truth plan were valid and sober. But this vapid excuse for a threat about suing me is masked by the usual rhetoric and window dressing that our president lives by everyday. You must live by venom and bite, or suffer an ignominious fate. This is why I think it would be impossible to unleash your identity on the public. You tend to be bold in private conversations and go incredibly limp in big moments. You are the Mets down the stretch. Give me the real shit and fuck all those people who can't take it. You're not running for any office for Christ's sake. Kick ass or go back to kissing Al D'Amato's feeble rump. For some desperate reason I have faith in you. I consider you my only credible source worth a damn. You can be a god, but choose to be nothing more than a mediocre commentator. Fuck that. Let the others rot. Take the road less traveled. Only a few people can pull that off. You are one of them. Don't waste your time being George Will.

Yours in vitriol,

jc

Date: 1/7/98 4:38 AM

Campion,

I'd rather be like George Will than some meat-hook hack of a writer better left in the gutter pissing in his pants because he's too inebriated and beaten by street trash to get up. What you are printing is not an accurate assessment of the situation. I was under incredible pressure at that fucking airport. I think my revised, better prepared, response had the appropriate amount of vitriol, but unfortunately any more would have rendered it unpublishable. I can ramble scathing editorials all day, but nobody would be reading them, so what's the point? I think you're much bolder on that sort of thing, but that's your style. Everything is black and white to you. There are shades of gray in this world, and the best thing to do at times is capture that. Goddamn it, if there were ever shades of gray on a public issue, its Clinton. That son of a bitch is making it hard for anyone to offer serious commentary, so all you get is bombastic gibberish. I was suckered into a jumbled hypothetical ramble by a third-rate journalist who would rather make a deadline and print the rants of a weakened man, than print anything resembling the truth. Who the fuck knows what the right answers are? If I had a regular gig with your rag, then I'd be a bit more outspoken, but unfortunately, I live at the discretion of the Republican party. A pay check and an affiliation are hard things to ignore in a time when money keeps you from random pistol whippings and Salvation Army handouts.

As for Nixon, I love to bring him up in every conversation— it just makes this horror show that much more palatable. I'm going site him in every-thing I ever say for the rest of my life. I had about 20 phone calls yester-day after this abomination of yours ran from a host of people putting in their own two cents. There were an equal number of those who thought I was a Clinton apologist, as there were who thought I was a right wing nut. These are people who already know my identity, and if I go down, you'll join me. There will be no place for you to hide in DC when I finish spreading the obligatory hooker/junkie rumors we peddle for fact here. I will come for you. And when that day arrives you'll wish you'd lost all your fingers in a farming accident and never even dreamed of seeing a typewriter.

georgetown

Date: 1/6/98 6:07 PM

Slickness,

The hack barb was below the belt.

Sorry about the diatribe before Christmas. I was under heavy sedation for this fucking cold I've had since Halloween, and then I had to fend off petrified editors who actually bought your Attila the Hun lawsuit bullshit. Actually, your retraction of my column was right on; informative and en-tertaining. You're just a pussy, that's all. I must admit my own nagging love and dedication to Tricky Dick, and I apologize for berating you for using him. God knows I do it myself in the weaker moments. But your fascination borders on obsession, and that is frightening to me.

Finally, who cares if anyone knows you're Georgetown. He has now become a man far more important than any government lackey. My readers rely on your lunacy to bring the biscuit home. No mercy!! Fuck the Republican party! Those scumbags had better be paying you top dollar for the kind of editorial anal probe you laid on their witch hunt. Where will they go when Big Bill is innocent as a lamb, smoking stogies in the leather swivel chair behind the oak desk Kennedy banged Marylin Monroe upon? This Senate trial is a fucking joke, and they should kiss the ground you trod upon for the literary blessings you bestow. Next time they try and calm you down, hit them with a First Amendment suit. I will be a character witness. It will give me a chance to try out new and improved expletives in a court room setting. I know these people, and they will be hearing from my attorney. Wait, aren't you my attorney? God help us all.

X & 0's

jc

Date: 12/8/98 7:12 PM

Campion,

I forwarded your comments to a friend of mine at the state department. This is his response :

Who is this guy? I like him! (Funny, I thought Dick Nixon died. I guess he faked his own death to become an ascetic recluse.) This Campion guy is angry, cynical, clear-headed, and articulate. I think I'm in love. To quote Moe, he makes you look like a pile of puke.

To be honest, my feelings about you and your fear of the GOP are very similar to his, except I try to be a little more diplomatic with you (if you want brutal honesty from me just say so). That's what I was getting at when responding to the highly digestible, yet libelous column, underneath all that psycho babble. I guess I'm the good cop to this guy's bad cop, the Sonny to his Cher, the Ronnie to his Nancy, the Chico to his Mr. Brown (from Chico and the Man, which incidentally is coming out on reruns on one of the Spanish channels. I'm so fired up!)

That crap about Clinton having the potential to be a great president is just that: crap (obviously you're not the first to say that). And discussing sex validates the liberal's distraction, and takes attention away from the legal issues. But I understand why you mince words in public and then back off. It hurts me to see you do that, but I guess the glorious end of getting in the door justifies your means.

My opinion, however, is that you'll get more attention at this point if your message has an edge, as long as it's well thought out and tough without being unfair or petty. Everything written now about Clinton is so mushy and noncommittal; look at the attention Perot is getting now because he has some balls (even if he is a senile kook; imagine if he could organize a thought!). The problem with politics and culture now is the lack of certainty; people are starving for it. Besides, the news cycles have gotten slow, nothing new has come out, so the media and public are looking for a kick.

How about a column talking about the Democrats' rhetorical roadblocks, bitching about everything; they should pick a story and stick to it, damn it! Or a column about this whole thing being the final explosion of the Democratic party, like a dying star; their last hope in Clinton is sinking fast. Or something about the fucking craven, brain-dead media, providing no historical or legal perspective on anything, just acting like a bunch of waterbeds for John Conyers and his every gripe. (This paragraph was my spleen venting).

I will give you the advice my grandfather gave me before he died: "If you have the consistency of the plot of every Three's Company episode, the unashamed pride of Pamela Anderson's breasts, the dogged persistence of LT chasing a quarterback while high on coke, and the intelligence of Rob Lakind, you will eventually win over the world, and more important, yourself. And if not, at least there's bound to be some loose chick out there who'll be impressed with you." As you can tell, my grandfather was a very wise man.

By the way, your little friend is wrong about you being the only credible source worth a damn; he obviously hasn't had the opportunity to bask in my genius. Set him straight, will you my good man?

tank

1/6/98 11:28 PM

Dear Sir,

I received the correspondence from Mr. Tank. This gentleman is my new hero. I wish to get very drunk with him soon, and hopefully get lucky. His references are oblique and dandy. I am glad I have raised his considerable ire against you and your kind. I thought all those dupes were brain dead over at state?

I hope to hear from this lunatic Tank soon and often, and if he is half of the insider he has displayed in this e-mail I've just read, I think we shall be fast friends. Is he a rumor weasel such as yourself? These are desperate times, my friend. We need to break the stories as they develop. I have no time to retract the crazy things which tumble from your brain. It is my job to place them in context to the current events which affect our very lives—and God help me, fill up 900 words a week.

Show some sympathy, and even more mercy. And if you choose to go the legal route I will take the brunt of it. Don't go after my paper. It's me and you, pal. Come hard. I don't expect the loser to live. This is not about us after all. It's about politics. It's about impeachment. It's about the future of journalism. aha! I have the First Amendment as my guide!

Peace to All
I have deadlines

jc

1/6/99

SHRILL FROM THE HILL: DEMO INSIDER RESPONDS TO GOP BACKLASH

My friend, Georgetown, has gotten far to many inches in this space. At least that's what a man I will now call Dibbs told me after a rather cantankerous phone call late at night—while I was pounding away on this infernal keyboard deep in the bowels of my bunker in Putnam Valley, NY. Georgetown is my only serious Republican source, and his record of correct predictions is staggering, but my left wing pals, whom I've apparently failed to satiate in print since my bygone college newspaper days, have crawled from the wreckage of their president to hammer me with rhetoric last heard from at the "People's Park" rally of '68 or '69. So in the interest of fairness, and more importantly, my own preservation within the cozy confines of whatever freak party arises in the next century, Dibbs gets his precious inches here and now.

JC: So are you guys afraid that if this trial lags on, the country, and those Democratic Senators you're counting on to block the two-thirds vote, will run for cover?

Dibbs: No. In a court of law none of this would have gotten past the grand jury stage. The president's lawyers have proven time and again he did not commit perjury. No one in the Senate could seriously consider sidestepping the truth about a liaison and ambiguous answers about sex as "high crimes and misdemeanors" which, by the way, the Constitution makes perfectly clear is the bottom line for removing a president from the office he was elected to by the American people. And I think the constant polls, no matter who runs them, have spoken to the first part of your question.

JC: I want to touch on the polls. Is it not true that the American people at one point were in favor of slavery, not allowing women to vote, prohibition, and vehemently opposed to putting Hitler out of commission?

DB: What is the point of holding elections if the person chosen is going to be hounded tooth and nail for six years?

JC: For laughs?

DB: Apparently.

JC: I'm told Gore's a shoe-in for 2,000, but the Dems believe someone will close the gap before summer. Tell me that vermin and his PMRC windbag of a wife is sent back to the tobacco farm.

DB: The Republicans have no one who can beat Gore. You know it, Georgetown knows it, and all your friends in the DC bullpen know it now. Gore will ride the momentum off this witch hunt. What is going on up at Capital Hill is political suicide for the GOP. Hope this was worth it.

JC: Will Gore separate himself from Clinton when he smells possible victory? Best bet says he'll dance on Big Bill's bones to become president.

DB: He needs Clinton. You're forgetting Hillary alone wiped out at least five senators and three congressmen. She will be instrumental in this thing. That's the beauty of this trial. Hillary has been bruised and battered worse than her husband, and she will pose the greatest challenge to the Republican surge in 2,000. Word I get is she will run for the Senate, possibly as soon as 2,000, and then president in '04.

JC: What the fuck are you saying?

DB: Hillary Rodham Clinton will run for the vacated NY Senate, and president in six years. Print it.

JC: If she doesn't dump Big Bill.

DB: No chance. It's a "us against the world" mentality inside the party now. Hillary rallied the troops when the shit first started to swirl about Lewinsky's testimony . We're afraid of her. You can lay your house on that. And she knows it. If she goes, the lines become blurred. Why do you think women come out in droves to defeat Republicans now? Plus, if Libby Dole tries to capture the female vote, Hillary will hit the trail.

JC: Getting back to the impeachment. Isn't there one Democrat in Congress who has privately told you that they wretched like a firehouse after standing behind Clinton and clapping for fifteen minutes after he was dragged through the political mire.

DB: Not that I'll tell you. But I will say this, everyone knows that this is a witch hunt. The Republicans, despite their better interest, hate Clinton so much they'll do anything short of putting a bullet in him. There are guys in bars all around town right this minute who are whooping it up on the embarrassment issue alone. They know he's not going anywhere. There has never been an endgame to this, and they don't care. They cannot help themselves. It's a disease, but they're the ones who are dying.

JC: It has to make you sick to defend this asshole. Clinton doesn't even care about the future of the party. He'll run this thing to the end. He lied to you guys as well.

DB: It was about an affair.

JC: Be honest, this doesn't embarrass you?

DB: We'll see who's embarrassed in two years when we get Congress back.
JC: And Al Gore?
DB: Hail to the Chief.

e-mail mania

Date: 1/14/99 1:08 AM

Campion,

What's the point of letting this Dibbs asshole waste crucial magazine space? The president's lawyers have proven time and again he did not commit perjury? Oh yeah, that's right. I was off the planet the day this happened.

Dibbs said:
"No one in the Senate could seriously consider sidestepping the truth about a liaison and ambiguous answers about sex, high crimes and misdemeanors' which, by the way, the US Constitution makes perfectly clear is the bottom line for removing a president from the office he was elected to by the American people."

Too bad it was good enough to oust 6 federal judges, not to mention the highest ranking enlisted man in the armed forces. There is a trail of dead bodies behind the Clinton presidency, and the sooner we recognize them, the sooner we can rid ourselves of this stinking low-rent scumbag.

And if the Republicans have no one who can beat Gore, I will drive my car off the cliffs of Mertile Beach. Tell that fucker Dibbs I'll bet money that Nixon's coffin would win against Al Gore in 2000.

And about all this bullshit of a witch hunt: I guess Clarence Thomas and the whole Long Dong Silver/Pubic Hair on the coke can wasn't? Fact is, everyone's got something to hide, and now it's the GOP's turn to slag some mud. In this case the slagging is made easier by the pig in the WH.

See, the problem with this schlub Dibbs is he's completely off the radar. Look back at how I've responded to the Senate trial, and how your pal, Georgetown has. Those are realistic viewpoints - yeah our side are being dicks, but so are the Dems. You've got to question someone who can't even admit the stupidity of his own guy. You want to be afraid of someone? Be afraid of the guy who thinks Al Gore would make a great president.

Finally, if the GOP has to fear that gullible hag in the White House, we're all in a heap of fucking trouble.

Please forward to Dibbs. Give him my regards...

Mr. K

Date: 1/15/99 2:33 PM

James,

Christ, who is this Mr. K? I don't think I possess a grasp of the vocabulary it would take for me to impart the utter horror I felt when confronted with the Neanderthal rhetoric you forwarded to me this morning. A man should be spared these kind of thoughtless bits of lunacy when relaxing at home with his family. Am I diseased? Am I guilty of some heinous crime that I should be subjected to such vicious brutality? I was afraid to shut off my computer. But for the love of democracy, I shall strive on, and attempt to set straight whatever biological mutation wrote that crap.

First of all, no one Mr. K listed as impeachable victims were elected to anything. Judges are appointed and the military has its own rules to which I wash my moral hands.

Dead bodies? I don't understand? If this man is referring to Vince Foster, then you are all as brain dead as I feared. Foster was a victim of his own battered conscious and failing id. His suicide was a product of the kind of pressure we in the land of milk and honey thankfully know little

about. And we are glad. Perhaps Mr. K blames the passing of George
Burns on the president.
Secondly, Al Gore will be the next President of the United States. Get
used to it. He's already picking out the curtains for the Lincoln bedroom. There is no point in holding an election in a couple of years, let's
just anoint him now and skip the massacre.

In grateful conclusion, remember, a good political junky and debater must
never underestimate the opposition. If you hope to win anything in 2,000
you have to admit how powerful Hillary is. You laughed at Bill and you are
crying now. Dealing with his wife is another level of hurt. But I will pray for
your dead.

Dibbs

Date: 1/15/99 7:41 PM

Campion,

Fair point by Dibbs. Perhaps if he didn't have his head so far up his ass
it wouldn't hurt. A Gore massacre? Clinton was lucky the first time
when Perot ate up the middle and the right and handed that cheap hick
a tainted victory. God forbid he actually captured more than half of the
popular vote. In reality the electoral college put Clinton in there. There
will come a day when the actual votes cast will be for candidate A and
the electoral votes will be in B's favor. Clinton was elected by the 42%
of the 48% of the people who voted. So in a way, the same people who
put those judges in are the same who put Clinton in. Plus, before those
judges ever get to that level, we the people had to vote them in at some
point which then enabled them to receive their appointments.

Did you ever read the list of the dead people Clinton's been directly in
contact with throughout his career? We're not talking normal numbers
here, where you can say it applies to everybody. I'm talking direct political contact. I thought I sent that information to you a while back. Huge
fucking list of people.

One point I agree with Geraldo on in all of this: Clinton's the baby boomer guy and stalwart republican. WWII generation types can't stand him. I see that in myself. The older I get, the more I hate these vacuous young assholes of the current MTV generation. And to think, I was one of them at one time!

And about Hillary. Dibbs must never overestimate her either. If Hillary's so powerful, why couldn't she get a national health care system up and running with a democratically controlled congress? Why does the public school system (of which she's SO concerned) keep sucking more and more money down the tubes with less and less results? Where's her power? You want to buy the line that it was because of her that a handful of congressmen won some seats? Explain Jesse Ventura. She campaigned hard against him, a real opponent. Talk to me about power when Hillary helps someone who's race ISN'T a coin toss, and maybe I'll listen. And where was all this power when it came to keeping her husband's zipper up? You know, the one with the political self-destruct button on it.

Here's your answer: We're living in a time when it's nobody's fault for anything they do. "My father hit me one too many times when I was a kid and that's why I raped and murdered all those college girls." Or, "Yeah, I axed that elderly couple to death but I've found Jesus." You've got people recklessly fucking each other and contracting deadly diseases or making babies they can't support, and what do we do? Feel sorry for them. Create a government program for them cause they're so goddamn stupid that honest-living hard working people have more taken out of their paychecks to support these weak motherfuckers. And the core baby boomers of this country, who would rather have someone else raise their kids than part with their SUV's, embody the selfishness that pervades our culture. Only in this kind of world can a Hillary and Bill have any power.

Nuff said.

Mr. K

Date: 1/16/99 12:11 AM

Mr. K,

Why is it when you drone on about these civic events it sounds like your spewing hapless right-wing rhetoric from some machine-head asswipe who has no original thought, or a boring text book from 8th grade history class? I think you should stop getting behind propaganda and start having your own thoughts. I'm not saying you're brainwashed (start the tune now) but you're views are so eerily similar to the usual obligatory "liberals suck" bullshit, it doesn't seem like I'm talking, or in this case writing, to a person, but an ad for ideology.

I love the flying dog dung that perpetuates the idea that everyone who votes is a dumbass who doesn't know a fucking thing and wants the government to save them. Where were all these dumbasses when they voted the Republican majority in '94? They wanted less government and less taxes. Are these the same geniuses who voted Reagan in twice on overwhelming numbers? C'mon, all these slick '90s' buzz words like "baby boomers" which pigeonhole everyone scares me. It's not that people don't know anything about government or politics, they don't care about government and politics. And the ones who do are donning fatigues right now with tree branches in makeshift helmets calling their congressman and hanging up, and communicating with 12 year-olds on the making of plastic explosives and Korn lyrics. They want to get laid, suck down brew, and watch fucking football and soap operas. The last time any of these poor saps put their fist in the air their leaders were cut down like dogs and they went into hiding with J.D. Salinger.

Finally, you have the balls to give me a lecture on voter IQ and throw Jesse Ventura into the mix? God Almighty could have come down and told people to vote against Jesse and he would have won anyway. This is why Perot got the votes he did in '92, the reason Clint Eastwood would win anything, the reason Chuck Heston is the president of the NRA, the reason so many people love those fucking laughably hackneyed "Rocky" movies. Celebrity rules. It is human nature to vote for the loudmouthed "every man". Now it is time for the "every woman". Beware Hillary...

Dibbs
1/17/99 5:12 AM

Dibbs,

Replace right-wing with left-wing and liberals suck with republicans suck in your tired diatribe and that's what YOU sound like. And can you please tell me what other sides there are to this story that I could've chosen from to avoid sounding like some mindless propaganda robot to you? Wait a minute. There is another side: the they-all-suck side. THAT'S the James Campion side. And that one is for sale to the highest bidder. Freelance journalists are the lowest form of land life. The only thing more despicable is the "anonymous source." So tell me, how much will it cost for that loon to crawl up your liberal ass and pen an "I Love Al Gore" piece?

Look, it doesn't matter to me that you and Campion are political whores. I wait for the usual balance he brings to his stuff. When it's not there, I'm disappointed. This whole ordeal has made me sad. I used to believe in things like grandma and apple pie, cherry bombs and anal sex. But, predictably. as soon as the Lewinsky scandal broke a year ago, the Clinton and liberal media machine spewed out all the same defend-the-creep stuff.

It's the 52% or more of the country that DOESN'T vote who are the dumbasses. And "babyboomer" isn't a buzzword, my liberal friend. A buzzword can't cause the collapse of the social security system. It's a fact that there are more people in this country between the ages of 35 and 55 than any other age group. The core of that group comes from the same era as Bill and Hillary. How else can you explain the collective apathy with what's going on? He's their guy, their age; and it's nice to know that he's as human and fucked up as they think they are. The country would've been outraged 30-40 years ago with all this. And think of the press 35 years ago. They knew the Beatles were fucking young chicks left and right, but they didn't report it. Why? We all found out about JFK after the fact, but where were the front-page bombshells back then? And there's two reasons why Reagan had two terms: Jimmy Carter and Walter Mondale. And the GOP '94 majority? Thank Clinton's retroactive tax hike and his other reckless bunglings combined with a spendthrift democratic congress for that.

You are right about one thing, dearest Dibbs. The problem IS that nobody cares about government. We should all be involved from the local level, where even crazier shit is happening, on up. Do you think things would've gotten so fucked up if we were all paying attention? Yo, c'mon!

By the way, I did not lecture you on voter IQ in regarding Ventura. In fact I didn't mention voter IQ anywhere, Slappy, so calm down. My point is, if Hillary's soooo powerful and scary, why didn't her campaign for the fill-in-the-blank incumbent in Minn. give Ventura the political suplex?

You beware Hillary. I got more important things to worry about.

The Supine, Mr. K

1/20/99

JORDAN & TYSON: AN AMERICAN SPORTS PARADOX

In the first week of January two of the most celebrated athletes of the better part of the past two decades wrote new installments in their careers. Michael Jordan, arguably the most influential sport's figure since Muhammad Ali, said good-bye to the game he revolutionized. The National Basketball Association's reconstruction from "Lock Out" madness will sorely miss him, but the world stage will miss him even more.

Meanwhile, Mike Tyson, the only prize fighter to even approach the curiosity and celebrity of Ali, was acting like an ass once again; cursing out reporters and trying to break a man's arm in a clench during his first bout back from a year's suspension. The boxing game has missed Tyson, but perhaps infamy will hardly notice.

Jordan and Tyson were both born in the borough of Brooklyn in the turbulent 60s'; Jordan in 1963 during the coldest winter in decades, and Tyson in the blistering heat of June three years later. Both would follow a path to sports dominance, seducing stardom and riches beyond their wildest dreams. The youngest Heavyweight Champion of the World at age 20, Mike Tyson became the epitome of "the sure thing". He was young and strong and unbeatable before anyone had even heard of him. On the other hand Michael Jordan was always a step behind, cut from his high school team and buried in a college system which used, but did not showcase him. He was taken third in the NBA draft and forced to use his burgeoning pristine athleticism to fight for respect among a league of cliques.

Tyson's star rose quickly. Jordan's star took time as a result of maturity and patience. Jordan did not win his first title until 1990, just a few months before Tyson began his tragic decent, losing his first professional fight to an unknown named Buster Douglas. The roots and subsequent struggles of two exceptional athletes with the same first name would clearly demonstrate the best and worse the America athlete could produce. Two heroes linked by time and headlines, but in reality, worlds apart.

Michael Jordan was rescued from the mean streets of Brooklyn in his youth, coming of age in the bucolic splendor of North Carolina with the love and guidance of his parents. He leapt onto the scene in spring of 1982 burying the winning jumper in the NCAA National Championship game. Two years later he helped bring home the last gold medal captured by American amateurs in Olympic basketball. He was drafted by the Chicago Bulls, a franchise which had never come close to a NBA championship. It took six seasons for Jordan's Bulls to reach the pinnacle of its sport, but he would go on to grab five more titles while winning six league MVP's along the way. Eventually everyone agreed he was quite simply the best to ever play the game. Michael Jordan was fire and grace, a prideful competitor with the uncanny ability to fly above adversity on and off the court.

Mike Tyson exploded from oblivion onto the world's stage with the very sheer brutality of the sport which bore him. Unlike a team or league sport which begs for the individual to subjugate personal ego for the collective goal, boxing is a game of force, asking only to seize the prize. Having grown up on the Brooklyn streets with no parental direction, Tyson bottled the rage of ten men, rousing an aging trainer by the name of Cus D'Amato to harness it. Unlike Jordan's glory in 1984, Tyson was denied entry into the Olympics by controversial decisions in the ring. He would rarely be denied anything inside a ring ever again. His first professional fight was a knockout, and nearly everyone after that. Before he'd even built a resume the boxing world had decided he was "the greatest of all time." Iron Mike was the specter of doom, the animal lust for blood in black trunks. He was the savage core of humanity come to conquer, and unceremoniously handed the keys to his own destruction.

Both Tyson and Jordan became men inside the fishbowl of fame and fortune. Both married; Tyson to a vacuous starlet, Jordan to the girl next door. Both battled demons; for Jordan it was always gambling, for Tyson, violence. But it was Mike Tyson who was inevitably defined by his weaknesses; the unbridled criminal, a viscous rhino stomping though the china shop. He was arrested, ridiculed, and jailed for rape. Even those who rooted for Tyson feared him. No one feared Michael Jordan, even those whom he beat into submission on the court every night. Everyone wanted to "Be like Mike". Jordan made movies with cartoon characters, Tyson was surrounded by them. Jordan built an empire on sneakers and cologne. Tyson lost his soul for money he would never see. When Jordan won championships, he wept. When Tyson won fights, he raged. When Michael Jordan stepped away from the game after the shocking murder of his father, he returned with a passion and respect reserved for a prince of fables. When Tyson begged for the right to showcase his talent after a prison sentence, he assaulted Evander Holyfield like a rabid dog. In the end Jordan walked away at the height of his sport and at the top of his game. Tyson hangs around for paydays while smearing his legend with aged embarrassment.

One week in January, two public lives born of athletics, but waned in opposite directions. Two men demonstrating both ends of today's sports spectrum.

1/27/99

IN DEFENSE OF LARRY FLYNT AND OTHER SCUMBAGS LIKE HIM

*"You can never go broke underestimating
the intelligence of the American public."*
- H.L.Mencken

*"Render to Caesar the things that are Caesar's
and to God the things that are God's"*
- Mark 12:17

It is customary for this space to espouse the ever popular theory that everything is fucked. Has been, always will be. Don't let anyone tell you how great the 1950s' were without hearing from African Americans, women, artists, and the remainder of those who might have had a friend or two of Eastern European persuasion. And don't listen to those boring Baby Boomers drone on about the love and peace revolution of the 60s' unless you contact those mired in drug clinics, veterans of cop beatings, and the poor suckers who worked on Robert Kennedy's campaign. In the grand tradition of this we bring you Lord Larry Flynt; publisher of smut and depravity, misrepresented patriot of the first amendment, victim of random violence, and enemy of Jerry Falwell.

Flynt, the 70s' poster child for vice along with disco and cocaine, has returned to relevance by recently airing the dirty laundry of Republican Congressmen, and paying a handsome sum for it. He is a businessman with an agenda, a politically motivated mad dog with capital and the use of a printing press.

As founder and publisher of Hustler magazine Flynt has the celebrity distinction of being both villain and hero; originally vilified for pushing Hugh Hefner's envelope, only to be exonerated by the Supreme Court. If you are not familiar with the contents of Hustler, it should not merely be described as pornographic, but the visual and verbal equivalent of a traveling side show, a freak compendium filled with the maggots which must eventually feed on a rotting corpse.

Unfortunately for those disgusted with Flynt's little black market carnival, they are surprisingly revolted further when finding out its maggots feed off the remains of a country once horrified by the very mention of sex.

It is only fitting that someone like Flynt rise from the muck of this senseless charade of a political Senate trial to start picking off the slugs and leeches who crowd the halls of this nation's capital. Salacious innuendo works well in a town where power is a free pass to the ol' boys network of character assignation, payoffs, and the daily mockery of law. If his hope is to save the president, Flynt only serves to illuminate the dark musty corners Bill Clinton has thrived in for decades.

Politically, this crusade may backfire on him and those Democrats who call the Legislative Branch their home. His flashlight theory may send the cockroaches scurrying to refuge, but it also brings the worms pouring from the can.

Larry Flynt is not a bright man. Anyone who has heard him speak on a myriad of insipid subjects can attest to this. He has risen to the status of Washington player on the same spite and fear that politicians rake out every summer to land on their collective feet in fall. Flynt is familiar with this terrain. This is a nation of the lowest common denominator. Polls indicate that although now nearly 85% of the American public think our president is a lying, cheating, lowlife hick with the credibility of streetwalker, nearly 75% want him to continue his job.

These aren't just the dumb-ass Generation X children or the whining retro-hippies the GOP blame for the uneducated sympathy of a criminal president. These are the survivors of Lyndon Johnson's blood lust in Viet Nam, the desensitized infants of Richard Nixon's reign of self-destructive paranoia, and the wounded underbelly of Ronald Reagan's economic lunacy.

Larry Flynt can do what he does because he is rich and famous. The rich and famous rule in this country. Why do you think O.J. Simpson is teeing up at a golf course near you, or Latrell Sprewell isn't serving time in an Oakland lockup? How do you think Jessie Ventura became governor of Minnesota?

Larry Flynt did not make his money in Russia or Europe with the dream of dragging the American Dream down with him. He made it right here in the good ol' US of A. This is a nation built on the blood and sweat of exploitation. We want to be raped, and fall all over ourselves finding out who else is doing the raping. The very freedoms abused by Larry Flynt have been tarred and feathered for centuries. In fact, there is something strangely wholesome about a publicity hound like Flynt going hard after the poor fuckers whose power they've handed him.

And don't let these sanctimonious trash sniffers like Bob Barr, Trent Lott, Dick Morris, Bill Bennett, James Carville, and Allen Dershowitz soil your television with their holier-than-thou rhetoric. They belong in the mud with Larry Flynt because he has skated on their leftovers. Blaming the messenger is as old as Greek tragedy, but blaming the guy sitting next to you at the slot machine for abandoning self-control is older.

2/3/99

ABSENCE OF THOUGHT: THE CURIOUS AND ASININE DEFENSE OF MUMIA ABU-JAMAL AND THE DECONSTRUCTION OF RIGHTEOUS PROTEST

Let's face it, I love to rage against any machine you'd like to present. I happen to be a big fan of the Beastie Boys. I'm not quite numb enough to fear a military police state where a citizen's rights are a billie-club-pistol-butt away from trouble. And no one who is familiar with this space has to ask my opinion of the good people who run the Meadowlands entertainment/sports complex. But, you know what? All these factions are way off base in their exoneration and protesting of the arrest of convicted cop-killer, Mumia Abu-Jamal. And, you know what else? It's a damn shame, because these amateurs have spent so much time defending this vermin that they've most likely overlooked some other poor soul who is truly innocent. Most notably, Philadelphia police officer Daniel Faulkner; the man Abu-Jamal gunned down in cold blood.

It's this type of misguided rabble rousing which dulls what might be considered a healthy "watch dog" mentality toward authoritarian abuse. Crying wolf alongside Whoopi Goldberg and Ed Asner, both dissenting voices against Abu-Jamal's arrest and subsequent trial, will turn genuine concern for certain cops who might take their power beyond the law into what Tom Wolfe once called "Radical Chic."

It's middle-class toilet paper protest tripe recycled like mouthwash from Rage Against the Machine—often regurgitated with the originality of a carnival barker—which dumps any real movement down some low-rent pubescent whine barrel. Hey, it's fine to protest and throw your freak flag into any revolution kick, but you, unlike the cloudy world of the Internet and video madness pumped through the MTV shredder, had better make damn sure what it is that you're raising your all-too willing fist in the air about.

At 4:00 am on December 9, 1981 Daniel Faulkner was on his beat and saw a car going the wrong way on a one-street way. When Faulkner pulled the driver of the car over, a man by the name of William Cook punched the officer in the face instigating a scuffle resulting in a third party shooting from Mumia Abu-Jamal. Five witnesses saw Abu-Jamal plug Faulkner in the back, and after firing several more bullets into him, blew his face off. Before succumbing to a painful death, Faulkner shot his assailant in the chest. Wounded, and eventually abducted close to the shooting with the murder weapon, Abu-Jamal was dragged from the scene shouting, "I shot the motherfucker, and I hope the motherfucker dies."

Anyone familiar with the violent contingent of this country's urban radicals this scenario is not coincidental. Cook is Abu-Jamal's brother. This was a setup in the tradition of a fractured revolt with all the subtlety and social wit of the Hells' Angels or the Black Panthers.

Abu-Jamal is guilty. Just like O.J. Simpson is guilty. Just like Bernard Getz is guilty. Just like Rodney King is guilty. Just like those rabid kill-geeks who beat him are guilty. For each of these rocky horrors there is some half-baked insipid protest attached to them like a parasite to a culture group. It is the twisted logic of the cowering dark edge of society to allow such criminal nobodies to even have a day in the spotlight much less represent a very real and pertinent issue. It is then that O.J. Simpson becomes Rosa Parks, Bernard Getz becomes the poster boy for white-male-rage, and Rodney King—drugged up and driving like a wild speed-banshee through rural neighborhoods—becomes the embodiment of a two-decade civil war between minorities and cops in LA. And because the crack dealers and thugs who pry on the California minority movement choose to burn their own city down, the actions of a desperate subculture suddenly become the voice of an entire culture.

We're already supposed to know that fringe schlock like Professional Wrestling, The Jerry Springer Show, Marylin Manson, Hustler Magazine, and South Park do not represent the whole of society. These pieces of pop culture reflect the underbelly of it. But when this mentality is subtlety moved into the realm of murder, protest, and a grass roots political movement it is not merely moronic, but dangerous. It is the only reason the pap smear of society like David Duke, Oliver North, Khalid Muhammad, and G. Gordon Liddy continue to run for office, host radio shows, and run rallies.

By the way, Abu-Jamal has published two books in his 18 year stint in prison, and if not for public outrage in Philly a few years ago, would have hosted several radio programs of his own.

If you attended last month's concert to protest Mumia Abu-Jamal's arrest you may have unwittingly damaged the very movement you hope to support.

Fear, anger, and revenge can cloud the goal of true revolution or even simple change.

So called icons, martyrs, and pathetic revolutionaries are reduced to blathering myopic psychos in its grip. Just ask your parents, who turned a self-centered goon like Bill Clinton into the Baby Boomer Messiah and got a fat southern bullshit artist instead. Don't let anyone tell you that you don't have the right to fight authority and all those nasty institutions that accompany it. You do. You also have the right to bury a real cause for outing police brutality, wrongful arrest, and abuse of power by hitching your wagon to snot-nosed rock stars with sports cars and mansions who find a need to tell you to rage and spit and stomp while they count the profits.

And of course you have the right to enact the very words of your heroes, "FUCK YOU I WON'T DO WHAT YOU TELL ME!"

2/17/99

LAST TRAIN FROM LITTLE ROCK

We the people, enduring this imperfect union, do here by fully admit to being its author. Yet, long before we were handed the torch, the original bearers suspended reality and stuck us with a fixed game. This republic, bound by these purple mountains and fruited plains, must finally conclude, in the waning moments of its self-proclaimed century, that although it is in God that we trust, what supreme being would bless this fucking mess?

And with such gibberish I bid farewell to the harassment, impeach- ment, embarrassment, and trial of William Jefferson Clinton, 42nd President of these United States. It was a slow blur, a skidding burn on the blighted history of America, but it was hardly a tragedy. Alarmingly, it was not, and remains so, hardly a wake up call for those of us still harboring allusions that a constitutional democracy falls terribly short of a true democracy. However, we have learned throughout the months upon months of this fiasco that neither life, or art, imitates one another quite like the blurry world of politics.

In life we are confronted with choices, and how we decide to rule on these choices will inevitably define us. As citizens, in theory, we choose our leaders, our civil servants, and send them to Washington to do our bidding.

In reality we are handed the rich, pompous, and the morally corrupt few who rise to grotesque levels of wealth and fame in order to make the cut.

Eventually we vote for the flawed survivors, and take the lesser of evils in order to root-root for the home party no matter what garbage it may spew. The ultimate hope is that our ideology emerges in the column with the least amount of blemishes. In the end we vote for whom we have little to no faith, but convince ourselves will do far less damage to our carefully crafted imagination. After all, it is our birth right as Americans to cast a ballot for the public official we will inevitably replace with another joker with a new and improved line of horseshit.

None of those creatures who skulk around Madison Avenue in their power ties and Armani suits selling security against loneliness and depression have ever known a fantasy machine that hums and burps like the one inside the Beltway. The ones who operate it are the mutant offspring of human failure still struggling to grasp the notion that no society can work within a structure which secretly cries out for anarchy while simultaneously begging someone to point it in the right direction; whatever that might be.

I have written hundreds upon thousands of words on this latest chapter in American history—most of it has been sprinkled with a healthy dose of sarcasm and satire—but in the end I am left with an empty feeling of disgust. As a professional journalist and amateur carnival barker I am barely moved by it all, only annoyed that something horrible and memorable didn't occur to shake my cynicism about governing bodies. But, alas, it was all just scripted for our pleasure like a hackneyed sitcom or a vacuous award show revue. Disappointed by the all-too predictable outcome, I crawl back to my typing device and struggle to encapsulate it without fighting nausea.

I can only muster this: Fear not future Americans developing in pre-schools, growing in wombs, or perhaps just thoughts in someone's eye; one day we'll get this thing down. The jumble of human emotion will take but a short respite in order to take the ores of this craft and swing them in unison. We will see the majesty of the concepts once dreamed of in dusty steam-fogged halls with the king's army breathing on the door. And remember, fine children of our making, even those poor fuckers didn't know a goddamn thing about what was going on. But they damn well sure knew that whatever it was they were forced to endure must change. We must honor their clairvoyance and praise their courage, but bemoan their fragile framework.

As we approach another century filled with criminals and despots and little smarmy flesh eaters with muted consciences and lined pockets, whom will no doubt try and screw up the works in the holy name of some patriarchal ego binge, we are relegated to pick our best and brightest from a muddy gene pool. We are, in effect, doomed. Do not make the same mistake.

Although, I fear you will.

2/24/99

THE SEDUCTION OF SENATOR RODHAM

From issue - 1/27 - 2/3:
"Hillary has been bruised and battered worse than her husband, and she will pose the greatest threat to the Republican surge in 2,000. Word I get is she will run for Senator of New York in 2,000 and president in '04."

So it was that my friend Dibbs told me over a month ago, to which I predictably answered with a carefully constructed barrage of expletives—and against my better judgment, sent to print where the wonderfully twisted people in copy ran with it.

It had been a long week, I was tired, and in no mood to follow up such babble with any credible ounce of journalistic integrity. Just the same, I was primed to sue the pants off that bastard if anything resembling a backlash came my way. Imagine my surprise when a few weeks later this gnarled slice of information turned out to be all the rage.

Hillary Rodham Clinton is contemplating a run for Senate and milking it for all its worth. It gives her front page status and the cover of *Time,* and remains the topic of conversation now that Kenneth Starr and his failed political bums-rush has gone away.

Those at the White House, more than interested at deflecting the bad memories of the last 12 months, now think of new and exciting ways to keep the martyred Mrs. Clinton in the news. But how serious is this rotten lunacy, and how afraid are Republicans of Ms. Rodham's final decision?

First off, the GOP, wounded like Custer's sucker troops at Little

Big Horn, should be frightened of the First Lady. She is poison as long as she doesn't mutate into a political animal. Presently, she is safe in her protected womb as a non-elected, yet caring, spouse of the most powerful, and apparently, completely invincible man in the free world. Ms. Rodham's rabid campaign stumping for Charles Shumer in New York five months ago was a roaring success. Even a campaign warmonger like Al D'Amato was road kill in its wake.

But if Ms. Rodham thinks that being Big Bill's Robin is anything like wearing Batman's cowl in a New York Senate race against a pit bull like Rudolf Giuliani, with a press corps that former Governor Mario Cuomo has called "the meanest in American history", she is sadly mistaken.

No one has to question Ms. Rodham's motives and moxi. Let's face it, she's been humiliated by her husband so many times she is numb, yet remains by Big Bill's side in excruciatingly embarrassing photo-ops while continuing to immerse her left-wing ideology into otherwise impotent moderate policies. She attached herself to a diseased host—but kept it alive long enough to wield some semblance of power—and the more her insipid husband tries to toss it all on the crap heap, the more she bails him out and resuscitates the patient. Now more than ever it's becoming obvious just where the killer instinct lies in this couple-by-convenience. Emerging from the shadow of the administration may prove it once and for all.

However, there have been rumblings in the Al Gore camp that Ms. Rodham's handshaking, baby-kissing, screech revelry will be needed when the Demo rally train gets into high gear. The party will need Ms. Rodham to be Hillary once again. But what the party has always failed to understand is that the Clintons don't give a fuck.

When the Democrats sent them to fry in George Bush's "Desert Storm" wake they plowed ahead like two crazy kamikaze kids and won the presidency. Since then Ms. Rodham has been Hillary to the core; a loving respectful wife and 90s' mom. Behind the scenes she's prodded and probed through the system with no chance of political retribution, all the while looking like she isn't too pissed about Big Bill's wild abandon.

No one has elected her to do anything, and Ms. Rodham doesn't owe the party a damn thing. If she feels like duking it out with a professional dross-slinger like Uncle Rudy, so be it. Moreover, without Hillary's Robert Kennedyesque campaign junket storming through the hinterland, the Democrats have little to no chance of retaining Patrick Moynihan's vacated seat. And the word I'm getting from Giuliani's bunker is that the very sight of a hatchet queen like Ms. Rodham will send Uncle Rudy spiraling into a race for Governor anyway. If my friend, Dibbs, and other Demo ilk just like him, have designs on taking back the majority on Capitol Hill, they had better hang onto existing chairs.

The real question remains: Why the hell would the defacto President of the United States want to take a step down and become a junior Senator?

Many close to the Clintons swear Hillary will not end up a faded memory like Nancy Reagan, perfectly happy to grow old with her hubby in respectful atrophy. If so, she'll want to stay in the public eye and effect future policy. Perhaps that would be better suited in Al Gore's cabinet or some other high-profile Washington gig. After all, a predictably nasty campaign would damage Ms. Rodham's current carefully nurtured Norma Rae image.

Surely, Giuliani, who barely broke a sweat painting former opponent Ruth Messenger as a nihilistic pornographer, will have little trouble digging up the mud of Whitewater. He would most certainly label the southern outsider as some mutant carpetbagger and regain the support he lost in upstate NY by trashing George Pataki in his run for governor against Cuomo five years ago.

The fact that an Arkansas lawyer, who has spent the last six years patching up a leaky presidential ship, leads a wildly successful NYC mayor in any poll right now speaks more about GOP fallout from the impeachment fiasco than anything else.

So for the political junky in us all we beg Ms. Rodham to fire up the engines and run. We can only hope she has a campaign maniac like Uncle Rudy lying wait. But who will blink first? For the First Lady none of this makes any sense, and the solid odds has her putting the kibosh on this media seduction when its legs begin to show fatigue.

3/10/99

JOE DIMAGGIO: 1914-1999

He was the best player on the most successful and revered sports franchise in America smack dab in the center its century. From 1936 to 1951, when the United States of America went from the depths of economic depression to the dawn of the golden age of capitalism, Joe DiMaggio played center field for the New York Yankees.

He was the child of Italian immigrants with limited social skills and a natural grace that belied his introverted fear of celebrity. Yet for nearly 70 years of his life Joe D. walked in the shoes of Ulysses. In the end he was the last of a dying breed: the untouchable American hero.

No one lived longer as a legend. As time wore on it was as if the Yankee Clipper had died some mysterious death as a young man. He retired long before the years eroded his magnificent talent. Then he became Mr. Marylin Monroe when she was the most famous woman in the world. DiMaggio was literally immortalized in song and story; Ernest Hemingway's voice of the old man crying from the sea for a chance to cast off with "the great DiMaggio", and Paul Simon's alienation of a Baby Boomer Generation devoid of heroes in the anti-hero landscape of the 1960s' casting their lonely eyes inside the haunting question of "Where have you gone Joe DiMaggio?"

Joltin' Joe was the best definition of the word "icon" found in the last 50 years of pop culture. He was the product of sports prose. Jimmy Cannon, Shirley Povich, and Grantland Rice waxed poetic about his graceful strides. The stirring spoken accounts of Mel Allen and Red Barber brought home his powerful stroke. He was the subject of the most awe-inspiring photographs in baseball history. Most of all, Joe DiMaggio was the last American hero created in the imagination of a populace devoid of television's prying eye. Other than those lucky enough to take the train to the Bronx and enter Yankee Stadium, or catch him on the road, an entire nation of sports fans knew the majesty and elegance of Joe DiMaggio like a reader might dissect the protagonist of a 19th century novel.

However, in the end, Joe DiMaggio will forever be remembered as a ballplayer par excellence. It has become fashionable in the latter part of the century for sports people to downplay his greatness on the field, just as, ironically, it had become common place for their predecessors to place him just below God for professional perfection. However, the numbers left by DiMaggio's considerable presence are irrefutable. As one of his managers, Casey Stengel liked to say, "You can look it up."

He followed the likes of Babe Ruth and Lou Gehrig with 9 World Series titles in 10 years, belted 361 home runs while striking out only 369 times. He carried a lifetime fielding average of .978; and in the Summer of 1941, mere months before the country joined the world at war, Joe DiMaggio dominated the front pages and radio headlines by hitting safely in a ridiculous 56 straight games.

"The Streak" is not only the most hallowed, and now with the homer-run record shattered, arguably the most difficult achievement in the history of sport. It was quite simply the final great American statement for a generation of young men who would leave their youth on battlefields two oceans away. And for three seasons, (1943-45) in the midst of a spectacular career, the Yankee Clipper joined the war effort alongside them.

Over the last few decades, while Joe DiMaggio was living out the legend of being named "the greatest living ballplayer", the part of him long forgotten in glowing prose and hero worship was his humanity. It slowly began to come to the foreground in not so glowing ways. A man who held the press in his back pocket for so long had begun to see his legacy take hits. Talk among close friends and former teammates often described DiMaggio as an isolated, almost paranoid man, who found demons in unfamiliarity, and jealousies behind every shadow.

The industry of being Joe DiMaggio (autographs, documentaries, ceremonies) seemed to eclipse the once world class athlete lost in the waning years of a century he once defined. Many argued that when succeeding Yankees' star, Mickey Mantle died so young a few summers ago, the outpouring of affection and remembrance would not be the same for an old-timer like DiMaggio, simply because so many who revered, or even saw him play, would no longer be around to mourn him.

Growing up in a predominantly Italian-American family in the Bronx, NY, and the first born son of an Irish-American Yankee fanatic who'd steal away on late-afternoons to enter through a rear gate into the Stadium to watch the mighty Yankees build upon a sports dynasty, Joe DiMaggio always had a place in the Campion household baseball discussion. My Great Uncle Vinnie held my Uncle Johnny in his arms and called for Joe D. to toss up a ball his nephew would unwittingly use in a neighborhood game. My friend, Steven Muratore from Brooklyn, took the subway to the Big Ball Yard in the Bronx to study the man's every move, as if witnessing a miracle at Lourdes.

Today, as thousands like myself grasp to find the correct words to place a man we have never seen dominate our national past time on the day of his passing, we reach back to that "greatest generation" to give us the slightest idea of what a black and white photograph might have looked like in living breathless youthful color.

HAIL TO THE CHEAT: A SORDID HISTORY OF PRESIDENTIAL SEXCAPADES

Bill Clinton may be only the second President of the United States to be impeached, but he is hardly the first to be rocked by career threatening salacious innuendo and a roving sexual appetite. From Gennifer Flowers to Monica Lewinsky, Slick Willie has been hounded and charged all the way to the brink of extinction, but for other philandering chief executives it wasn't always that way. Many never even felt the sting of their actions or were called on the carpet, (no pun intended). There were the few who found their private lives probed, (once again no pun intended) had their run for the office, and in some cases, their time at the helm hampered; but for those who survived long enough to serve under the moral code of the ultimate office these musty skeletons forever rattling in the closet have caused their share of embarrassment and incrimination.

Big Bill may forever be remembered for his wild libido and a penchant for the odd oval office oral pleasure, but he's just another link in the long chain of powerful men with dark bedroom secrets. Here is a complete list of those beloved lecherous politicos and the women who threatened their crown.

Thomas Jefferson - Member of the first continental congress, author of the Declaration of Independence, 3rd President. (1801-1809)

Often recounted in song and story (see the musical "1776") as equipped with an insatiable sexual appetite, Jefferson, according to several biographies, ran around with a married woman named Maria Hadfield Cosway while spending time in France as minister of foreign affairs in 1786. Fourteen years into his marriage Jefferson was so smitten by the beautiful young blonde that when the short romance ended he wrote several love letters complaining of "sever pangs" without her. But it was an article written by a jilted political rival named James Thomas Callender which jolted a young nation during Jefferson's first term as president. The piece revealed several children Jefferson was to have fathered as a result of an ongoing affair with one of his slaves named Sally Hemings. Several partisan newspapers at the time perpetuated the rumor by running quotes from "witnesses" who had never met the president, and although not one had substantial evidence, word traveled fast. Despite being inundated with questions and accusations, Jefferson never made a formal denial during his presidential tenure or throughout the remainder of his life.

It had all been more or less passed off as political mudslinging until 50 years later when the son of Hemings, a middle-aged man named Madison, claimed to be the son of Thomas Jefferson. Jefferson's daughter, Mary, coming to her late father's defense claimed it "morally impossible." Since then only two of numerous Jefferson biographers, Fawn Brodie and Page Smith, have given the story any credence. It wasn't until last fall when a team of European geneticists led by Dr. Eugene Foster ran a series of tests on the Y-chromosonal DNA samples of 14 male descendants of the Hemings and Jefferson families. The conclusions published in the November 5 issue of the British journal "Nature" finally laid to rest that indeed the man who stood guardian over the Louisiana Purchase had a long and apparently productive sexual affair with one of his slaves. Eric Lander, a leading DNA expert at MIT told the Columbia-Missouri Tribune last year that "the almost 200 year dispute is now settled."

The findings also confirmed that Hemings became pregnant at age 16 while acting as maid for Jefferson's own daughter, Mary, seven years before Jefferson's wife, Martha died in 1782. As scholar, Joseph Ellis points out in the same Tribune article, "There is a world of difference between a slave and master at the close of the 18th century and a married man and a White House intern at the end of the 20th."

Andrew Jackson - Hero at the Battle of New Orleans, 7th President (1828-1836)

Rachel Donelson Robards, known as something of a vivacious free spirit, married a young Andrew Jackson in 1791. The only problem was that Rachel was already married to a man named Lewis Robards. Although Jackson was a lawyer, both he and his new bride plead ignorance. Robards, whom Rachel had described as extremely jealous and possessive, not only took the scandal to the public, hounding Jackson's burgeoning political aspirations, but sued Rachel for divorce on grounds of adultery. After the divorce was finalized the Jacksons remarried three years later.

Well documented in James Marquis', "The Life of Andrew Jackson" Robards' revenge was apparently sweet and lingering. In 1806, due to the repeated harassment the couple endured as a result of this mess, Jackson murdered fellow attorney, Charles Dikinson in a duel over remarks Dickinson made about Mrs. Jackson. Besieged by charges of bigamy and adultery from the opposition throughout Jackson's campaign for president, Rachel did not live to see the happy results. Already suffering from a weak heart she died suddenly in December of 1828, only a month before her husband's inauguration. Andrew Jackson, heartbroken, and sure that relentless public derision murdered his wife, never remarried. Until his death he believed the negative press and public humility killed her.

Martin Van Buren - 8th President (1836-1840)

Van Buren lost his wife to tuberculosis 11 years before he took office. Peppy, and seemingly always on the make according to biographer, Denis Tilden Lynch in his "An Epoch and a Man: Martin Van Buren and His Times", six years later he courted Ellen Randolf, the granddaughter of Thomas Jefferson. Randolf was half his age and already engaged. She declined. He remained single during his presidency, but in 1851, at the spry age of 68, Van Buren popped the question again, this time to 40 year-old Margaret Sylvester. Although flattered Sylvester declined as well.

James Garfield - 20th President (1880-1881)

According to biographer, Allan Peskin, Garfield had what is described as a brief affair with a woman known only as Mrs. Calhoun in the fall of 1862. His wife, Lucretia, an intellect and former teacher, discovered the liaison and charged her husband with yielding to "lawless passion." In a time when these indiscretions were considered less newsworthy, Mrs. Garfield forgave her husband and the affair was never a factor in the 1880 campaign. In fact, Garfield was traveling to his wife's side when she was diagnosed with malaria when he was assassinated.

Grover Cleveland - 22nd President (1884-88 1892-96)

In 1871 a woman named Maria Halper, a 33 year-old widow, left her two children in Jersey City and moved to Buffalo where, according to all historical accounts, took several lovers including young Grover. Three years later she gave birth to a son, and although Cleveland did not believe he was the father, took responsibility for the boy by agreeing to pay child support. While nursing the child, Halper, not exactly a font of motherhood, began drinking heavily. Cleveland won a court case to wrest the boy from her "care" and placed him in an orphanage. Halper landed in an insane asylum, but upon release a few years later she kidnapped her son. She was quickly abducted and eventually young Oscar Folsom Cleveland was adopted by a well-to-do family.

Little did Cleveland realize he would be running for the nation's highest office ten years later and his opposition, James G. Blaine and the press would hammer the details of this fiasco home. The cry of the day "Ma, Ma, where's my Pa? Gone to the White House, Ha, Ha, Ha!" badgered Cleveland throughout the campaign when he admitted to the sordid tale. Proving how much things haven't changed; despite being raked over the coals, Cleveland won his first of two nonconsecutive terms by 1% of the popular vote.

Woodrow Wilson - 28th President (1913-1921)

Considered the perfect spouse and a rabid religious zealot during his marriage to wife, Ellen, Wilson spent his first year as president prowling for a replacement. Only months after his wife's untimely death he was discovered in the company of Edith Bolling Galt, a widow herself with the distinction of being the great-granddaughter of the famed Pocahontas. The president was so taken by the striking Mrs. Galt that he asked her to marry him a little more than a year later. Though the couple tried to keep the engagement a secret word surfaced and scurrilous rumors spread that the two conspired to murder the first lady. Describing the burgeoning relationship a typographical error in the Washington Post at the time read, "The president spent much of the evenings entering (entertaining) Mrs. Galt." Typically, several other accusations of prior infidelities, which were never substantiated, made the rounds. Just the same, the couple married and Wilson was elected to a second term.

Warren G. Harding - 29th President (1921-1924)

Harding, by any standards, was a grade-A philanderer. Stuck in a seemingly loveless marriage to a "somewhat masculine" woman whose badgering sent him running to his poker buddies, he had two lengthy extramarital affairs simultaneously. The first was in 1905 with the wife of a close friend named Carrie Phillips. Neither Mrs. Harding or Phillips' husband suspected. The two couples often traveled together. Two years into what amounted to a 15 year romp, Phillips left her husband to live in Germany where she became politcally involved. A few years later she threatened to blow the whistle on Harding, now a senator, lest he vote against America's involvement in World War I. Harding called her bluff, she relented, and the two kept at it for a few more years until the Republican National Committee sent her abroad with a $20,000 payoff to avoid any chance of a scandal disrupting their man's presidential run. Monthly payoffs to Phillips continued until Harding's death.

Moreover, twelve years into the Phillips affair, Harding began a fling with a blonde cutie who was 30 years his junior. Nan Britton first developed a crush on Harding at age 14 when she draped her bedroom walls with his campaign posters. She wrote him five years before Harding became president from secretarial school and he helped her find a job at US Steel Corporation. It was seedy union from the start, complete with hotel trysts and intimate meetings in a 25-square-foot closet near the Oval Office. Britton eventually gave birth to the president's daughter, but they kept it a secret from the world. When the

Hardings passed on she unsuccessfully tried to extract funds from the family trust by blowing the lid off the whole story with her 1927 book, "The President's Daughter" which was dedicated "to all the unwed mothers, and the innocent children whose fathers are usually
not known to the world."

Franklin D. Roosevelt - Father of the New Deal, Commander and chief of the free world, 32nd President

Roosevelt's extramarital affair with Lucy Mercer was one of the more blatant and well-attested among all those who've studied his life. Even those who covered the White House and prominent members of the government knew of it, but all kept the secret. Ironically, Roosevelt's famously strong-willed wife, Eleanor, originally hired Mercer as own secretary. Stumbling upon love letters years later she threatened divorce. FDR ended it, but the trauma became a watershed event in the life of one of the most active women of the 20th century. From that point forward Eleanor decided to spend next to no time with her husband and live a life of constant public involvement. This allowed Mercer to reenter his life, and according to political historian, Joseph Aslop in "FDR, 1882 - 1945: A Centenary Remembrance" she was privy to diplomatic and military secrets during the most volatile moments of world history. The relationship continued until Roosevelt's death for she, and not Eleanor, was by his side when the president drew his last breath.

Dwight D. Eisenhower - World War II hero, Mastermind of the invasion of Europe, 34th president (1952-1960)

While Eisenhower was in Europe saving the world from Nazi tyranny he was continuously being photographed in the company of his personal assistant and driver, Kay Summersby. Andy Rooney, then a reporter for Stars and Stripes described her as "wonderfully attractive, bright and beautiful." The future first lady, Mamie apparently knew of the possibility her husband was getting extra R& R action, but all accounts were only alleged until the release of Summersby's autobiography, "Past Forgetting: My Love Affair with Dwight D. Eisenhower" in 1975. Merle Miller's biography of Harry S. Truman quotes the president with having destroyed a correspondence between Eisenhower and General George C. Marshall in which Eisenhower revealed his intention to divorce his wife to marry Summersby. Marshall threatened to "bust him out of the army" if he did. When the war ended Eisenhower returned to Mamie and the two shared the White House throughout the 50s'.

John F. Kennedy - Prince of Camelot, Martyr of a Generation 35th president (1960-1963)

Kennedy was quite simply the king of swing. From the time he discovered women JFK didn't miss too many opportunities to love 'em and leave 'em. As a powerful, young, rich politician he ran wild and free with an array of women, not allowing a little thing like marriage to Jackie to impede it. There was even rumors of a first secret marriage to socialite beauty, Durie Malcolm which was never annulled. Seymore Hersh's recent tome, "The Dark Side of Camelot" quotes secret service men as first hand witnesses to a parade of hookers and chorus girls being whisked to and from Kennedy's hotel rooms and standing guard at the door of the White House pool where sex parties with his brothers, Robert, Teddy, and a host of friends ran for hours. Government officials were often turned away and an elaborate lookout system was devised to alert the participants of Jackie's imminent arrival. Several escape routes were formulated to get women in and out of private rooms surrounding the oval office. The book also serves up a plethora of testimonials by jilted lovers caught in the web of the president's charm and lies.

Most notably, Kennedy spent quality time in Hollywood in the company of Frank Sinatra, a host of gangsters, and, of course, Marylin Monroe. The starlet's affair with Kennedy is the most infamous, but hardly the only lingering liaison. There was a stripper by the name of Blaze Starr which has surfaced in many books dealing with Kennedy's assassination, linking her with Jack Ruby, the man who eventually killed the president's alleged murderer, Lee Harvey Oswald. Then there was a painter named Mary Pinchot Meyer, who mysteriously died during Kennedy's first term, an expensive call-girl, Ellen Rometsch whose known affiliation with the Communist Party threatened national security, the mysterious Alicia Darr Clark, who was allegedly paid $500,000 for her silence during the 1960 campaign, and many others. The most notorious secret union of the Kennedy presidency involved a woman named Judith Cambell Exner, who along with also being the girlfriend of known mob boss, Sam Giancana, admittedly ran cash from the Kennedy campaign to the Mafia in return for key votes in Illinois. In her autobiography, "My Story", Exner describes being caught inside the machinations to assassinate Fidel Castro, the planned invasion of Cuba, and the surreptitious payoffs to billion dollar manufacturers of military weaponry. The FBI and CIA knew nearly every detail of the Exner affair, and because of this many Kennedy biographers believe had JFK lived and been elected to a second term he would have been in far bigger trouble than Bill Clinton could ever dream.

Lyndon B. Johnson - 36th president (1964-1968)

Only one biography of Johnson, Robert A. Caro's "The Years of Lyndon Johnson: The Path to Power" alleges that the ornery Texan had an affair on "Lady Bird". Caro tells of a 30 year tryst with a woman named Alice Glass who had been a companion of Texas newspaper publisher, Charles E. Marsh. She supposedly broke off their relationship because of her opposition to the Viet Nam conflict which ironically also cost Johnson the office itself. Of course, a roving eye and an unzipped fly is hardly the tip of the iceberg for presidential crimes and scandals. The world of politics has changed a host of inexplicable ways over this country's 220 plus years, but one ingredient has not. This is a government for the people and by the people. We are human. Politicians are human, and humans screw up, especially humans cursed with power. If nothing corrupts like absolute power than the type of ego and temptation which accompanies the presidency is tantamount to mainlining pure speed chased with a gallon of coffee. One thing is for certain, the world's most successful democracy has produced some pretty wild characters to lead it, and in each case the people have chosen him. At the end of this, the American century, we can only look at ourselves; our strengths and weaknesses as a people and know that we not only get the government we deserve, but one we produce. And if the President of the United States is a sexed crazed maniac who would sell the highest office in the free world down the river for a blow job and some heavy breathing on the phone than we have only to look in the mirror.

3/24/99

KOSOVO: END GAME OR FOREIGN POLICY DISASTER?

The United States of America loves a good civil war. We had one here nearly 140 years ago and apparently can't get enough of them. We poked our noses into Korea and Viet Nam, dabbled in the Middle East, and lately, will place troops just about anywhere some lunatic or Third World faction misbehaves.

As I write this the war machine behind the North Atlantic Treaty

Organization threats begins air raids on the mess which presently resides in the former Yugoslavia. But what is presently developing in a southern province of Serbia called Kosovo, the last remaining facsimile of a republic left to the ravaged ashes of a nation raped by the fall of the Soviet Union, is more than mere internal fisticuffs.

True, the Serbians and ethnic Albanians, who inhabit the region, have differing convictions on the birthright of their land, but it is the powerful presence of one man which has changed all that.

A political monster by the name of Slobodan Milosevic, with the charm and international etiquette of Hitler-meets-Stalin, summarily relocates or murders thousands of ethnic Albanians in the great name of hallowed ground. Presently, one million refugees from Milosevic's tyrannical romp spread thought the rest of Europe at a record pace. This vile scourge of humanity is sufficient enough evidence of a burgeoning evil which has been causing mayhem in this volatile region since 1989.

The irony lies in the eerie fact that what could be this country's last European military campaign of the century mirrors its first. World War I became a reality for the US in these very same Balkans where Eastern Europe began its role as violent centerpiece for two international conflicts and a Cold War. Since the end of the latter the hatred between Croats and Serbs in Bosnia has come to a head, necessitating U.S. intervention, and causing the Clinton administration to deflect criticism from Western Europe, Russia, and within.

As the missiles fly and the bombs begin to fall only Russia stands against the liberation of the citizens of Kosovo, something which could halt peaceful relations between the former Soviet Union and the US. If the first strike fails to put the fear of God into Milosevic the likelihood of Russian military involvement increases. Word of impending NATO aggression caused a midair U-turn by a Russian ambassador to the United States and a warning of "mistake" by the otherwise politically impotent Boris Yeltsin.

This risk will certainly become more dangerous with time, simply because a fractured poverty-stricken Russia is a dangerous enigma. But if the history of this region teaches us anything, it is that waiting too long is folly. The strange parallel to America's original head-in-the-sand policy in the face of Nazi Germany's "ethnic cleansing" policy is obvious, and could once again lead to a greater loss of life.

There doesn't seem to be any humane alternative to Milosevic's murderous reign but force. However, the question which begs an answer, is what will the epilogue to this latest military action be? Of course, there can never be solid answers. Assurances in war are an absent plea.

The White House likes to use phrases like "achieving a durable peace" and "returning autonomy to the people" but no one seems to have a clue to the extent of America's responsibility after the bombing ceases. The past two administrations have had follow-up problems in Iraq, and the military still waits for this president to settle the issue of Bosnia — which was supposed to be completed by Christmas of 1996 — but continues with no end in sight.

Unlike the ambiguous Bosnian policy, and the seemingly endless Iraq muck, the commander and cheif has the support of Congress and the rest of Europe. The future of a war-torn ethnic and geographical land literally stands in the balance.

Threats and bombing are not enough. Is this country prepared to physically, financially, and politically rebuild Kosovo, and protect its survivors into the next century? Is this administration, which has demonstrated without fail that its foreign policy is at best duplicitous, and at worst stupid, willing to remove a potential Adolf Hitler threat to civil rights in Eastern Europe despite the protest from a world power with no negotiable leadership?

If recent history in Iraq and Bosnia are any indication this is gearing up to be Bill Clinton's biggest mistake as the 42nd President of the United States. However, if there is an end game to this latest show of military muscle, then the only mistake was waiting this long to act.

3/31/99

GINSBERG WAS RIGHT

"I saw the best minds of my generation destroyed by madness, starved by hysterical nakedness, dragging themselves through the negro streets at dawn looking for an angry fix."
- Allen Ginsberg
"Howl"

This was all Willie's idea at first. It wasn't as if I didn't see the humor in it—nor could I ignore the potential for sending another cheap column to the editor's desk replete with expletives—but it is my commitment to covering the story, and not judging it, which inevitably moves me in the direction of all things bizarre. And when all is said and done, every experience to date involving my demented burly friend has proven lucrative for this space.

This time, Willie, only two months removed from serving three months in a minimum security lockup for his incendiary comments and erratic actions in a crowded Denny's last year, was hell-bent on trying to add to his ever-increasing rap sheet.

Willie is not only good for deadline business around here, he is also a favorite among my readers, who predictably fashion him as somewhat of a folk hero. People have accused me of making him up, but the last guy who charged me of this (you know who you are, Mr. Red Bank) received a first class visit from Willie right after he'd served time for conspiracy to commit assault and battery on a relatively innocent Mexican gentleman whose only crime that day was to ceaselessly lay on his car horn. Mr. Red Bank wrote me some wise ass letter to the effect that the whole incident was fabricated—which I found unprintable but noteworthy—and after having Willie read it, I sent him to the address marked below the e-mail. I'm still "dealing" with Mr. Red Bank's attorney, but that is a story for another day.

The phone call came late at night as it usually does. When I'm working on a larger project, I might be up staring at the blank computer screen praying to every god possible that someone will interrupt the incessant ticking of the clock above my head, but this time I was roused from a dead sleep.

Willie's voice is ordinarily a low growl around noon to about six when the heavy drinking begins—then the tone takes on an almost inhuman quality—by the time 2:00 a.m. rolls around the sound is nearly unrecognizable. From what I was able to ascertain through the burps and syntax of his slurred speech, Willie was feeling left out of the latest chic Amadou Diallo protests going down daily at One Police Plaza. In his weaker moments Willie is a huge Susan Sarandon fan, and when he learned she was busted for sedition, he could hardly contain himself.

Willie is at his best when sedition is mentioned, so it seemed a natural progression. I thought I also heard him say it would be a great story if he could lead a charge onto the mall in front of the station, and get what he later described as "big-time press once again."

Having abandoned all hope for a normal journalism career long ago, and having to toss out a minimum of 800 words for the good people of this publication, my first resonse was simply, "Why not?"

Most of history's best mistakes have been launched with those two little words, and considering that nearly every time Willie had come into contact with me he ended up in court or behind bars, it was a rather heady decision. However, it is one I had to make.

I hadn't even seen Willie since he took that overdose of Viagra and proceeded to run amok in Denny's demanding to see "black folk." No one there cared much for the way he ran roughshod over the salad bar, and when the police came they made me explain it. So whenever I'd heard from Willie while he was inside, or when he was serving his parole, I steered clear. I wasn't even sure he was finished with his parole when I picked him up at the West 4th Street subway station, but he flashed me what looked like bogus paperwork signed by an ex-marine stating he was some kind of war hero and needed slack. "They're not fucking with Audie Murphy's ghost downtown!" he exclaimed, sliding into my passenger seat.

Seeing him in that state unnerved me. I was starting to regret my rash decision to even answer the phone, much less drive into Manhattan at dawn to let a jabbering ex-con inside my automobile, hand me a crudely forged legal document, and drone on about leading a booze-crazed charge on the NYPD. To say trouble flashed before my tired eyes was dealing in understatement. "Trouble" is normally a luxury for journalists. As a group, we care little for fallout. But Willie seemed more tense than usual, and by the way he was wringing his hands, I knew this was more than some third-rate journalistic exploitation.

"Do you realize that in the last two weeks nearly 1,200 people have been busted for protesting police brutality and violence?" he began. "Where the fuck were we?" I thought I heard him say "we", but he would have had to be totally mad to think a respected professional like me would engage in such lunacy for anything less than the cover of Time or a fat check from the National Enquirer. I had no answers, only a silent prayer that he hadn't seen my Mumia Abu-Jamal piece last month. "And I read that pile of crap you wrote about my bro, Mumia!" No such luck, I thought, grabbing fast to the steering wheel. "I hope someone at that fucking rag of yours tore the cops a new asshole for riddling that poor fucking African with 41 goddamn bullets!"

Now, it seemed, I was the enemy. The car's interior took on a steel cage aura, and Willie's snarl became far more threatening with every block. Everything will be fine, I began to plan: I'll arrive uneventfully at the station, then kick him out of the car and scream something in the avenue of kidnapping. They would have to believe me. Surely no one would believe I'd willfully let this maniac into my car and drive down to the center of policedom to cause a half-baked ruckus. Willie is a raving loon, I thought, juiced to the gills, and armed with a pogo-stick length police record. I'm an insignificant columnist just trying to do my "job."

But when we reached the mall there wasn't a soul in sight. Word we got from a chuckling officer was the truly hip and pissed were up in the Bronx at the courthouse where the accused police personnel were being indicted for second degree murder. The disappointment at the empty mall, his already aggravated state, and the fact that murdering police thugs repeatedly shooting an unarmed man was only good enough for second degree murder, sent Willie into a paroxysm of rage hardly seen this side of Rasputin.

"Revenge for O.J.!" he screamed, flailing his arms like a wounded animal. The officer backed away and pulled out a radio. "Attica!" Attica!" Willie bellowed, his voice echoing around the empty square.

"There aren't any television cameras or press here," I told Willie in a feeble attempt to calm him. "You're press, you dumb fuck!" he yelled at me, striking blue veins bulging from his forehead. One thing about Willie, no matter how far his mind bends, he never forgets my profession.

It was all true. I am a journalist. And that certainly was my car parked outside police headquarters which had just hatched this raving corpulent lunacy. The police, finally having earned a measure of peace after two weeks of media circus time, were in no mood for it. They subdued Willie as best they could. "Use the tazer on him," I instructed. "Do you know this man?" one officer called out as they dragged poor Willie away. "Yes," I calmly answered. "Once, before the streets beat him down. He was my friend, but Ginsberg was right. 'The best minds of this generation...'"

4/6/99

THE KOSOVO EDITION

No military campaign launched by the United States of America has ever reached completion without the aid of ground troops. Those familiar with the war-addled history of this country—from the American Revolution to the Civil War, from Europe to Asia to the Middle East—understand this all too well. What is now being referred to as the "Crisis in Kosovo" will not be different. That is unless it is yet another innocuous muscle-flexing foreign policy faux pas for the Clinton Administration or this feces of a man in charge of these atrocities backs down in a predictable cowardly fashion..

The present bombing of Yugoslavia has done less to weaken the power of war criminal/murderer, Slobodan Milosevic than it has nearly to splinter NATO, speed up the eradication of Albanian lives, put the Kosovo Liberation Army under international scrutiny, and further piss off the Russians, Italians, and Greeks.

The polls have varied on how the American public sees this government's latest foreign rescue mission. When this thing heated up a month ago, 74% of us did not want to get involved. Now more than half see it as imperative. It will be interesting to see where that number goes once American casualties start mounting.

Meanwhile, thousands of Kosovars continue to live in refugee limbo on the Macedonian border. The pictures and video are horrifying: Women giving birth in freezing rain, elderly couples clinging to each other against gale-force winds, men lifting their daughters onto escaping trucks.

One bit of information which hasn't eluded our citizenry, but may have slipped past the politicos at NATO, is that although this had been ostensibly an alliance operation, it is once again American strength which greases the wheels. More than 80% of the fighting machines flying over enemy territory and dropping tons of grade-A missiles, are U.S. property. The soldiers captured thus far have been American. The more you read about NATO, the more you must substitute USA. Let there be no mistake, without American military materials, weapons, and expertise, there are no NATO operations.

We are in deep now. It is far too late for any treaty backtracking by Milosevic — evidenced by Big Bill's stern rejection to the Serbian president's weak attempt to curb bombing by dragging holiday sympathy and a release of prisoners into the proceedings. There is no point to a NATO, or any democratic presence in the Balkans, without an end game here. And any talk of allowing the ethnic Albanians back into the country without protection is leading lambs to the slaughter. Milosevic is killing hundreds of people, including his own beloved minions, as you're reading this.

There is always the nasty little quandary of taking Milosevic out through covert means. But we know how that works these days; couldn't get to Saddam Hussein, not going to get to laughing boy. The CIA has been reduced to advanced photography and phone tapping. Coups d'etats and assassinations are apparently beyond them now.

Increased bombing on key targets in Belgrade has shown a U.S. commitment to finishing Milosevic's power base, but his real strength comes from Serb ground forces which lay in wait for a NATO invasion. Once again, let that read American troops, and a few straggling European factions. Getting Europe to defend itself has been a ridiculous endeavor for more than a century. This gets done only if the U.S. Army says it does.

All of this means the poor bastards who wanted to earn extra money

Fear No Art

for college, avoid a career at McDonald's, and the precious few who aimed to "be all they can be," will soon find themselves on their bellies in Yugoslavian mud. The Serbs will fight. They are used to fighting. This is what they do. But unless they are confronted, and Milosevic realizes that the U.S. means business, there is little reason for us to be there.

This space has been consistent in the moral imperative department of this mess. Germany got away with expulsion and genocide for too long before anyone stepped in, and politically the Balkans is a far too dangerous strip of land to allow a psychopath like Milosevic to disrupt. It is the gateway to Russian soil and too close to Western Europe for peaceful comfort.

Before this campaign is done, American credibility in Europe, and relations with the splintered remains of Russia, will lie in the precarious balance. Handled swiftly with justice may mean a bump in the millennium road, but bloodshed, and the slightest hint of defeat, could spell trouble in this volatile and significant area well into the next century.

4/21/99

CYCLICAL PAIN: CHILD ABUSE IN THE 90S'

> *"fuck you*
> *and your untouchable face*
> *fuck you*
> *for existing in the first place*
> *who am i*
> *that i should be vying for your touch*
> *who am i*
> *bet you can't even tell me that much"*

> -ani difranco

So I sit in my television bunker and watch CNN throw visions of this latest school massacre atrocity at me in a horrific violation of my sensibilities. Today its Columbine High School in Littleton Colorado. October of '97 it was Pearl, Mississippi. Two months later it was West Paduch, Kentucky. Last March in Jonesboro, Arkansas and Springfield, Oregon in May. Tomorrow down the street. Infants with automatic weapons. Children with plastic explosives— Generation Z on the rampage once again, seeking vengeance for pieces of fractured youth that used to have us running for the bottle or the joint or the syringe.

Doesn't make the least bit of sense. Makes all the sense in this world. You remember the pain of being a lump of personality clay. You don't remember neatly transferring teen angst for a bloody stomp through the musty halls of Sunshine High.

Politicians call it an epidemic. Pacifists blame the guns. The NRA sights the lack of discipline and empty prisons. Religion blames violence in music and movies. Psychologists cram the airwaves with cute 90s' buzz words like *grief counseling* and *post traumatic syndrome*. The media asks the president for neat governmental solutions. The public write their congressmen for legal actions.

Put metal detectors in gym class! Fill detention halls with psychiatrists! Take away the army toys! Sue Marylin Manson! Find those money grubbing fuckers in Hollywood with their high and mighty box office numbers and string them up!

Hyperbole is the bouncing baby of panic. Americans are good at panic. It is human nature to place blame and wonder why; but somewhere in the center of those murder-zombies clad in black ski masks and long trench coats rests the remnants of a pristine soul. Before these kids hunted minorities and jocks, and everyone who pushed them into the shadows of pubescent hell, there was innocence.

Once these young minds couldn't differentiate between *us and them*; the same eyes which scoured classrooms for "human debris" to cut down in cold blood. Behind those eyes is a mind which puts *niggers*, *kikes*, *fags*, *wops*, and the *evil woman* in place of another soul. Where once the undeveloped brain was a clear white page, now the prose of hatred scrolls from the pen of ignorance and alienation.

On April 20, 1999, eight months shy of this century of enlightenment—when humanity reached beyond the Renaissance for extraordinary achievement—two boys heralding the birth of Adolf Hitler crawled from the depths of something called the "trench coat mafia" to open fire on imagined enemies. Nazi youth with grenades, rifles, and swastika tattoos; these were not the crazed and warped, economically deprived, urban survivors we read about every morning in the papers—they are far more frightening. These children scare us because they are the offspring of the privileged, the middle class drones mowing our lawns and delivering those very same papers to our doors.

There is no denying the presence of evil in these kids, but did it creep into their heads during the odd acid trip, or channeled from a rap video; or did those poor abused kill-machines gather the mental ammo right at home or next door at the neighborhood picnic.

The manifestation of violence from hatred is delicate. It is nurtured as much as the trip from love to philanthropy. What happens on a dim Tuesday just outside of Denver should not be looked at as an aberration as much as a culmination. We are lucky more children don't take to the streets with savage vengeance for the abuse, distrust, and pain we substitute for understanding, and the garbled misinformation we trade for teaching.

We have wrought the fallout rain of our own selfish pouting. We conveniently forget the dumb brutality of our own wounds riddled with the twisted juxtaposition of money, friendship, lust, greed, and sweet confusion. We don't hand down the weapons of bigotry and intolerance; we hand it over. It isn't a devolution like the Bible preaches in all its patriarchal cynicism, it is a cyclical passing of misfortune.

The great Arthur Koestler once noted that change isn't a forward graph, but a spiral in and out of time. These children have a piece of you and me by mere experience. We have all been there before. It might not take a village to raise them, but only a few of us to fuck them up. Those unfortunate victims of the Littleton tragedy aren't the only casualties. Something like this can tell us more about ourselves then we wish to admit. And unless we realize that those are our children lying dead in a pool of blood in math class then we are doomed to live in a place where the most damaged psyche with the biggest fist rules the day.

4/28/99

GONE FISHIN'

His name is Cedric Batch. I know because he told me, sitting as he was, in a comfortable nook resting between two overturned canoes on a rock at the edge of Lake Carmel, New York. He was one of those anachronistic sorts; not quite out of time, but beyond the rush of things. I know this because he told me so, while throwing his rod outward and pulling the reel inward, a plaid fishing hat perched shoddily upon his graying head.

"Want a beer?" he grumbled. "It's ten-thirty in the morning," I answered. "Too late fer ya?" he smiled. The sound of Leon Redbone crooning a prewar ditty from a mud-crusted radio wafted above our heads causing the geese under the adjoining dock to squawk as they fluttered over the glassy lake.

Cedric caught my attention with his high-pitched melodic whistle, a blade of sound that cut through the traffic behind me as I walked along a stretch of route 52, winding and careening through the hills of Putnam County. When I approached him he almost seemed angelic, like a ghost from a childhood I never knew. I told him that I'd never fished, grew up a city kid unaffected by mosquitoes and poison ivy. He laughed as though I'd been tortured and deprived, left to choke on smog and crime.

"Ever walk barefoot in a field of cow shit, boy?" he asked. I told him I never had the pleasure.

Then Cedric pointed at me with a knowing grin, figuring I'd soon be asking questions and prying like all the others who've passed by to break his silence. It was apparently easy to notice my fascination with his placid demeanor in the face of this turbulent world; a long way from strategic bombings, high school violence, and the urban din he finds so abhorrent. It was from this tiny place of peace that he looked at me like some beacon in a pea soup fog.

"World ain't no different than it was twenty, thirty years ago," he whispered, tugging on the fishing rod with the deftness of a man who could do so in his sleep. "In my time, we always thought that we didn't have much time to go. We thought the bomb would get us in the end."

I am often uncomfortable in these places, and I told him so. I like it loud and bustling, clock ticking with someplace soon to go. Cedric Batch didn't look like he had anywhere soon to go, flipping open his cooler and shaking the ice from his beer can on this lazy Wednesday morning.

"Retired?" I asked him.

"For some time now," he said. "Bored out of my mind."

Of course, he was right; I did have questions. I wondered what a man in a fishing hat and suspenders, far removed from anything resembling a rat race, might think of children going on a killing spree in Anytown USA, or the U.S. army primed to ship another generation of young soldiers to some god-awful stretch of land in the great name of foreign policy.

"Everybody's time comes," he said. "I went to Korea for what amounted to little. But I was proud to go, and I didn't suffer none. And luckily no one I knew died or anything. We were, how you say it, stupid then. We were young, believed anything."

And now?

"It's a shame what's happening to those poor people over there, but I don't know if American boys should have anything to do with it."

"What about those kids in Littelton?" I asked, as the geese returned with a flourish, most likely scaring away any possible swimming prey.

"Could not believe it," Cedric croaked, "Still don't." For the first time his expression hardened. It was as if he were awakening from a dream that I, unfortunately, interrupted. "How can anyone that young have so much rage in 'em," he began again, furrowing his brow. "I seen people with the weight of the world on 'em go nuts, really nuts. But teenage kids, high school kids, wanting to shoot up the school? Never would have thunk it. And where'd they get the stuff to make bombs? And how the hell did they do this with nobody knowing?"

He stopped for a moment, even placing his trusty rod beside his lawn chair and lowering Leon on the radio. "There is something scary about what people envision, you know?" he said. "Somewhere they have these ideas, and then they go as far as carrying them out. It's one thing to want to do something that horrible, but to have the anger to get up and do it with all that planning. It's scary."

I left Cedric Batch between those canoes with the glistening ripple of water shining in his blue eyes, and a hint of sunburn forming under the corners of his fishing hat. I bid him farewell, shook his wind-hardened hands, and headed home to write these words.

He checked out of the circus long ago, and I was sorry to offer up so much lingering sawdust. He told me to consider fishing. Fishing isn't my thing. I prefer the bustle, clock ticking, with somewhere soon to go.

5/5/99

LUNACY RULES: ON THE STREET AND IN THE BLACK WITH *THE PHANTOM MENACE*

Editors Note:

Two weeks ago Mr. Campion spent an evening outside the United Artists Union Square NYC location in the hopes that he could be better educated on the cinematic cash-cow phenomenon known as Star Wars Episode 1: The Phantom Menace. *It was never his idea to be confronted with those camped out on the street waiting to purchase tickets to an opening-night showing nearly a half a month away. Most of the people Mr. Campion saw had been more-or-less lying on the sidewalk for almost a week, trading eight hour shifts with their rabid compatriots. Below is what is left of the report he promised; most of which was received in the news room around 5:00 p.m. on the 5th of May, 1999.*

Tuesday May 4 - 2:33 a.m.

The bodies are strewn everywhere. Children and parents huddled like refugees in the breezy dark. A slight sprinkle of rain washes over their sleeping bags and makeshift tents. Umbrellas tilted against buildings and canvas awnings give the impression of a small, temporarily displaced society. It is Woodstock of the damned; a purgatory of souls crammed into groping orgies of mother warmth. My first thought: How far removed have we become at the end of this millennium that we can allow a social recluse like George Lucas to send us scrambling for asphalt refuge? Suddenly, my trance is broken by movement. My God, one of them, a young man, somewhat confused, perhaps sleepy, is approaching. His mood is tense, hands wringing like a speed freak.

boy: Coffee guy?

JC: What?

boy: Are you the coffee guy? The last one said he'd send out another guy four hours ago.

Four hours? Who waits for coffee for four hours? His faith is unsettling. There is something not quite right about the gleam in his eyes, this science fiction reject searching for an answer to those singsong echoes in his head by attending a two-hour Hollywood fantasy. Another one stirs behind a deep blue Nationwide bank blanket wearing what appears to be a garbage bag under his ragged Yankees cap.

guy: Hey Bill, get a hold of those Hasbro talking figures?
boy: The only thing left after that midnight raid on FAO Shwartz is a few damaged Obi Wan dolls.
guy: None of those Lego microprocessor-based Droid developer kits?
boy: Are you shitting me? I saw some poor sap loose a limb five minutes after the doors opened. Made that goddamn stomping at the Who concert back in the 70s' look like a Quaker picnic.
guy: What about Nintendo or Sony Playstation games?
boy: It was a massacre. Those left for dead were the lucky ones.

It is hard for me to admit in print but these people frighten me. Yet, no one here senses my fear. This is good. No point in showing weakness now, not in this ghetto of middle class America meeting at the Mecca of media hype and careening toward the end of this insane century. There isn't one lousy passage in the Bible which can soothe the desperation felt on this street. It is palpable, undulating, a life unto itself. One might deem it excitement, even pure adrenaline; but the conscientious Red Cross people know better.

Sam: This is a movie opening, right?
JC: Yes, in three weeks.
Joe: So, like, Harrison Ford, or that fucking Wookie thing aren't showing up?
Sam: Or that hot Princess Leia?
JC: Not to my knowledge. Although the guy in the T2 sweatshirt claims there will be a UFO sighting before dawn.
Sam: Look at all these kids. Isn't it against the law to drag minors out here?
JC: Not if they're accompanied by an adult. It's MPAA law.

The line goes on forever, spilling across Union Square like a winding caterpillar afraid to slither up a reed for fear of swooping crows. It's always the predators which keep the grand ballet of nature rolling along. Where do these Lucasheads stand on the food chain? Are they better than us? Are they in tune with something we can never understand? Something pristine, almost perfect, as if erected by a higher mind. Perhaps the man presently clutching at my foot knows the answer.

man: I have no one to spell me. It's been three days. Save my spot, mister? Please, God! I need food, and rest. I haven't seen my children since Easter. I traveled for six weeks from Texas to get a ticket to one of the digital showings.

In a rare moment of emotional weakness I acquiesced to his pleas. His two week growth of beard and rancid odor alerted me to his true plight. He was in for the long haul, hunkered down for the duration; and one look at his featured spot at the front of the line told me to do right by him. After all, he is my fellow man, however depraved and deranged he'd become by this lunacy.

JC: Go! Clean yourself up! Show some dignity in this world of groveling drones!

man: Thank you, sir! God bless you and your kin!

He limped away as I settled into his spot. It is almost four in the morning and no one here has the answers I'd come for. Except for the kindly Spanish woman motioning for me to lean closer.

woman: Did that man expect this theater to show Star Wars in the digital format?

JC: Whatever.

woman: This theater isn't one of those. That's why we've all come here. You should get a load of the line at that one.

Too late for that pathetic madman. By the time he gets the bad news there may be nothing left to rescue. Before the poor woman could blink I looked both ways up the long avenue and headed for the subway. Ah yes, the subway. Refuge with the normal psychopaths, underground where they belong.

5/19/99

HILLARY, RUDY, THE NY SENATE RACE, AND THE FUTURE OF NATIONAL POLITICS

The word I'm getting from New York Democrats whom I'm apt to trust up here is that the first lady has already started running for a Senate seat in 2,000. Major evidence points to Ms. Rodham showing up at Demo fund raisers and picking the brains of the same insiders I bug on a daily basis. It was enough to land me on the phone for nearly thirty straight hours of mind-numbing politico speak last week.

For the uninitiated, getting anything on the record out of people in office is tantamount to pulling the teeth of a starving Bengal tiger with chopsticks. But those milling about civil servants like to chirp. And chirp they did this past weekend.

All agreed that Ms. Rodham's decision will effect the party's fleeting hopes to keep the White House in two years. But in order to double-check these loose cannons I always go to my Demo snitch Dibbs, who months ago pulled the *Rodham for Senate* story out of nowhere and paraded it in front of me like a prom dress. He owed me a follow up, but predictably didn't return my calls following Rudy Giuliani's sarcastic boast to run for an Arkansas Senate seat, prompting upstate Republicans to cheer so loud it altered lake-effect weather trends.

However, for the core of the GOP, Uncle Rudy's precarious standing in the state after his bums-rush of the governor is lukewarm at best, and permanently damaged at worst. The last thing I remember Dibbs telling me is something I stupidly refused to put in print; "Giuliani's only chance to win that Senate race is for Hillary to run."

Two days later it made far more sense, forcing me to curse my very name for blowing off this hot, and apparently, valid news. Another key GOP source, my always lively friend, Steve from Albany, sent me a garbled fax which simply stated, PATAKI TOLD ME LAST NIGHT THAT THE ONLY WAY HE'S STUMPING FOR THAT SCUMBAG GIULIANI IS IF CLINTON COMES ANYWHERE NEAR THIS STATE.

Sure, I suddenly remembered, Giuliani sold his soul for the Big Apple back when the future governor needed him. He's been a party dead man for years. Uncle Rudy chose Mario Cuomo over Pataki and immediately felt Republican wrath.

That's the way it was five years ago, and as far as I know, no one in the GOP power ring of New York state has changed their requiem. Of course, I can't get solid confirmation on this since no one at Gracie Mansion will talk to me after my rabid GOP pal Georgetown sent the mayor's office a copy of my 4/14 column where I thoughtlessly quoted an obvious crazy man describing the NYPD as "kill-freaks".

However, for the Democrats, New York state is small potatoes now. As stated in this space before, if Ms. Rodham runs for anything she will not be around to rouse the troops next summer for what looks to be a Bob Dole-like Al Gore national campaign of little substance, and even less effort. Even if Gore tries to separate his ticket from Big Bill in the realm of pussyfoot bullshitter, his hands are already bloody with this throbbing political fiasco going on in Kosovo. The Dems need the First Lady stumping for Gore next summer, not wasting time fending off allegations of real estate fraud from a master mudslinger like Uncle Rudy in New York.

Here's what I got out of Dibbs last night:

JC: Who's advising Hillary?

Dibbs: Never mind that bullshit, did you see that paltry turnout for (Geraldine) Ferraro this week? The President comes sweeping in and gets booed on the tarmac at Kennedy! This Kosovo bombing is killing us! And, Jesus, if I have to hear Gore go on another goddamn minute about pornography on the Internet heads are going to roll.

JC: What about Hillary?

DB: (James) Carvelle called her three times from Israel last week.

JC: Who is running this defacto pre-campaign though, the White House?

DB: Money's coming from National funds, not taxpayer money. So don't push me in that direction. But just let's say the Clintons won't be paying any tabs. She's not a politician. Public property, but not a public servant. First Lady is like Mickey Mouse in Disneyland; focal point, not foundation. But right now she's potentially a dangerous factor to both parties.

JC: She's running.

DB: Why the fuck would she go to Albany? Land deals? Legal convention? Are you even paying attention?

JC: Is there anyone in the party who doesn't want her to run?

DB: No one's on the record yet, but you can bet your ass when she starts stumping across New York this fall there'll be negative leaks from inside.

JC: Tell me about the Giuliani fallout.

DB: The way the Democrats see it, he has two choices, and both are not inviting politically. He baits her into running, which is exactly what he's doing already, because he knows he has no shot against anyone else. Everyone in New York state hates this guy. Check polls in Montecello and Syracuse lately? And now with all this NYPD crap he's losing big numbers in the city. He needs a fucking carpetbagger from the high plains to make him look like a pit bull fighting for the integrity of New York, otherwise Pataki will let him swing in the wind.

JC: You guys think you can beat him?

DB: It's New York state or the White House. I don't think we can have both. We cannot keep the executive branch without Hillary's full support. And if the New York campaign gets ugly, like if Giuliani starts bringing out the "Commie bitch from the South" routine it will draw attention away from Gore. The party is tied to the Clintons the way Reagan held the GOP by the balls in '88. Hillary saved the Lewinsky scandal in the public's eyes. We need Bill, but we need his wife more. Especially on a national level. She's serious about running in New York, and I'll tell you, that scares the hell out of us.

5/26/99

OPEN LETTER TO MY WIFE

editor's note:
The author, scheduled to be married on June 12, and feeling extremely
humbled by the very idea that anyone would hitch their wagon to someone so
completely strung out on wanton anxiety and utter paranoia, wished to take
the opportunity to address her through the one medium that hasn't failed
him. The following is "a dedication to the one and only; capable of receiving
the most love that one self-absorbed, egotistical, ranting lunatic could mus-
ter for a woman."

Dear Erin,

I know how we got here, because the moment I had you in my sight
all the rest of this nonsense we humans incessantly belabor became a pile of
nothing compared to three minutes of your time. It's just that when a man is
faced with sharing a life that cannot be considered by anyone over the age of
fifteen as normal, there begs to be a moment of reflection. I mean, why on this
spinning rock would someone like you even have me?

I noticed one particular thing about you from the very beginning that
appears troubling. You don't fear me. Fear is an acquired trait by anyone who's
spent any "quality" time in my diminutive, but obnoxious, presence. Yet, you
tell me you fail to see that person, only the good and true, and I wonder if this
is any indication of true love or a major flaw in your personality make-up.

Anyone who hangs around with a writer should be given the highest
medal bestowed. We are lonely, depraved, and twisted sorts; running around
the living room humming tunes we might have heard as infants in an attempt to
wrest the right words to describe what street vendors could muster in minutes.
Never mind a freelance journalist, with our empty pockets, and pathetic sources
calling at all hours of the night to send us on wild goose chases through the
back alley of some bullshit story which will most likely land us at the slippery
corner of slander and libel. Then when the bug hits we go back to that infernal
book we always seem to writing, to shape up the manuscript and wade through
seemingly endless pages of incoherent crap which once passed for brilliance.

But, of course, you knew what you were getting into, you poor ador-
able thing. I can still see you standing on my porch in your sweat shirt and
pajama pants, looking like a grounded angel just in from Satan warfare. You

came to my hovel in the woods and brightened my life with art and laughter and these friggin' cats. I'm still waiting for a better gesture from someone somewhere. I suppose if I'd allowed myself the grief I'd still be waiting.

And maybe that's the point of this whole marriage thing in the first place. Finding something you weren't even looking for. Who knows where to look? Who knows what's there when it's found? Who the hell even knows what "it" is?

The whole idea of true companionship had been lost on me. The isolated don't date. We just poke our heads out of the chamber we've constructed, get the lay of the land, then rush back in for more self-loathing. Let's face it, who's going to pick me up and dust me off the way that you do? Who is going to heal those wounds, the ones the doctors can't see, or the tax man can't heist, or the priest can't bless with a few hollow words? I don't deserve any of this. I should be banished to a remote island in the pacific and left to dig for fallacies with a tea spoon.

I wish you all the luck that karma provides in this life. You're going to need it with me; and my big mouth and low tolerance and thoughts so ridiculous and occasionally off the deep end they belong in Kierkegard's toilet. All this stuff which follows me around like bad odor is all yours now.

But God help you, I love you so. I love you because I simply have no choice. I love you because without it I'm a cold intellect with cable TV, an old varsity letter, and an unfinished manuscript. Most of all I love you because your the best damn friend I ever had, and I've had them all over the goddamn globe. But, most of all, you love me. That's why I'm writing this for a two week deadline. By the time it hits the stands we'll be out of town getting hitched, and it'll be too late for you to change your mind.

Sincerely,
your burden

Dear Voter,

When you are finished reading this, run to a telephone and call your Congress person. Tell he or she
that if the government's idea of umbrella parenting is
threatening, censoring, or making final creative decisions
on film, music, and other forms of art and entertainment,
then his/her time on Capitol Hill will be short. Tell them
you are good and sick of bringing this up every time some
murdering little cretin decides to shoot up Happy High. Tell
them that by now they must know that all the warning stickers, ratings, bully tactics, and pedantic sanctimonious
rhetoric by pandering politicians do not, and will not, ever
serve as a substitute for discipline and education between
misguided humans and their mush-brained children. Neither
fear or laziness are good enough reasons to screw with the
always politically flimsy freedoms of speech, expression,
and choice.

While you're at it, why don't you tell the reactionary pain in the ass that even though the publicity
hounds over at the NRA and the odd annoying talk show
host are making all the noise about the latest Juvenile Crime Bill, you are well aware of the lesser
known $2 million "investigation of the creative poli-
cies of entertainment companies." Remind them that
it is YOUR tax dollars being pumped into a MyCarthyesque
witch hunt on video games, movies, and television shows,
while the offspring of the stupid are waiting to blow
their tops and kill our children.

Sure, they'll tell you this sneaky Big Brother maneuver is
aimed at the marketing of violent images toward those
children, but your response will simply be that the only
people in favor of such back-alley shenanigans is the
frightened knee-jerk set suffering from acute societal
compunction, and the lazy, uninformed, self-centered morons who keep pumping out kids with little to no idea how
to raise them.
About this point in the diatribe you'll be getting

the bums rush or the fancy speech about protecting our
children and taming the wild and out-of-control Hollywood
money machine from using the weak-minded as fodder to sell
soda pop and Rap records. They'll throw out the obligatory
knock on savage video games like "Doom" or irresponsible
Devil worshipers like Marylin Manson. (I'll tell you, I wish
I had a fucking dime for every time some Bible-thumping vote-
grubbing monger gives that mediocre musical combo free publicity) But don't let these pusillanimous drones tell you
what you can watch, how and when you can watch it, what you
can or cannot listen to, and who will be in charge of setting
the bar on too much sex, violence, and otherwise goofy
behavior in fantasy land. And even if you don't think that
darn Marilyn Manson is art, that's your valued opinion. But
we don't elect officials to do this kind of thinking for us.
They, of course, have enough problems keeping Howard Stern
in line.

The recent outbreak—some say epidemic—of child violence has not only brought the obligatory Republicans, but now the petrified Democrats out in force.
The white-elephant liberals and dying-breed conservatives refuse to go toe to toe with the big campaign
money potential of the NRA. Music, dance, and theater
is all good fun, but this is a nation, like all the
others before it, built on the trigger and the itch. God
forbid some of these macho brutes lay low when junior
starts building bombs on the Internet. Instead, it's "SHUT
DOWN THE INTERNET!" Kid blows his brains out listening to
heavy metal. It's "CLOSE DOWN THE RECORDING INDUSTRY!" But
take away their guns? "NEVER!"

Not that I favor any tweaking of the Constitution—and you
may haggle all you like about regulations, permits, and
waiting periods on the subject of guns—but I love it when
the Second Amendment set scream and yell that goofballs
like me cry about the First Amendment while disregarding
their untouchable slice of rights. Although, I think a
demented juvenile is far more dangerous with a semiautomatic weapon than he is armed with a video game.

Even our morally damaged president—pushed through
the polls on the power and blather of the same Hollywood he
now attacks—is spending precious CSPAN minutes waxing poetic
on the parameters of the "R" rating. Not since the Tipper/Al
Gore PMRC torch-bearing days of the early 80s' have we seen
this much Washington attention paid to the entertainment
business. And with a presidential election churning in the
wings for next year, there will doubtless be more yelping and
whining from mud-hungry politicos praying for a piece of the
easy-target pie.

The gory results of this fiasco may inhibit future
film makers, writers, or musicians from having their
say in a growing societal paranoia the likes of which
we may not have witnessed since the racist backwater
hell raising that went on as a result of a white girl
dancing with Frankie Lymon on the soon-to-be-can-
celled Alan Freed Show. And this will not do.

It must be said that no one with half the reason
provided by the human brain can argue that most of
the crap Hollywood and the music industry cranks out
annually is neither fit for beast or fowl, but in all cases
it should be the viewing or listening public who should
decide this. Once the government starts poking its grubby
fingers in the art business, visions of Josef Goebbels
dances in one's head. Remember, governments will historically use crisis to start yanking rights away faster than
you can crack the preverbal whip. And the first, and in
most cases easiest, place to start is the arts. Sure, now
it's just a dumb horror flick or a rap record. Then the
next thing you know your mail is being checked.
It is time people in this country start taking responsibility for their actions, their kids, and their
rights. Start parenting. Television is not Uncle
Buck. A video game is not the baby-sitter. And if you
have a 10 year-old listening to thug-posers singing
about pistol whipping their women, rip the goddamn CD
out of their hands and punt it into the gutter. Let

the government protect our borders, lower taxes, and get back to excepting bribes between self-imposed raises. And while you're at it, let them know that just because Mary Sunshine and her date didn't use a condom, you shouldn't have to feel like you're gearing up to live in a police state.

You can conclude by telling whoever allows you to stay on the line this long that it's high time the government figures out how to deliver the mail, deal with national health care, vote honestly on term limits, and impeach a president. Leave drama and tunes to the initiated. Tell them there are far too many of these moral majority loudmouth doomsayers clogging up their phone lines and fax machines, and now it's our turn. They claim to know all about those left wallowing in all this unchecked media muck. Now it's time to hear from us.

This is no joke. This is your freedom of choice and expression at risk here. The chic maneuver when the war on drugs and guns reaches mystic proportions is to point the finger at the art and entertainment community. And unless those who cherish their liberties in this arena speak up or there will be ever-tightening government controlled regulations on theaters, television and radio stations, production companies, record companies, and the hazy realm of the arts.

I'm sick of being the only pain in the ass bugging these righteous fuckers. Get off you butt, get your hands out of that bowl of Doritos, put down the goddamn Martini, and raise the hell of your forefathers; or be treated like a weak, pathetic child begging to be protected by the fear police.

Luck Be With You,

jc

6/2/99

RED SCARE REDUX

Let's face it, we miss the Soviet Union. Once the Berlin wall came down in living color on CNN the good people who sink our tax dollars into nuclear tonnage were going through the inevitable junkie shakes. This is, after all, a planet juiced with an overload of competitive male syndrome which needs a bad guy target. So, in the grating tradition of Joseph McCarthy, Alger Hiss, and the peppy people who brought you the "Duck And Cover" jingle, we bring you Red Scare II. Sequels and spy rings excite us. Goddamn it, we need it so.

Sufficient enough time has now passed since California GOP senator, Christopher Cox emerged from his seven-month probe of leaks and lapses in U.S. defense against Red China's alleged "espionage ring", which has been reportedly rolling along nicely since the late 70s'. Of course, this has been predictably followed by Republican attacks on the Clinton Administration and Democratic rebuts to the tune of "this was all Ronnie Reagan's fault," along with everything else below the eroding ozone layer.

Even presidential front-runner, George W. Bush, has the audacity to check in on the issue despite the fact that most of the spying was apparently done on his father's watch in the late 80s'. House Majority Leader, Dick Armey is doing his best Newt-speak, asking for the heads of National Security Advisor, Sandy Berger and Attorney General, Janet Reno. Congress scrambles to simultaneously blame and save face by whipping up some bogus $288 billion defense spending bill which will doubtless be drop-kicked off capitol hill by the military-loathing draft-dodger current president.

And the Chinese, fresh from their daily civil rights massacres, have laid down the ground work for prime time denials and accusations of racism and bold faced lies.

But in the end this is all foreign relations putty in the hands of the right boys. Problem is the right boys used to run around the halls of the Central Intelligence Agency. Now those are empty halls, filled with musty boxes full of microfilm and James Bond posters, while smart-ass dingles in the Middle East and the Balkans flip Old Glory the bird. True spying in this world of media frenzies and intelligence leaks is dead. Everybody knows everything about everybody else.

Why do you think the American public is even privy to this mess? Do you think for one minute if there was a national crisis, or this truly was the "worst lapse in national security in the country's history" it would be in your handy Time magazine right now? This is only a discussion because some hayseed in Kentucky can presently download Chinese nuclear secrets off the Internet as fast as some Asian egghead can transfer top secrets to Beijing.

Sure the Chinese are spying on us. And we're spying on them. And, news flash, the Russians are still spying, and the Arabs, and Chechs, and those crazy drunk fuckers running Disney right now. And whatever poor sucker settles into the oval office next January will be the fall guy. This is not news, its history. However, what is fast becoming news is the damaged relations with China this country will suffer as a result of this public blameathon by Mr. Cox and his Clinton-hating ilk. Wrap that nasty bit of FYI around a charred Chinese embassy in Kosovo, and you've got yourself a cute foreign policy disaster on your grubby paws.

But alas, Chicken Little fans, word from experts around the Natural Resource Defense Council is that what the Chinese have learned about our ability to fry any nation on this spinning sphere is minimal. Reports have clearly shown that China has had most of this information for the past 15 years and has failed to do anything with it. Right now, the big bad Red Menace has 20 warheads to our 6,000. And if the financial track record of Communist economies are any indication, China will be a vast wasteland ten times over before they can threaten anything larger than Newark, NJ.

The moment Richard Nixon stepped on that getaway helicopter and bolted from the White House lawn in the summer on 1974, Red China was on alert. Before his brilliant political sojourn two years earlier, the world's second largest communist nation had gone unrecognized as a international player among the United Nations. But Tricky Dick changed all that, and in the process awoke its tyrannical government to the ways of international surreptitious intrigue. Then he resigned in disgrace, leaving a void in communication that ripped through a truncated Ford administration, which gave way to a laugh-a-minute Carter foreign policy farce, and finally the Reagan new-bully-on-the-block run—still talked about in some circles of the machismo set as the *golden age.*

All the while the Chinese have been spying us. Now, 12 years and two administrations later, we uncover spy rings. Folks, this is not a lapse in national defense, it's a glaringly slow recognition period.

6/23/99

ATTIC REVELATIONS ON COLUMBUS AVENUE

The last thing I needed on my honeymoon was a frantic phone call from my good friend, and Republican insider, Georgetown, somewhere around 10:00 p.m. We were comfortable in my fifth floor Mayflower Hotel room just outside Chinatown in windy San Francisco when the desk informed me that "a frantic sounding gentleman was very interested in contacting me." It was freezing by the bay, and my hearty wife, Erin, and I had just recently burned 2,000 miles through Arizona, the California desert, and somehow survived two manic days in LA. We had neither the need or gnawing compunction to face this. The voice on the other end reminded me of why I didn't bring a cellular phone, beeper, or goddamn white flag on this jaunt in the first place.

"Hang up on him," Erin moaned. But the nightmare was just beginning. Georgetown was full of "low-down", he said, "couldn't wait", he cried, "had to impart", he pleaded. Something about Al Gore's trip to Northern California, a gay rights parade, and a miscreant relative who was competing in the infernal X Games, all of which was to commence the next day.

"I managed to make it through 90% of this trip without being hounded by paranoid anonymous sources," I croaked out, tattered from warm beer and a series of hotly contested games of billiards with this newlywed crazy woman who was now threatening to hang me from the hotel ledge if I didn't hang up immediately. "What makes you think I'd give you five minutes of my time?" I moaned.

"How much do you know about Junior's plans to canvass California?" he asked me.

"George W. Bush Jr.?" I asked.

"Yes," he exclaimed, "'The Master'. That's what we call him now."

"The man hasn't been out here since his father was president," I reminded him.

"Nobody on my end of the party seems to know what to make of this guy," he began. "I knew you were going to be here, and I'm sure those morons at the Chronicle have cooked up some cynical background check on him while giving Gore a pass."

"You're in town?" I asked.

"Me and you, right now," he whispered sinisterly.

"O.K., listen," I croaked. " I need sleep."

"C'mon, meet me somewhere. On your turf."

Georgetown knew all to well about the demons which bubble below my surface. I'm a sucker for political dirt, even thousands of miles from my computer, and a few inches from my betrothed. So meet we did, for 15 excruciating minutes at the top floor poetry attic of the City Lights bookstore at the confluence of Columbus and Market; cradle of the Beat Generation, Yippie insurrection, and more banned radical literature than could be peaceably confiscated at a Texas cookout.

There is something about huddling for a chat on those type of demons amidst the musty fragrance of a classic bookstore. My turf indeed.

The City Lights looks the same as it did seven years ago when I last sat thumbing my way through reams of anarchistic dribble. The golden city had taken a beating since then. Homeless line the urine stained streets, and the best you can say about the air is "thick." But the City Lights still stands on that infamous slant, across from every bar a writer could ever want to end up face down, crumpled unconscious in a shady rear booth with dreams of a life without deadlines and wackos like Georgetown and his rabid ilk.

But it is the summer before a national election summer. And for the first time since Dick Nixon fucked the bell curve, the race is wide open. If my prime GOP source says he needs confirmation on his front-runner, and frankly the odds-on favorite to become the 43rd President of the United States without ever opening his mouth, then it was time to turn our attention to one George W. Bush. After all, the worst thing you can pin on George's boy is that he is the latest Colin Powell political mutant; presently untouchable, unflappable, and looking like something the Republicans haven't seen since Newt Gingrich cracked that canary-swallowing grin of his in the fall of 1994; a winner.

"Gore's been out here, what? ten, twelve times?" Georgetown asked, appearing eerily collected in the dim light of the room, his head perfectly framed below a Lawrence Ferlinghetti calendar. This belied the obvious strain in his voice as he attempted to piece together potential cracks in G.W.' s apparently impenetrable facade.

"What else do you want?" I interrupted. "Bush will own Florida and Texas, and most of the southern border states. Clinton carried them without trying,, but Gore might as well not spend five minutes anywhere near those places without serious security."

"Yes, but we know California and New York puts Gore away."

"Fuck Gore," I lashed out, catching him off guard. "He will lose to

Dollar Bill, and then we'll come after you and that robot Texan."

"Bradley?!" He chuckled, almost too confidently. "He won't have the balls or the money to deal with the Gore machine. Don't throw me any wild cards! We've got all the poll numbers now, and Hillary hasn't even abandoned ship yet."

"What about this garbage I'm reading lately that conservatives are bolting the party for some third string has-been like Pat Buchanan or Orin Hatch?"

"They'll never make it out of New Hampshire," he smiled.

"New Hampshire, is a long way off," I said. And too far from this quiet place at the end of my honeymoon, interrupted by a man whom I foolishly trusted to give me insight, not drill me like a prison stooley. Al Gore was due in town in less than ten hours and the Gay Pride Parade was gearing up below us, but The Master was nowhere to be found. If a man so completely immersed in the party's innards was puzzled by G.W., what chance did I have for concrete answers; half asleep and faced with an ornery woman back at my hotel. This was no place to find myself, in the company of a confused Republican insider contemplating the preternatural consequence of his party backing a mystery man for President of the United States. So Erin and I practiced the fine art of the ditch, leaving Georgetown in one of the hundreds of bars in North Beach before heading to Las Vegas. That's the only place that matters in a presidential race before the last 14 desperate months.

The demons and pollsters will have to wait.

6/30/99

HATE INC. - IT'S NOT JUST FOR SKINHEADS, NEO-NAZIS, AND FAT, STUPID WHITE GUYS ANYMORE

If you have yet to hear about a lively organization called the World Church of the Creator, then you have missed out on the newest and hippest way humans have devised to perpetuate violent ignorance. Of course, the clever dregs who skulk around its halls of overt loathing want to be discovered on their dime, beneath a dazzling sheen of well-devised witty rhetoric. However, a multi-state blood bath and eventual suicide by one of its rabid members might have shed some unwanted light on things.

You see, this past Fourth of July a 21 year-old member of the WCOTC by the name of Benjamin Smith celebrated the anniversary of America's independence by systematically slaying and wounding nearly 20 blacks, Jews, and Asians before shooting himself.

Hiding behind the hazy guise of organized religion, the World Church of the Creator is one of many new "hate groups" systematically popping up all over the fruited plain. Its chapters have increased from 13 to 41 throughout 17 states in the last year alone, and when the FBI comes a-knockin' after something like Benjamin Smith's murderous joy ride, it's leader claims innocence behind the laws which protect churches from government oppression.

Unlike the obvious cross-burning, hood-wearing mania of the atavistic Klu Klux Klan, and the reverse psychological bombastic march of the sporadic Black Muslim movement, it operates with a surprisingly conservative approach.

The World Church of the Creator's 27 year-old brain child, and current chief of fear peddling, Matthew F. Hale wasted no time clogging the media lines with denials about his "religion" advocating such an aggressive or violent solution to his group's hate-speak. Yet the late Mr. Smith, a student of three prominent Midwestern universities, and the son of upper middle-class parents from an affluent suburb of Chicago, fits the perfect description of a World Church recruit: Young, educated, energetic, articulate, and left drifting in the wind with no sense of purpose or direction.

Mr. Hale, like his automated killer, Smith, lulls the senses into neutral. When listening to him address the media there is always the disturbing recognition of all things normal, like Johnny Varsity trying to make good in an otherwise cold and indifferent world, when just beneath the surface there is an alienated dweeb taking out gym class with a Tommy gun. Below the surface of his carefully chosen words Hale queers the stomach with talk of white dominance and sub-humans crammed into the ever-present ego-bloated propaganda of Old Glory, mom, and apple pie.

Hale has heralded in the dawn of fashionable abhorrence. The days of the bomb threat, random arson, and lynching loonies with their confederate flags and swastika tattoos will soon be passé. In their place will be white collar yuppie zombies with a fist full of forefather misquotes and manipulated Bible verses rallying at the local mall with Senator Dumbfounded.

The World Church of the Creator has learned well from the special interest groups which slither their way into the country's consciousness nipping at the heels of our legal and political systems. The power and pomp of the religious right, the NRA, the plethora of civil rights groups which lobby and effect elections and law making have burst out of the closet and onto the scene in the last few decades. The subtle, and often times saturated press and degree of celebrity these groups receive serve as free publicity for causes both true and warped.

Hale, and many others yet to be identified, will have you believe that the perpetuation of hate among religions and race, which has enjoyed a healthy run for thousands of years now, cannot possibly lead to violence. Meanwhile, the United States government is busy tracking down horrible images in movies and song as "little-boy Stalin" is whipping up the middle class jocks and over-achievers into a savage frenzy.

Let's face the disgusting facts; there are enough lonely, angry people out there for every twisted group dynamic to satiate. They have a right under the law to practice their white supremacy trip, but it is high time the rest of us stop fingering only the whooping rednecks and gothic fascists with hunting jackets and brown shirts, and be wary of the vipers in power ties who wish us a nice day and light the fire of discontent under every vacuous dolt our precious education system spits out like human sewage.

7/7/99

CUTTING THROUGH THE INDIE HYPE IN THE LAND OF NO PRINCIPLES

*"We need to clean out the pollsters and consultants and the spin doctors
and the bloated staffs who tell us what to say, how to say it, when to say it,
and how long to say it."*
> - Senator Robert Smith of New Hampshire
> upon renouncing the Republican Party
> to become an Independent 7/20/99

And thus Mr. Smith bolted Washington. Or so he would have us, or
the Republican Party believe. It was the Senator's grandstand mere weeks
before the all-innocuous Iowa Straw Poll, when the GOP will scramble to
fish the losers from George W. Bush pond and get on with the task of dismantling Al Gore as the horrific spawn of George McGovern. Smith could
very well be headed for the U.S. Taxpayers' Party, or some other conservative think tank organization for several pertinent reasons, not the least of
which is that Bush, the GOP Golden Boy, has yet to stamp the party ticket on
such perennial sticklers as abortion, gun control, and tax cutting 101.

Usually this space would applaud such blatant rebellious revelry and
rain praises down on any Washington lifer giving up the gravy train for a solitary walk on the wild side, but Mr. Smith, although fiery, ambitious, and wholly
serious—Republican Party Chairman, Jim Nicholson has long feared other
staunch social and fiscal conservatives such as Pat Buchanan and Steve Forbes
will abandon ship, yanking key votes from Bush and putting Gore, who he has
deemed as "the most extreme liberal in a generation" in the presidential
driver's seat — is just another political hypocrite.

Having a third party is as vital now as it was 140 years ago when
Abraham Lincoln's little experiment buried the Whigs and landed the first
Republican in the White House. And if the Clinton scandal taught us anything, it presented the best case to date that a two party system cannot rouse
even a modicum of impartiality. But a retread like Smith attempting to derail
his party from following the Democrats and drifting further to the middle is
not the best of concepts. Certainly, anyone who has gotten fat on this political buffet can't be the right animal for such an experiment.

What Smith is conveniently forgetting with his staged pejorative rant is that the convictions he holds so dear rest comfortably in the arms of special interest groups instructing militants like himself what, where, how, and why to think. Let's face it, although they are quick to point out that Democrats follow the special interest parade, most Republican candidates have little choice but to bow to the Religious Right on abortion and anti-gay sentiment, the NRA on guns laws, and the ubiquitous corporate money lenders who clamor for tax cuts.

Smith, like all conservatives since the first Bush settled his fanny in the Oval Office, are angry that the party no longer carries the full burden of the tried and true American values. Now that desperate Republican strategists go to the Clinton drawing board and follow the twisting wind of public fancy, those married to personal concrete beliefs feel betrayed. They wish to perform the impossible illusion: rest the Dems from the White House while distancing themselves from politics as usual.

Smith does have a point. George W. Bush—the man most likely to take the country—and his former party, into the 21st century has shown himself thus far as nothing more than a vacillating campaign tripper like Bill Clinton. But his attack on the system that wrought such a beast is capricious at best.

The Republican Party is as split now as the Democrats were when Reagan ruled the land. No one in the GOP seems to have a clue what any of their candidates stands for, or if it is necessary that they stand for anything but the achievement of total victory. There is a sense now that George W. Bush may never ostracize a single American if it risks a chance at the big prize. Big Bill pulled into New Hampshire nearly eight years ago with the same plan and everyone doubled over in infectious laughter. Eight years later they can't yank the bastard out of the Oval Office with a pair of super-sized birthing tongs—and those doing the yanking know precisely why. Except, apparently, Senator Smith.

Bush has not shown the slightest inclination to alienate women voters with any Right to Life rhetoric, the confused taxpayer with any fiscal leanings, or the NRA with antigun talk; and with power polls a-poppin' in his favor, he ain't about to start. He has become the machine who will defeat Al Gore by simply not being Al Gore.

Robert Smith can start a ground swell for a new party, but he fails to see the historical writing on the wall. Not even Clinton's middle-of-the-road halfhearted moderate bullshit ever truly tugged at his liberal soul. Once Bush trounces Gore he will bark the way the old dog usually barks. Oddly enough, he doesn't need the ultra right wing sector of his party to get the job done. G.W. has enough desperate GOP pirates to lock up the nomination before

Limp Bizkit hits the stage at Woodstock.

Robert Smith is no maverick. He is full of shit. Just like George W. Bush would be if he wasn't smart enough to keep it to himself.

7/14/99

TECHNOLOGICAL ISOLATION & THE CULT OF CELEBRITY

Commenting on a photograph of Jackie Kennedy crawling on the back of the limousine which carried her murdered husband, Lenny Bruce once remarked that contrary to Time magazine's description of the image as "the first lady bravely helping the secret service man aboard the car" the poor woman was just trying to "hall her ass out of there."

In his own satirical fashion, Bruce thought that by presenting the image of a phony icon in place of a normal human response to a horrific tragedy, it only left the rest of us feeling inferior to "the brave super woman in the picture."

Thrity-plus years later we once again fight confusion and grief when the son of those stricken people dies suddenly before his time. The grief is simple, a human condition brought on by the knowledge that no matter how rich and powerful we become, someday we'll all be gone. The confusion is in why we grieve with such unabashed sorrow for famous strangers.

What if you felt nothing when you heard that John F. Kennedy Jr.'s plane was missing? Beyond the understandable concern for another human life, their family, and the normal sense of utter mortality connected to a seemingly untouchable young, rich, powerful, good-looking couple and another young woman, what if you just shrugged your shoulders and went out to continue your life? Should you feel guilty for not weeping, conjuring up images from Camelot, or spending countless hours listening to talking heads wax poetic about these strangers while hours of file footage rolls across your television screen?

The minute yet another Kennedy died in the icy waters off the New England shore a few weeks ago, those of us familiar with the latter 20th century penchant for placing images ahead of humanity were reminded how much our conscience produces such powerful collective grief. Humans have always placed Lenny Bruce's "super person" in place of the ordinary person in the realm of celebrity. Thus when the superhuman is slain, it makes the rest of us seem pitifully mortal.

It is an easy mark for the media to regurgitate the tragic loss. Often politicians and artists are raised to inconceivable levels of impossible perfection leading to their inevitable fall from grace, which in so many ways is far more interesting than the plastic god created in their fuzzy image in the first place.

It was eerily fitting that wherever you turned throughout that blistering hot weekend in mid-July there was a TV report, radio update, and newspaper headline echoing the terrible news that three young people in the prime of their lives most-likely lie dead at the bottom of the Atlantic Ocean. After all, John F Kennedy Jr., the pilot, knew no other life but the one spent on page one.

He was born and raised in front of cameras. He failed and triumphed in bold print and living color. Above and beyond anyone else responsible for fame in the vacuum of media wilderness, JFK Jr. was America's version of the "Truman Show". The more we knew about him, the less we knew about him; a personality erected from our collective conscious.

Ironically, JFK Jr. became a prince for a nation built on the disdain for royalty. He was handed this title by parents, who so brilliantly seduced the technological age. Despite volumes of reality injected into the otherwise Teflon image of 36th President of the United States, there is still the indelible image of Jack Kennedy's significance on a generation of Americans.

For those nurtured on the powerful influence of television, JFK was a shining knight in the court of Camelot. These children of the medium created a fantasy world of friends, neighbors, and family, and awaited a new hero. A generation of isolated minions traded in the urban neighborhood with its corner grocery and stoop discussions for suburban fences and air-conditioned play rooms. It was in this social canvas that the painting of the New Frontier came into focus. By the time JFK stepped onto the campaign trail in 1960 nearly half of America felt a closer rapport with Lucille Ball and Desi Arnez than their neighbor twenty feet away.

When the Kennedys stormed the infancy of the television political campaign like ravenous wolves, their first born was just an infant. By the summer of 1960 JFK was the image of a bright, young, strangely unblemished political crusader heralding the age of promise and prosperity, and his family followed as a distorted reflection. A piece of glorious fiction staged for an era made for, and produced by, the power of television.

The Kennedys' carefully formulated image was neatly packaged for that flickering box nestled in the corner of our living rooms. The film footage of a toddling John John crawling around the oval office and White House lawn became as important as the president's famous rocking chair or million dollar smile. That is why we felt close to a boy we hardly knew, and why a nation was so crippled by that black day in November of '63 when those poor children were left fatherless by an assassin's bullet.

It was in the blinding glare of celebrity that the Kennedy family became a beacon of postwar affluent America. It stands to reason that when their lives were so suddenly torn to shreds in that spotlight, their eldest son became a nation's orphan.

Americans have identified with John John because they too felt abandoned with unfinished business. That is why Jackie took her children away from us, sequestering them from the peering eyes of the lonely and disconnected in an attempt to give them a normal sense of self beyond the icons so easily sculpted for failure in the face of unreachable potential.

It was not long after her brother-in-law was gunned down in Los Angeles that Mrs. Kennedy remarried, changed her name, and gave the proverbial finger to a generation who craved the remaining pieces left of her fractured family as ghoulish Camelot souvenirs.

Now we mourn the death of the boy left behind by the savage realities of a violent world. He was our technological child of a bygone golden age, which existed entirely in our imagination. Now he is gone. JFK Jr. was a celebrity by birthright, the same way we eventually became his grieving friends when he died.

7/28/99

R.I.P. WOODSTOCK

Like all things attached to aberrations and miracles, the legacy of Woodstock must be allowed to rest in peace. It has become sadly apparent that to revive its memory only unearths actions barely resembling anything to do with the word peace. Glaring examples of capitalism run amok in the form of

90s' sponsorship, and potential record sales eclipse any homage to a time and place so rare it defies explanation even now. For if Joni Mitchell had been walking down the road to Rome, New York on the weekend of July 24, 1999, it is more likely she would have seen less a child of God, than a Baby Boomer fallout.

Whatever those who put together Woodstock '99 might have thought—or offered up as an excuse, following three days of disgusting accommodations, ridiculous overpricing, lewd and abusive behavior, blatant acts of violence, looting, and arson—it can simply be summed up as the day the piper came looking for his check. Somewhere between MTV, pay-per-view, and ultra-hip.com, the ripped-off, starving, unwashed, poser revolutionaries who were bilked by this sham enacted their vengeance on what surely has to be the last of these hapless revivals.

Thirty years ago, a couple of rich kids got lucky. All they wanted was to make a few bucks on a burgeoning music culture born out of a Summer of Love and a stockpile of recreational drugs. The small town known as Woodstock, nestled in the mountains of Sullivan County, New York seemed as good a place as any to have what was fast being known as a music festival.

Home to artists for most of the century, and by the Summer of '69, host to musicians including the patriarchal Bob Dylan, the town of Woodstock served as a mini-nirvana for those starved for an image to summon the crude, but sometimes charming lifestyle begun in the streets of the East Village in NYC and Haight-Ashbury in San Francisco. The Woodstock Music and Art Festival didn't turn out like the rich kids planned (Actually, it didn't even take place in Woodstock, NY, but in nearby Bethel), but it could've been a whole hell of a lot worse.

Nearly three decades later, other rich folk, coupled with corporate America and the record industry, decided to press the odds. A 25th Anniversary weekend went relatively well a few towns south in Saugerties, NY five years ago, and now it would take place a few miles southeast. But it was more than decades and miles which separated the 350,00 lost souls who descended on Max Yasgur's farmland in the Summer of the moon landing and the Amazin' Mets, and nearly 230,000 suckers crammed into an abandoned Air Force base last month. That was a distance made but for one element: luck.

It should always be noted that the original Woodstock festival was supposed to be a profit venture. Sadly, for the rich kids financing it, the thing turned into a financial bath before the end of day-one. More than half the kids who piled into the festival waltzed over downed fences. As a result of the unchecked influx of flower children there wasn't nearly enough toilets, water, or space. The New York Thruway, a winding stretch of road as long as the

Mississippi River, was closed. Humanity outweighed the blue print ten times over. Then came the torrential downpours and random dissemination of tainted LSD.

But something significant, some might offer magnificent, happened over those three miserable days. Through it all, the people survived. Better yet, they thrived. What originally was supposed to exploit them, deteriorated into something which transformed them. For all their antisocial rhetoric, the hippie generation formed a mini-society which laughed in the face of convention by embracing its most ardent qualities. This was the story plastered on the front of the *New York Times* on the Monday morning after.

Crazy kids with heads full of drugs and hardly a stitch of clothing or a dollar to spare supported each other for three days of "peace and music."

Like Kennedy's Camelot, Woodstock has been retrospectively lifted to epic lore. But for those who found themselves there it was nothing short of a disaster area. The Who's Pete Townshend still speaks of it in horrific terms. Filmaker Martin Scorcese, who worked the sound for the award-winning movie, has often described it as surviving war. Bad acid, bad weather, bad well water, and creeping sickness turned fields around the stage into Gettysburg without the rifles.

Yet, the world continued to wonder if those hearty souls showed the rest of us a thing or two about the glow of the human spirit., where behind the myopic harangue of civilization there is a ring of collective truth about brotherhood, caring, and the simple, but significant, act of lifting the person next to you out of the mud and back on stride.

The world knows now it was nothing but dumbass luck.

People would love to blame the senseless violence and looting of this year's version of Woodstock on the music, the artists, the culture, or those empty-headed youngsters whose only sense of self-respect and responsibility eludes them. But if you find yourself in Limp Bizkit or Korn right now, a few months, maybe years, from eating stale bread in your no-heat apartments, you're taking any gig, especially a high-paying, high-profile one. And if you need to scream and yell about how much life sucks to a rapid-fire beat and three chords to make a buck, may the good Lord bless and keep you.

Ironically, many feel that the acts not allowed to perform during the original Woodstock allowed for the vibe to float rather than sink. There was a reason why the Doors, with their radical calls for the break down of reality barriers and invisible social casts, were left off the bill.

When the rebellious Satan clan known as the Rolling Stones were told not to come, Mick Jagger decided to host his own festival on the hills of San Francisco which resulted in the blood bath forever known as Altamont.

But in reality the music didn't have as much to do with the tragedy of Altamont as the fascist violence of the Hell's Angels and the hippie misman-agement which inevitably led to infamous killings and another type of bell which tolled for the Baby Boomer peace and love era.

All of this had been conveniently forgotten until the pathetic display of raging capitalism, apathy, and finally violence in Rome last month. Only this time ignorance cannot be used as an excuse. As the weekend unfolded it seemed far more attention was paid to draining patrons of their cash than pro-viding decent camp areas, ample toilets, showers, or any presence of security. The hundreds crushed in mosh pits could have been prevented. The overflow of human secretions hindered somewhat.

By the time the miscreants began looting the evil money lenders and setting fires, Woodstock, as we have come to know and love it, became just another example of humans misinterpreting compassion for luck. Those stum-bling into a wonderful mistake and sliding through relatively unscathed 30 years ago achieved a level fortune rarely reached in the annals of humanity.

The luck ran out in August of 1969. For the rest of us there is only an empty vessel of suffering at $169 a pop.

8/4/99

SUMMER OF '99: GOD HATES US

> *sunlight...*
> *she loves me*
> *i mean it's serious*
> *as serious can be*
> - Perry Farrell

Welcome to the summer of '99. We is hot, very hot; getting burned and dry as a desert road. Like a country music lyric, seized engine, and the charred remains of Atlanta; so very dry. We is losing it. We fight and grab and honk our horns, and some of us get crazy with the guns and the fists and the words which blast and ping from street lamps to beach heads. It ain't letting up. It's taking us down. We in hell.

Did we do something wrong? We didn't want it to rain on our picnic, Little League game, or boat ride. But we didn't expect a reverse Noah. Hottest July of the century in New York City with one half inch of rain. Three inches too few for sweet water relief. Con Ed puts the brown out to us. Government puts the rules and the screws to us. Sears is empty; out of air conditioners, out of fans. We is out of patience.

Weatherman shrugs his shoulders on every network. Meteorology has no answers. Science is futile in the wake of such utter oppression. Television has no answers. Selling us beer and pantyhose. Can't move, can't lift a finger to help my brother. Want to crawl into the basement, below the earth to the cool, cool, soil. Away from the sun, beating down on us. Coast to coast the heat is real, and the days long, and hotter by the minute. We is punished, oh Lord. We take back all the sex, drugs, and Willie Clinton. We is sorry.

God hates us. Put the whammy on humans in the waning moments of this millennium. Show us your infinite mercy, oh Lord. Your children are dying. Over 150 this summer from the heat alone. Stop your summer revenge, oh Lord. Save us from this goddamn heat.

Sorry Lord, didn't mean to use your name in vain, but you have to understand we ain't as lively as we used to be. No time for 40 years in the wilderness. Can't be bothered now. We're not even sure you is. After all, look around. Things is screwy. Not like we planned at all. But who has the time to deal with it. We need to zip between continents with our cd rom and our cellular phones and our e-mail madness.

Give us a break. We'll take anything below 90 degrees for more than 48 hours. We will denounce all the bad things. We will spend less time in front of the computer screen, away from the porn and the bottle and the joint, Lord. Save us from your summer. Spare us our much deserved wrath. We won't read the Weekly World News any longer, Lord. We'll ignore those wide-eyed southern preachers who claim to know you, Lord. No holy man in the world can stop this heat. How about if we will swear off Jerry Springer and Hustler and CNN, and give some of our paychecks to those poor souls baking in the streets or stuck in that country we can't pronounce? You know the one, Lord. The one you abandoned when you were blessing America. That is until now.

Call of the dogs, Lord. Turn off the heat! We were supposed to party like it's...

Sorry Lord, that guy who used to be Prince, he's nasty. I think it's his fault. Maybe it's the church, the military, my congressman. Maybe Jerry Falwell attacked the wrong thing, or Chuck Heston is saying something else stupid somewhere. Sinead O'Connor says she's sorry. Ozzy Osborne says he's sorry. Woody Allen, Jesse Helms, Kathy Lee Gifford and those horribly dysfunctional cretins she plopped out in order to parade them on our TVs every morning, are all repentant, Lord. Is it the NYPD, the Gotti family, those idiots who turned Woodstock into Saigon? I promise to no longer vote for those purveyors of evil; politicians. I'll vote for.....Well, let's just say I won't vote anymore. Just do something about this heat, and about the rain. Lord, we need the rain.

Your plants and animals need the rain. My cats are miserable. My wife, who is freezing in 70 degree heat, is melting. My parents can't go out of their house. My friends don't call anymore. Dehydration is the word of the summer, Lord. The doctors like to come out of the woodwork and tell us they told us so. You know, about the weight, and the smoking, and the excessive masturbation. Never mind about "global warming" and that friggin' ozone, already. And the priests, oh Lord. The wackos and the doomsayers; they say we're heading to your judgment, punching the clock. Natural disasters, Lord. Not fair, I say.

And maybe you say it's just hot, get over it. Even though records fall, and lakes dry up, people drop dead all over the place because it is not just hot, but fucking hot! But God, if this is the last days, and we're paying the price for the wrongs of our ancestors, we can take it.

It's just real rough down here, Lord. We take the disease and the war, and the really bad Ricky Martin crap. But we is a tough breed. But I guess you know all about that, Lord. We're nothing if not clay figures of your grandiose image, left to biped across this continent in the hopes that somehow we'll figure the easiest way out. And, you know, Lord; some days it gets hotter than others. So, I guess we'll take the heat.

How 'bout some rain?

e-mail mania

Date: 8/10/99 4:30 PM

Eric Hauser
Press Secretary
Bill Bradley For President

Mr. Hauser,

Al Gore must be stopped.

He is a lapdog Washington cretin with the credibility of a street pimp. His wife makes my skin crawl and if she is allowed to run unchecked through the White House we may as well sell the rest of our military secrets to the Chinese at half-price. I hope you realize that you presently work for one of the few people who can cease this terror from being unleashed on the American public. Are you prepared for true battle?

I am the main nerve for news, politics, and social issues for the Aquarian Weekly. Mostly freaks, drug addicts, the unemployed, or musicians read my column. However, any points of interest for the young voting public in the NJ, NY, Conn. area can be targeted through me—and anything short of all-out violent revolt or taking a slow boat to Australia, I am most likely going to endorse your candidate forcefully. It is in your best interest to keep me well informed. I would like to receive info and credentials to any appearance of Mr. Bradley or his tri-state campaign in the coming months.

This is mainly a liberal or independent publication. Yet, nearly every one of our readers would like to see Al Gore tarred and feathered, and hung from a flag pole outside the Vince Lombardi rest stop. And lest you think this information unworthy of your attention, I personally receive hundreds of letters a week to this end. These are people who are jacked to vote for anyone but Al Gore. Jesus, man, G.W. leads in most polls dealing with the 18-25 set. What are you people doing about that? These are free votes for Bradley, and I can bring them aboard. It's a harmful existence, but we cannot be weak. And if your boy can't stop that inane creature of hypocrisy I shall back whatever the Republicans can muster.

Let's work together on this and you can sweep the tri-state area in the primaries, and we won't have to worry about me painting the Democrats as "the home of pathetic losers and dipshits."

Also, it is imperative that your candidate address issues pertaining to the federal government's annoying penchant for sticking its nose in the arts, from film to music. An extremely sticky issue with myself and my readers. First Amendment rights and all that.

I can also be of use to you in the mudslinging department. Just last week I received nude pictures of your opponent with a donkey. Take from it what you will, but I was told it was the result of a campaign photo-op mishap that would have already been circulating the Internet if not for death threats and five-figure cash offers. Yours free for the asking.

Also note, it is optimum to fax the newspaper's office when you send me e-mail. You will find it to be an effective way of working your points in other parts of the paper and getting a cover next summer or fall. Until I hear from you all...

Never Surrender,

James Campion

Mating Rituals:
"A Study in the Habits of Humans and the Search for Sex and Companionship at the End of the Second Millennium"

by Professor Garth Dillweed
as told to James Campion

Nature is a funny thing. It must build upon itself with mysterious rules which are never constant, yet thrive in perpetual motion. In order for a species to survive in this mess it must create others like it. Birds, insects, reptiles, algae, and all the mammals that walk the earth all possess an instinct for the mating process. The Mating Ritual is a consistent and fail-safe natural conduit between the male and female for the express purpose of simplifying procreation. The human being is just a small part of nature's grand frenzy, however, unlike the other living beings which inhabit this planet the human does not have a single tried-and-true way to connect its inevitable bond and satiate the sexual appetite. In most cases the male fumbles to find the unique while inevitably leaning onto the cliché. The female struggles to fuse emotion with lust and ends up with frustration and eating disorders. The greatest argument for those who subscribe to the Creationist Theory is that after millions of years in the arena of sexual compatibility the human being is the only creature left on earth that has no fucking clue what the hell is going on.

In the spirit of this seemingly endless conundrum the following is a synopsis of several male of the species who have spent the better part of their youth on the hunt. Each one has different agendas and styles with a variance of results. Through constant observation over months of study the hope was to gain crucial knowledge of how they have pursued a sexual encounter despite having no fixed plan of attack. The details and results of these specimens caught in their natural habitat through separate incidents with the women they desire may very well serve as an analysis on human existence at the end of the millennium, proving no matter what lengths humans have achieved in the great evolutionary chain there is very little chance it will translate into one true Mating Ritual.

Subject One: The North American Dweeb
Lester - 27 year-old of no fixed income, hairstyle, or fashion sense.
Occupation - Computer Programmer.
Hunting Territories - The Internet, dating hot lines, library.
Success Rate for the past 24 months - Very fond of left hand.
Best Feature - Familiar with prime time lineup of Science Fiction Channel.
Worst Feature - Developed a theory of pragmatic equations in the white man's dance patterns.
Best Intro. Line- "My IQ is higher than the national debt."
Worst Intro. Line - "Are you aware of the inherent kinks in Windows '98?"

Although it is true that the North American Dweeb feels more comfortable in environments of his own making, when searching desperately for a mate he will occasionally move out into society. Here the Dweeb is usually reduced to fodder by the stronger more primitive of his species, but risking life and limb is little consequence to finding a potential mate. Preferring the anonymous method, the Dweeb must eventually complete the connection by roaming from his cushy lair and check the results of his inquiry. After slyly working a young woman through a chat page on the Internet, in which he claimed to be on the verge of inventing a cure for hiccups with toothpicks and a dust buster, Lester set up a meeting at the local diner. Buying a new shirt became almost an afterthought to the possibility of cologne.

Object of Desire: The Timid Clam
Celeste - 25 year-old quiet soul with smoldering id, near-blind prescription, and an alarming amount of wool skirts.
Occupation - Secretary.
Grazing Territories - Health food stores, doctor's reception office, Shoney's.
Prospects in the last 24 months: Wrong number, Aunt's landscaper, guy who smashed into her Honda.
Best Feature - Never gets lost in New York subway system.
Worst Feature - Been known to read during dinner engagements.

Celeste had not spoken to a man who wanted her this bad since she was inadvertently left in charge of a keg at the company picnic. Upon the moment of Lester's invite she had phoned nearly everyone she'd ever known looking for advice and perhaps a way out. Thumbing through the latest issue of Cosmopolitan for enlightenment she happened upon a quiz that when sufficiently answered revealed that if she did not walk, ney, run to the diner later that week she would be doomed to living in one room apartments with more cats than the health board could allow without a permit. The Timid Clam is not one to ignore premonitions and will listen to magazines above and beyond common sense and her own parent's advice. Before her next breath Celeste began the reconstruction of her hair at once.

The Meeting: The Olympic Diner

Lester, in grand Dweeb style, arrives four hours before the impending date. His greased hair cannot defy the excessive odor coming from his cologne. He settles into a booth in back when eventually Celeste enters almost three hours early. She is impressed with his promptness and scent. When she finds out that he'd saved a few bucks by rubbing a CK ad from a magazine onto his neck Celeste is downright smitten. Although the Timid Clam is the perfect mate for the Dweeb she instinctually sniffs him out. Unlike his brethren, the European Dweeb, the North American does not shy away from this ritual, making it an even better match. The two talk amid constant interruptions from the waitress. For a single moment Lester seems to fall for her, but then turns his attention back on Celeste. Love may be in the air, but neither can truly tell beyond Lester's cologne.

The Result: No Match

A few weeks into the budding relationship Celeste's prescription changes once again and upon receiving her new glasses she begins to date the waitress from the Olympic Diner.
Lester goes back to the drawing board managing to hook up with a heavyset woman who loves Star Trek.

Subject 2: Forever Erectus
Brad - 26 year-old beefcake with tree-trunks for arms and very little neck.
Occupation - Personal Trainer
Hunting Territories - Health Club, train stations, beach.
Success rate for past 24 months - Can open his own service.

Best Feature - Looks like he can hurt anything.
Worst Feature - Takes Narcissism to new levels.
Best Intro Line - "Has anyone ever told you that you have great defini-tion?"
Worst Intro Line - "You gonna finish eating that?"

Like Big Foot and the Loch Ness Monster the Forever Erectus is a legend, a freak of nature better left to the imagination of science. Most males have heard their mothers mention the idea of using a stick to beat off future female intrusions, but parents of the Forever Erectus actually provide him with one. The best way to describe his miraculous success with the opposite sex is to try and imagine Bill Gate's bank statement. Moreover, the Forever Eerectus is so completely incapable of monogamy—destroying all theories that humans were meant to mate with one partner a lifetime—that many of the experts who contributed to this experiment took their family savings and sunk them into condom futures. Admittedly, Brad has not used the word love with any real intent since cancellation of "American Gladiators."

Object of Desire: Curvitous Delecti
Tami - Luscious blonde with unusually large breasts for waist size and teeth that put the Osmunds to shame.
Grazing Territories - Anywhere people draw oxygen.
Prospects in last 24 months - Local college lacrosse team, Larry King, suit salesman/drug dealer who needed mother figure.
Best Feature - Knows more about abdomen muscles than 85% of medical community.
Worst Feature - Thinks Albany is a country in Bermuda.

The Curvitous Delecti is the most sought after of all women. To most male of the species she is considered the perfect catch; gorgeous and vacuous with just enough brain power to procure a beer from the refrigerator mere moments after masterful falatio. Aside from errant giggles better suited for the preschool set the Curvitous Delecti is a gem, but just as dangerous to hold onto. She has the attention span of a marine and the loyalty of the French. This often creates dilemmas for lesser species, but for the Forever Erectus it is nature's ultimate showdown.

The Meeting: Bally's Fitness Center

Brad eyes his prey with the cunning of a tiger. Tami knows immediately that she is being watched by a Forever Eerectus and begins to flirt with subtle body movements. The other humans in the sizable room can also sense the impending connection, and in a telltale sign who is king of the jungle, they disperse when Brad moves in. It is hard to breathe when the tension of two highly dangerous stalkers of the mating world are about to pounce. The one trait of a Curvitous Delecti, which is glaring in such confrontations, is the timely pelvis bend before the male approaches, giving Brad a long and intimidating look at her firm buttocks. Most men shudder in the wake of such perfection, but Brad plows ahead with a compliment and engages in a conversation on body parts. Tami is not immediately taken, but cannot resist. Soon the room fills with noise which drowns out Brad's banal, if not effective, come-on. He has apparently succeeded again, but, as Tami winks to her other boy-toy from across the room, how long?

The Result: No Match

Brad doesn't make it to the club's coffee shop before hitting on another woman.

Tami forgets about Brad when she realizes that she hadn't completed her five thousand sit-ups.

Subject 3: The Crinkled Collectanecktie
Jake - 28 year-old male of slight build and throwback hairstyle. Known to his tribe as Hubbs.
Occupation - Advertising
Hunting Territories - Local clubs, work-related parties, Laundromat.
Success Rate for past 24 months - 14 dates, 3 relationships, 1 failed girlfriend with demented mother.
Best Feature - BMW and flexible wardrobe.
Worst Feature - Believes life is more important than it really is.
Best Intro Line - "You look like someone from Melrose Place."
Worst Intro Line - "On a scale of one to ten, how bored are you?"

It is an accepted theory among most scientists that the Crinkled Collectanecktie is a common wedge between both ends of the mating scale. Although extremely dangerous to himself when searching for a mate he can also be cunning and suave, in some cases even able to get laid with little to no effort. He may work well in sober encounters, but prefers the lubrication of alcohol when going in for the kill. Money, looks, brains, or even timing mean nothing for the success or failure for the Crinkled Collectanecktie. Jake is the perfect example; showing more exceptions to rules than the rules themselves he has managed a rather formidable sex life in the face of all odds. His interest in Monica began when he was abandoned by his friends in a night club and saw her from afar. Chucking all inhibitions he asked her for a dance. Monica agreed, and despite witnessing Jake's poor attempt at this ritual, decided that seeing him again in better light with less of a buzz was not such a horrible proposition.

Object of Desire: The American Beauty
Monica - 25 year-old tightly wound woman with a sheath of hair, endless legs, and not known to run in any particular pack.
Occupation - Fashion Designer
Grazing Territories - Mall, health club, Mom's house
Prospects in past 24 months - Three admitted dates, very good friend who happens to now be gay, 1 very persistent man whose inability to take a hint far exceeded his driving skills.
Best Features - Could make most males confess to the JFK assassination by smiling.
Worst Features - Believes that most males can read.

There is not much more to say about the American Beauty than has already been stated in song and story. She possess grace and brains, the kind of woman a male could bring home to the Mom. Usually the sentence, "What the hell is a girl like that doing in this dump?" follows the sighting of such a creature. When Monica's friends advised her to kick Jake swiftly in the groin, she only laughed and followed him to the dance floor.

The Meeting: Luigi's Italian Cuisine

Jake spent a week's salary on this evening; flowers, car wash, a new suit, and dinner. Monica plays the reluctant, but appreciative, lady so magnificently that halfway through the meal Jake forgets most of his motor skills which she luckily finds cute. Monica had already forgiven him for asking her if it was raining out while standing in a downpour. They had decided to eschew the movies and take a walk in the park where Jake nearly blew the date by asking

Monica if she were adopted, but made up for it by asking if she wouldn't mind a peck on the cheek. She blushed and planted one right on his shocked lips.

The Result: A Match

Jake is ecstatic he has a date for New Year's Eve.

Monica is rounding up bride's maids.

CHAOS IN MOTION IV

Push the inevitable.

Anarchy cannot be perpetuated.

Everyone knows nothing about everything.

Anyone knows everything about nothing.

Help stamp out stupidity.

Rape is worse than murder.

People don't live after murder.

Lift the ban on normal people in the military.

It's time for another tea party in Boston.

SOMETHING CAN ALWAYS BE LEARNED FROM DISSIDENCE

History repeats itself

There ain't nothing new.

This has all come before

It spirals into view.

Put credence in things unpopular.

Women are the ultimate underdog.

Security is for sale.

Drugs are the product of boredom.

Drug addicts are boring.

Time reminds me of the clock

Not the other way around.

Everybody is a television.

Dracula had less lives than the NY Post.

Understanding rebellion is not enough.

Time to put that wall back up in Germany.

The truth is lost.

Find it.

Demand RESPECT OR RECEIVE SOMETHING ELSE.

There is danger in patriotism.

Hug instead.

Lenny Bruce was framed.

Obsession is good for the soul.

The past is just wasted future.

Live Loud.

Feel something new today.

Stick with me I'm bringing down the T.

8/18/99

FEEDING THE PIGEONS

The man with his finger jammed firmly on the pulse of the Democratic national interest for the next 14 frenzied months was sitting across from me, rhythmically splashing four types of spices all over his mound of shrimp goo at a prime table of the Simka Indian Restaurant on East 78th street. Dibbs, as he has been known in anonymous terms in this space, is a proud, if not misguided man. He refuses to admit defeat for his boy, Al Gore, despite the ugly numbers coming from every poll involving his prime Demo competition, Bill Bradley, or the man setting the early national pace, George W. Bush.

Yet he seemed to exude more grit than my GOP pigeon, Georgetown, who was last seen accosting me from a teetering bar stool in the eclectic North Beach area of uptown San Francisco and wondering out loud whether Bush jr. had the balls to admit he didn't know what the hell he was doing.

Georgetown needed only minutes to remind me of the utter futility of the Iowa Straw Poll, which had been completed less than 24 hours before I got the call from Dibbs about the loyal opposition. Neither man had put much credence in a curious institution which did little more than keep the doomed Phil Gramm campaign alive four years ago, except, of course, to prove that the Bob Dole campaign was in dire need of what turned out to be useless retooling.

Dibbs, fresh from a trailing tour of the Clinton's house-hunting in Greenburgh, NY and a front row spot at the Dali Lama's Central Park visit, did not hesitate to hoist the red flag in response to the plummeting poll numbers regarding not only Ms. Rodham's faltering "listening tour," but the enigmatic mess Al Gore refers to as an early "umbrella campaign."

It was Dibbs who blew the whistle on the Senator Rodham mania last winter. I fingered him for a mindless shill and waited to address it too late, something he reminds me of with incessant messages daily. But the calls ceased the minute I received a peculiar fax from a radio station in Syracuse listing numbers from a questionnaire which emphatically stated that central New Yorkers would sooner impale the First Lady with a rusty harpoon than have her represent them.

As for the White House, Republicans are working from the outside with a expansive field, but their golden boy, G.W. Bush is running on high octane fumes. Dibbs has been following the Gore cruise through the Midwest with special interest; a promotional tour which continues to ignore the news that Bill Bradley is whipping their boy among those who posses anything beyond an 8th grade education. He still sees no reason why the vice president won't get the Demo nomination and pummel Bush jr. in any debate once the issues start to appear.

But what of the issues facing the next presidential election? The usual litany of bullshit from tax cuts to gun control to health care, none of which will be seriously addressed by the survivor, will take the forefront on this, the first open election for president without an incumbent in 12 years. Evidence of this is splattered all about the history of American politics, and more than a year before we choose the lesser of evils the true test of the campaign trail—a savage gaggle of male ego and posturing—here is the crux of my more than an hour long conversation with Dibbs.

JC: Hillary is doomed.

Dibbs: Doomed? Who's she running against? Has Giuliani declared yet? (Rick) Lazio's their only hope and he pulls out waiting for this guy, forcing Pataki to back a man he hates. Who's doomed?

JC: What can you tell me about a Hillary timetable on announcing.

DB: Waiting for an opponent, pal.

JC: There is no way Giuliani is making the first move.

DB: You answered your own question.

JC: What's wrong with Gore's approach so far?

DB: Honestly, I think there is something to the "Clinton Fatigue" syndrome. It won't be a factor come next summer, but right now, it hasn't helped.

JC: The president has been lukewarm on this thing.

DB: Well, Gore is stuck between the jagged rocks. He can't distance himself from the Clinton crap and follow it up with, "Let's keep a good thing going" without talking out of both sides of his mouth. The White House wants him to ride the wave, but those people haven't been out on the stump for a long time. Gore's getting the backlash. You see, people always want change, but they don't know what kind of change. Bush says he's for change, but beneath that none of us see anything more than Republican pandering.

JC: Team that's ahead doesn't go on fourth-and-long.

DB: Let's see Bush survive scandal. He isn't a Washington outsider like Clinton was. For Christ's sake, his father was president! The GOP fossils will not accept cocaine abuse.

JC: Unless they want to win.

DB: They don't want to win. They'll ruin this guy's chances.

JC: You have dirt on the cocaine stuff?

DB: We have four guys on staff who partied with Bush at least once. We're waiting for denials. We think he needs to hold a press conference.

JC: To name dealers?

DB: At least contacts.

JC: Are you even considering Bradley?

DB: Let's wait and hear from him. Attacks on *Meet the Press* won't cut it.

JC: Ed Koch tells me the only chance you guys have is Dollar Bill. He was on Fox News last week screaming that Gore is already a dead man. Someone in the Pataki office got drunk with Cokie Roberts and swears she has it on record that if Tipper Gore becomes first lady she'll turn the White House into censorship headquarters. The Gore's think music equals Satan. NBC's Washington affiliate has video of Tipper trying to slit her wrists when Fleetwood Mac played the inaugural ball in '92.

DB: So what? We have sworn testimony from Bush's junkie girlfriend from college.

JC: Yeah well, I get more crap from PETA depicting Gore as some Stalinesque animal killer. It could be time to abandon this sinking ship, shake your hair free of this "Clinton Fatigue" and attack the Bush machine with a real contender.

DB: We're giving Gore until Christmas to shake Bradley by ignoring him completely. If he has to actually deal with him it will weaken the incumbent issue and we'll be forced to reinvent this thing as two new guys who want to tweak the system and rely on the voters to go with the party which has kept them in the pink for nearly eight years.

e-mail mania

Date: 9/1/99 10:43 PM

Mr. Campion,

I can see the headlines now:

Gore and Bradley, together! The new dream team! Enough charisma to wake any sleeping baby or excite a roomful of old ladies!

Vs.

McCain-Dole, The Good Guy and Perky Gal. He was locked in the Hanoi Hilton for seven years and her marriage to Bob has been just as excruciating.

Bush evaporates quicker than Gary Hart as the allegations pile up of womanizing and coke snorting. Bush: "I swear, I don't remember any of it!" The Reagan defense, this time also true, but in vain, since G.W.'s parties were always the greatest. Dan Quayle fights to the bitter end, securing a sympathy spot at the convention, in which he forgets his wife's name during his speech. Pat Buck threatens to join the Reform party and is mysteriously kidnapped, never to be seen or heard from again. Gary Bauers is revealed to be a cross dresser, and Forbes flips out during the debates, ranting about his late father Malcolm. "He did not have sex with Rock Hudson!"

At the last minute, Jesse the Body and Jesse the Reverend form an unholy alliance and win as write in candidates!

Buzz

Date: 9/1/99 1:20AM

Buzz,

Excellent assessment of the upcoming races. I have heard much of the same. Ventura want to lock up all pansies and Forbes is spending millions on a smear campaign for Bob Dole. He misses the old pro. Are you as connected as I suspect? Or have you been over to see Dr. Feelgood again? Nevertheless, I must pick a bone.

Why the fuck should Dollar Bill taint his outsider, rebel from the streets, image by hooking his diesel up to Satan? Bradley will crush him in the primaries. I will personally see he wins the tri-state area alone. When I'm through with Gore he won't be able to get his parking validated in Yonkers. It's over. Admit it. It was a nice run, but Clinton should have run Gore out of town if he thought for one minute he'd have a chance in hell of keeping it going. Get with the winner!!! I'm registering Democratic if this wave keeps up!! Sure, word is out that I receive a ridiculous pile of literature from every Socialist faction known to civilization, and I'm the only crazy fuck who voted for John Anderson AND Ralph Nader! God help us all Buzz, I need a winner besides the Yankees; who, by the way, will be crushing anything that cheap fraud National League lays up as a sacrificial lamb. When the World Series is finished they'll be starting a religion after whatever survives.

jc

Date: 9/2/99 2:01 PM

sir,

I remember it well, back in 1997. J.C : "I will personally shoot Gore if it even looks like he will become the next President." Will it be a prophecy...fulfilled? Otherwise, you must ingest! Show some guts and take matters into your own hands. And when you end up a patsy for all time I will cry foul! "Poor Jimmy, he was my friend," I'll say. "He never showed signs of anything violent. Why, the Ramsey's are a festering clan of killers compared to him." Then when they beat you to death in prison like Dahmer, we will all rejoice in your memory. Two great Americans assassinated by fate. Aaron Burr would be proud.

Remember my friend, my memory is long. I recall the egging of school buses. Some insane gibberish you penned having something to do with molemen running around a basketball court in Freehold, NJ. And don't think I'll leave out the endless drinking in unknown village bars with the dreck of this earth. I cannot forget how I came to your aid when the cops caught you running wild in the woods wearing nothing with a burlap bag. When they finally dragged you to the rotting leaves behind Mrs. Potter's house you were screaming something about independent candidates!

Loser indeed.

Buzz

Date: 9/2/99 11:54 PM

You can't prove it. I'll deny it all. I am not a killer, but a LOVER! The only question the authorities have ever had for me is — what do you love?? You, my misguided friend, are mistaken about Al Gore. He is my friend. I love the environment, and suck up to PETA daily. And I am quite happy with warning stickers on rap records. Having never smoked a single cigarette (inhaled?) I can truly say I now weep for the vice president's late sister. But it is a matter of national security and the preservation of freedom of which we speak now. Sometimes innocent people end up hurt, or in the case of the Clintons', dead. Did I just write that? Look what I've become in the glaring light of your bleary accusals.

If you persist in spreading these ugly rumors culled from our close friendship I must seek legal restitution. There are important people who will want the contents of video tapes revealing you as a harsh drunk who would think nothing of abusing musical instruments. Especially those that are off limits to the lunacy you practice under the sheath of darkness and fog of drink. Most times when these ugly things form in your unconscious, you, perhaps we, are quite inebriated and surely incapable of memory. That is the tact my attorney will take in the event you finger me as an assassin. Bill Bradley will decide the fate of Al Gore, not the irresponsible rumors spewing from the bowels of NYC.

8/25/99

POLL ME

It's bad enough I must endure reams of meaningless gibberish from every political party under the sun, and nightly phone calls from a lunatic named Barry at precisely 8:01 reminding me that Libby Dole will sign any tax cut put in front of her if we're all drunk enough to elect her president 14 months from now. The good people at Gracie Mansion hate my guts because of erroneous rumors passed on by the misinterpretation of this column. The Sons of Pataki, Peekskill order, have sworn testimony from six witnesses in the governor's clan that I drank all the wine at the dais before a fund raiser in March, and in turn have used my name to strike rage in the heart of my pal, George.

And it isn't getting any easier dealing with Al Sharpton now that anyone who "handles" him gives me 40 minute lectures on his chances for legitimate office, and how much he loves everyone now. My buddy, Tom Leighton, the Marijuana Reform Party candidate faxes his weekly facts, figures, and assorted propaganda to a local radio station in White Plains under my name. Since, no less than four interns and a late-night adult/contemporary DJ have asked me to score them weed.

I receive nasty letters from Abu-Jamal apologists who call me a police lap dog and hate mail from thugs who defend the actions of swastika-painting cretins allegedly working in tandem with the Ossining police department.

All my sources threaten to sue me like clockwork once another column hits the stands filled with their misguided blather. Not the least of which is that ingrate Georgetown, who besides trailing me through most of California, continuously mails caustic letters to Chuck Shumer using my name.

And did I fail to mention that my parents are pissed at me for idle comments made as part of an interview I granted to Amazon.com about my book, "Deep Tank Jersey". Seems neither of them thought it particularly funny that I credited my craft to lying in order to escape "severe retribution and punishment".

Now I open a letter from US News and World Report, whose promotional department has apparently ignored five years of my refusing to receive their periodical. It seems I'm to represent the over-30, white, male with random answers to some asinine questionnaire. But a deadline beckons, and there is forever a space to fill, so here goes.

How would you rate Bill Clinton's performance on domestic matters from 4/ 99 until now?

(Fair) People are still working. Taxes are still high. Kids keep killing each other at an alarming rate. And my next door neighbor drinks a case of Wild Turkey a week while trying to shoot my cats from the cherry picker teetering atop the idling fire truck in his driveway.

International?

(Poor) There are still a few countries left without U.S. troops stuck in it. The Chinese are intercepting my cellular phone calls. France still stands.

Do you believe president Slobodan Milosevic should be allowed to continue as leader of Yugoslavia?

(Yes) As long as he does it disemboweled and hanging from a pole in the village square.

Rate the candidate in order of whom you think will represent the Republican party.

G.W. Bush - Best stash in Texas. Libby Dole - Hates taxes? Steve Forbes - Rich guys are silly. John McCain - Never ceases to make me chuckle. Pat Buchanan - Guffaw. Dan Quayle - There's always room for the stupid.

Do you believe that airline passengers should be compensated through the Airline Passenger Bill of Rights when flights are delayed, canceled, or overbooked?

Passenger Bill of Rights? The entire business is run like some fascist regime, or at the very least, insurance companies. A leather-faced, uniformed, menopausal vulture on the Continental Airlines pay roll tried to extort $100 out of me for a goddamn duffel bag. And when I vehemently refused, treated me like a war criminal and sent for security to rough me up. Needless to say I traveled 700 miles out of the way to save the money on principle.

Do you think the NY Stock Exchange should be open for trading until 10:00 p.m. daily?

Why? So those yuppie geeks at home trading on the Internet can cram up cyberspace all night? Come to think of it, why not? Let the Japanese sweat a little more.

Do you believe that the U.S. should continue to offer trade benefits to China, even though it's been accused of stealing nuclear technology secrets?

Stealing secrets? Never mind forced abortions, a mockery of civil rights, and the incarceration of anyone seen enjoying themselves.

Do you believe that the U.S. should have stronger warnings for its tourists who travel to dangerous destinations?

Nah, let the bastards guess. I did.

Do you believe the government should prosecute the person who sold guns to the two students who opened fire at the high school in Littleton, Colorado?

Let's start by jailing the parents of all mutants.

Do you believe U.S. companies should be allowed to sell sophisticated military equipment to the Chinese?

I thought they had all of it already.

How do you plan to prepare for Y2K?

A case of Corona, six limes, a Cuban cigar, my wife, and my three cats all lounging in a tent pitched in the backyard. Let the good times roll!

9/8/99

CONGRESS IN WINTER

The legislative branch of your government has returned from their annual lengthy summer recess with hopes to get back to the business of the people. This usually means gumming up the system with maniacal rhetoric and useless jabbering which will likely amalgamate from the ugly to the savage resulting in yet another widely predicted shutdown of government. No one on either side of the political fence knows what party would favor that type of lunacy, but one thing is certain among the braggart elite: before this latest gnawing and gnashing of fangs concludes political blood will be shed.

The order of Congressional "business" this time around is monumental for not only the next decade of fiscal prosperity or damage, key legal ramifications, and how this government will view crippling political issues like gun control and health care reform, but will doubtless carry the final year of the Clinton Administration and shake the campaigns of warring probables for the White House.

As of the first full week of September Congress must debate, whine, scrap, and finally vote on whether they should conduct the investigation of the FBI and attorney general, Janet Reno's obvious torching of the Branch Davidian compound in Waco six years ago. Also included on the agenda; campaign finance abuses, gun control and juvenile crime bills, and how to divide the reported $3 trillion federal surplus among tax relief, federal programs, and the always popular debt relief over the next ten years.

This building fracas must be handled carefully by both parties. Although word has it that Republicans will try to jam tax cuts through at any cost, they must dance around gun control. Both issues have, and will, be used ad nauseum by George W. Bush in his burgeoning campaign by summer. With Bush Jr. leading in all polls down the line, giving in is no option now. Similarly, the Democrats cannot be too bold on campaign finance issue, seeing how it's plagued Al Gore in the past. They must also deflect investigations involving a sitting attorney general, and the continued nasty whispers about billions of Russian dollars being laundered through the Bank of New York under Clinton's watch.

It is a sticky time, when the polls may lie and the backlash is hard. The American people are fickle. What could make you the cock of the walk in September could turn you into Hugo's Hunchback by Christmas. Constituents push for one issue while hiding from another. We want a tax cut, but we tremble at the doom-struck rants of Allen Greenspan. We hate the violence, but we love our guns. No one returns calls, media types horde information, and the political wind shifts hourly. It will be hard to get a gauge on this from the shills on CNN and the confused over at the New York Times, but before long we'll all want results. Any results.

The Waco mess gets all the press for now. Although no one I've talked to for six years believes for one minute that the FBI knew what they were doing down there, and followed that up with the most vague and shameful cover up in recent history. It is the single reason for the tragedy at the federal building in Oklahoma, and growing suspicion about the government's penchant for choosing brute Marshall-law force over negotiating in any instance. But Reno will either resign in disgrace or survive on the same miserable bilge Reagan pumped after the Iran/Contra affair. "Hey, ya gotta do what ya gotta do in times of national crisis." So it would behoove Congress to shovel this over to another incompetent independent investigation and clear the floor for the real deal; tax cuts and gun control.

The pressing question will be how many Democrats will keep a straight face while debating a lame duck tax-cut issue knowing their president will veto it the second it leaves the hill. The White House has more than instructed the denizens that anything above $300 billion won't be acceptable, unless Gore and Bradley slug it out in the muck and Bush Jr. looks like he will carry November of 2,000 somewhere in June. Then the smart political move has Clinton signing over a future fiscal disaster to his successor.

And expect to hear more crap about this "extra" Federal funds than the perennial favorite, gun control. Few in Congress believe there will be anything but lateral moves on this issue. Trent Lott and Dick Armey say all the right things, but no Republican will risk the conservative vote or NRA power unless there is a party decision on how far Bush Jr. will lean left to gain independent votes—and how many of those votes Pat Buchanan will take with him when he heads to the Reform party.

Anything short of a government shut down is expected. That is the main reason Newt Gingrich is sitting in divorce proceedings at the Cobb County courthouse rather than further burying the GOP. The Dems have enough problems, not the least of which is Gore being booed like a Hun during a Labor Day parade in downtown Washington. All these issues are hard line, and in the shadow of a presidential election year, nobody wants to tip the political boat. However, this is Washington, and there is always a chance for a miracle. Although I think it was Goethe who said, "Mysteries are not necessarily miracles."

9/15/99

EDUCATION IN AMERICA

> *"Thinking men cannot be ruled."*
> - Ayn Rand

> *"We blew it."*
> - Peter Fonda to Dennis Hopper
> in "Easy Rider"

While the damaged souls on Capital Hill mind-swell on the wildly inventive ways to improve the state of education — such as metal detectors, prayer groups, and history books updated past the Reagan Era — we here at the Reality Check News and Information Desk offer the following comprehensive study into the fractured dismantling of the well-informed American child. Backed with statistics, both enlightening and gruesome, there is always hope that such an animal still exists in the waning hours of the American Century. It is with our deepest regret that we must remind those with any sense of national pride or positive outlook on the future that a planet ruled by talking apes is still at least a millennia away.

According to the rough numbers compiled by a group of fatigued college students from Pace University, subsisting on ham sandwiches and Mountain Dew for fourteen straight hours on 9/9/99, 37% of all students entering High School this year expect to be introduced to sex and drugs long before correctly identifying their congressman. (20% of the remaining 63% have been-there-and-done-that and plan to use the next level to stay out of prison and the military). Meanwhile 62% of High School graduates entering college believe drinking a keg of beer with less than half-a-dozen dorm mates in an eight-hour period counts greater in the scheme of campus survival than having a minor-to-deficient grasp of the periodic table of the elements.

Less than 17% of High School students can name half of the state capitols or conjugate a verb in another language, but 88% of the same students polled are proficient at locating a variety of celebrity nude photos using news groups on the Internet. The same group boasted nearly 90% success in getting a hold of their father's handgun in a pinch, but less than 20% could pick out Albert Einstein, Hitler, or Jesus in a lineup.

All the teachers polled were reluctant to formulate a usable hypothesis on this disturbing data; but many without nervous conditions, hypertension, or drinking problems believe the system's failure lies in the diminishing number of parental beatings being administered.

With apologies to the malnourished few from Pace, it has suddenly become chic to denigrate the public education system in this country, with so many families opting for private schools, tutors, or ROTC sweatshops. But can any of us still young and frightened enough to remember what a farce even half-a-day of school was? We are abused, desensitized, mutants with a minor grasp of the obvious, and an even less handle on daily survival. Can you blame us; being ushered through an utterly senseless maze of standardized testing, Beowulf readings, and gym classes. Therefore, we breed the stupid.

Currently, there is far more legislation being considered, voted on, and passed concerning the burning of cloth with stars and stripes on it then the proper funds to educate young Americans. Daily stories of kids being tossed out of school for wearing a Star of David, blue hair, or not complying to some petty rule continues unabated. College tuition is through the roof, yet millions of us leave these institutions with more of an ulcer than a true understanding of what we can do to either be useful parts of a society, or at the very least, less likely to be seduced by a Don King production.

If we are naive enough to believe that a robotic curriculum aimed at policing rather than enlightening is the answer, then we can leave the act of educating to the public school system or the church. This waltz of lazy ignorance has produced a false sense of security in leaders and systems in the first place; a line of thinking which has resulted in the raising of carnival barkers, con men, and celebrity fodder to the status of role models and focal points in an age of deceit and corrupt laziness not witnessed since the fall of Rome.

The purest acts of self-discovery or simple research on subject matter which may define our culture is dying a slow and painful death. It's not the fault of the government or school administrations if they've become lax. We allow it. Instead of droning debates on cross-cultural heritage curriculum, or handing out condoms to infants, how about stimulating their psyches or broadening their sense of motivation and self worth with challenges beyond, "Sit down, shut-up, and turn to page 123"?

Of course, there are exceptions to many of the hideous details found above. I had some wonderful people offer up countless moments of learned passion which helped me along the way. And to them I will be forever grateful and in their debt. But I was also cheated, just as you were, are, or continue to be. Now is the best time to demand knowledge so another generation avoids becoming the product of inferior education. Waiting for someone or something else to do anything about it is the way of the stupid. The way, apparently, we are now headed.

9/22/99

REFORM PARTY FUN

"The Republicans need a new pit bull. Pat Buchanan will dust off his rumble-act soon, but with the snub in San Diego at the convention in August of '96 serving as the last straw, he will likely abandon the party ship for an independent run."

Reality Check
Issue : 6/2/98

As I write this, one Pat Buchanan, scourge of philosophy, master of hyperbole, and prime-time crackpot of latter century American politics, is the focus of begging by pertinent Republican officials to remain a member of their party. Fresh from a rousing performance on "Face the Nation", where he defended the literary self-inflicted wounds of his book, "A Republic Not An Empire", Go-Pat-Go has once again become the media's whipping boy. But what has been a constant theme in this space for over a year has finally hit the core of the George W. Bush campaign: If Buchanan leaves his present place in the Republican pantheon for a run on the Reform Party ticket, he could pull key conservative votes along with him, wreaking the same havoc Ross Perot did on Junior's dad in 1992.

The priceless subplot of all this surrounds the Reform Party's steadfast denial they want anything to do with a publicly branded, racist, isolationist, ultra-right-wing maniac. Beyond former party vice-presidential candidate, Pat Choate, who salivates at the chance the Reform Party would nudge a debate viper into the arena, party officials fear Buchanan would tip the boat so far right only the KKK, inbreeds, or Pat Robertson rejects would dare vote for him.

Even so, the fun begins with the party's wide-open auditions for a candidate. Despite having a powerful bedrock contingent, $12 million dollars in its coffers, and grabbing a monumental 16% of the national vote in the '92 presidential election, the Reform Party has become the refuge of the disenfranchised loon.

Founded by the deranged Perot, the Reform Party has gone from anti-trade, anti-big business, antigovernment "watchdog", to a wide open forum for the radical celebrity. So far, its front-runners include wrestler-gone-governor, Jesse Ventura, vacuous, rich guy playboy, Donald Trump, Hollywood power-broker and once leading-man, Warren Beatty, and just about anyone with a chance to turn heads by name alone. Each personality, although notable, cause some problems ideologically.

Ventura is a fiscal conservative, but a social liberal. Warren Beatty, who leans toward nothing if not a Democratic run, is a staunch 60s' liberal. Ventura has called Beatty a socialist, but loves his old buddy, Trump. The Donald has no ideology, but boasts a far more sordid past than George W. Bush and Bill Clinton put together.

No one working for the Reform Party has any allusions about actually winning a general election with any of these colorful dupes, or with a resurrection of Abe Lincoln for that matter; but all names, especially the always entertaining Buchanan, gives them an angry voice crying out from the wilderness. And if the prime candidates won't listen, their parties certainly are. The GOP needs to keep Buchanan in the fold, and let the Reform Party choose a more liberal candidate to chew into the Bradley/Gore vote, and the Dems want him on the trail as an independent to skew the gaudy Bush numbers.

Buchanan needs a new home for his Bible-thumping, flag-waving rhetoric. He sights late October for an announcing date, but this space has learned that it's a done deal. Intercepted faxes from the Buchanan camp to Reform Party officials as early as June which warned of a healthy debate on pro-life vs. the party's pro-choice stance seals it. The only question which needs to be answered is how much carnage this will inflict on the middle-of-the-road, "ain't interested in alienating anyone" Bush campaign.

Buchanan has many enemies in the Republican Party. Bush hates him, and still blames him for weakening his father's run for the presidency twice. Buchanan's vitriolic speeches have consistently wounded the GOP over the years, becoming a public relations nightmare in the wake of the Reagan wave. His name still evokes chilling memories of a Spiro Agnew press conference, for whom Buchanan wrote every below-the-belt word. Bill Buckley has called him an anti-Semite, and George Will has trouble keeping a straight face whenever confronted with him.

Buchanan has no other choice but to take his show on the road. Whether the Reform Party is the place for Buchanan to pitch tent is yet to be seen, but it will not be his call. Go-Pat-Go wants in, because he feels regurgitated by a Republican Party which has sat on its laurels since the glorious winter of '94 when the 104th Congress had so much promise, but ended up being a dumping ground for a Clinton comeback.

But if Buchanan doesn't strategically deflect his book's WWII revisionism and apparent ethnic bashing, no one but circus freaks and stooges collecting bombs on the Internet will touch him with a mile-long poll. Beyond Go-Pat-Go's obligatory early blip on the political screen, the Reform

Party will be stuck with a Barry Goldwater retread and further its cause as comedy relief in an already laughable field.

9/29/99

BILL BRADLEY-THE BEST MAN, THE WORST JOB

Suddenly the vice-president has a fight on his hands, and if Al Gore doesn't wake up to this fact soon, his automatic nomination for president will disappear. Former senator, and basketball star, Bill Bradley, is starting to gain numbers in the polls, which has brought him income comparable to the party's heir apparent, and a growing list of support from high profile party members. Not to mention that while Bradley is presently viewed by key Demo focus groups as a scholarly Jimmy Stewart, his opponent, besides appearing as a vapid dullard whose transparent attempts at "image retooling" is beyond regrettable, believe Al Gore to be nothing more than a mendacious Clintonian vapor trail.

Bill Bradley is the first quality human being within sniffing distance of the highest office in the land since Jimmy Carter shuffled from Georgian obscurity to feast on the carcass of Richard Nixon. Granted, he has flip-flopped on major issues, and does seem to have that peace-and-love 60s' mentality which is easily punctured, but compared to the usual Washington fare, Bradley is a decent, highly intelligent and compassionate man who truly cares about the country's most pressing domestic issues.

Bradleys' honesty is almost alarming. When questioned about his use of drugs in the wake of G.W. Bush's cocaine denials, he not only told a national television audience that he smoked pot several times, but wrested a similar confession out of Sam Donaldson.

Al Gore likely avoided recreational drugs, but would mainline grade-A Peruvian slam if he thought it could gain him some major numbers in New York and California. In the face Bradley's "quiet, intellectual every man", the VP comes across as a bargain basement panderer. He has even failed to reveal a sincerity about the issues he claims to champion; environment, health care, or gun-control. Although he should be skating toward a breezy nomination as the vice president of a two term commander-and-chief in relative economic heaven, Al Gore is damaged goods. Early returns sight that if Gore were to run against anything the GOP throws out there short of Bebe Robozo, Al Haig, or the bastard son of Jim Baker, he'll be dog meat.

The system which produces things like presidents and senators usually eats candidates like Bradley alive. But this is a new era in American politics. This is the age of the wide open closet doors with skeletons dancing naked for the paparazzo, and Bradley finds himself in the cross hairs. The very idea that he even presents a threat to anyone outside a school board is an encouraging development.

There are many more clear reasons why Bradley could upset Gore and stand a better chance against the ambiguously pertinent political locomotive that is George Bush Jr. in a general election, not the least of which is the ambitions of Senator Rodham.

The First Lady's run for NY Senate was launched by the retirement of the well-respected, Daniel Patrick Moynihan. On September 23, in front of A DNC crowd more shocked than dismayed, Moynihan stood firmly behind a Hillary run, but followed the Ed Koch hue and cry that Al Gore is unelectable. Trouble for Gore is twofold: While straddled with the daunting task of distancing himself from the notorious "Clintion Fatigue" it will be virtually impossible for him to stump without the force of the Whitehouse. Yet, Senator Rodham, and her soon to be civilian hubby, cannot serve two masters; the party and her campaign. People may be sick of Big Bill now, but by his final term the nostalgia for a president becomes campaign gold. Without major support from the Clinton Machine, Gore will be fortunate to get a traffic ticket in Washington by spring.

Right now Bradley has gone from quirky outsider with a couple of NBA championship rings to full-blown thorn in the side of whatever Gore is parading around. The national numbers lean favorably toward Gore, but that could sway on the New Hampshire primary, which is definitely up for grabs. The dead heat in New Hampshire poll numbers by press time could only be swayed by the one avenue Gore in which excels; the debate. But with Bill Bradley's growing mellow confidence, chances of reducing him to the stammering muppet Dan Quayle was in '92, or the befuddled moron that was the last vestiges of Jack Kemp in '96, is highly unlikely. Bradley's dealt with Jerry West, Oscar Robinson, and Earl the Pearl, and anyone who knows a lick about hoops knows that Dollar Bill is far too cool for that kind of cheap trash talking.

Bill Bradley is a rare breed. He clings to a hint of character and integrity and still has a chance to win a major office. The cesspool that is American

politics doesn't deserve him. He will most assuredly come up short, which is
why he is the best man for the worst job.

10/13/99

POLITICS & ART: A QUESTION OF BIGOTRY, TASTE, & THE FIRST AMENDMENT

The city of New York, with the approval of the mayor, signs over an
allocation of funds for the arts each fiscal year. This is done with the assumption that the local government will not be critiquing said art. So, when the
mayor decides he isn't fond of, or pains to define this art, there is the usual
furor. Those receiving the funds hypocritically cry that government has no
place in deciding the type of art it pays for. They have no problem taking the
money, but are shocked when the patrons want to close the store.

Rudolf Guiliani, in dire need of the conservative, religious right vote
in the outer reaches of New York, threatens to pull state funding for the Brooklyn Museum of Art if it continues an exhibit called *Sensation*. Uncle Rudy
sights the desecration of religion, insensitive images of animal abuse, and the
always popular pornography as his reasons. The most notorious piece, a painting called *The Holy Virgin Mary* by Chris Ofili, has brought the expected slew
of angry Catholics to the forefront. Native African, and devout Catholic himself, Ofili argues that his piece, festooned with elephant dung, is a celebra-
tion of eternal life and God. Uncle Rudy thinks its offensive nonsense.

Those familiar with the First Amendment, which Guiliani has sworn
to uphold, do not care what he thinks. Uncle Rudy says they should start caring, especially if they want to see these images in a publicly funded museum.
For instance, the privately funded Whitney Museum will soon be displaying
the mother of all Christian-taunting pieces, *Piss Christ*. However, the mayor's
moral outrage on that one is silent.

The Brooklyn Museum stands to lose $7 million if Uncle Rudy gets
his way; but, of course, he won't. Guiliani has fought over 100 First Amendment cases since becoming mayor of the "art capitol of the world" and has a
grand total of one victory. And since that one had to do with porn and school

zoning, it was a lay-up ruling. This is a museum, and in the wonderfully gray area of artistic integrity and sludge mongering, the museum will out.

Uncle Rudy is playing the victim. Ironically, his fingerprints are all over the smoking gun. He approved the money used, in his opinion, to offend nearly half of his constituency. He has no case. This attack on the Brooklyn museum is as much political pandering as it is saving face.

Meanwhile, a predictably huge number of people stood in line for hours to whisk past the *Holy Virgin* painting on the exhibit's opening weekend. The power of negative publicity has always been good for these kinds of things. But despite its noisy feedback, *Sensation* brings up curious questions about the fine line between social bating and free expression.

Those defending the Catholic-bashing element of Ofili's *Holy Virgin*, with its feces stained portrait of a beloved religious icon hanging mere feet from explicit photographs of naked buttocks and mutilated cows, would like to know where the standard of abuse ends. Would a painting of Martin Luther King smeared with dog shit be summarily defended? How about a charcoal rendering of Anne Frank boffing a Nazi? If these images bring vomit to the bottom of your throat, then maybe they have a point.

Is the legitimacy of art the degree to which it represents negativity toward humankind? The Swastika is a work of art. The Confederate Flag is a work of art. Both have horrific connotations to Jews and African Americans, and still carry a very deadly image. But those in the corner of free expression can argue that using those symbols in art can do more for the eradication of their demented ideology than any political or social stance. They may also argue that the view point of the artist is subjective. What one person may see as disgusting may very well be beautiful to the next. Who then should decide?

It is noble to want tax dollars to fund the arts. After all, our money goes to such frivolous and destructive government endeavors, it is somewhat refreshing to see provocative culture, if not at the very least, emotional awakening having its place. But if accepting these funds means compromising the integrity of the artist, perhaps there should be a separation of art and state. The marriage of a rigid political monster like Uncle Rudy and some artistic freak from abroad goes a long way to defending that theory.

The broader quandary in these sticky First Amendment battles is the very realistic possibility that a government allowed to delve into free expression is one step away from a police state; something Uncle Rudy has been accused of envisioning for his city. Cleaning up the homeless and attacking pornography is admirable, but where does this myopic holier-than-thou attitude end? It is important to remember that it wasn't too long ago that public libraries were censoring books. And no amount of hurt feelings can undo the damage that kind of fear can induce.

10/20/99

LAST RIDE FOR THE GIPPER

Editor's Note:
Mr. Campion felt it necessary to respond to an e-mail he'd received from a
reader that felt "disturbed" by the "dismantling of a great man" which the
writer believed takes place in the pages of a controversial Ronald Reagan
biography by Edmund Morris called "Dutch".

Of course you should be disturbed, my friend, but not by some over-
blown, self-absorbed rendering of a human billboard like Ronald Reagan—be
disturbed for the level of worship we have reserved for creatures of celebrity.
Certainly, Edmund Morris should not be the subject of your disturbance. Morris is trying to sell books. Fairness is not the aim of historians, only agenda. I
can mail you six books by learned scholars who would contradict each other
vehemently on the same fact. History is a slippery rock to tread upon. Sometimes considering the source is a fruitless endeavor left for teachers and patri-
ots to ponder. Dick Nixon was a deranged criminal with little regard for things
like laws, but he was right on the nut when he said that history would finally
judge him through the eyes of its authors.

Morris may paint a riveting picture of the 40th president of the
United States by delving into his enigmatic psyche, but in the end, he is an
Englishman. I had to live in this country during the fairy tale that was the
Reagan Administration. And anyone who wasn't scarred by it were either
failing to pay attention or doing the scarring.

Although I've received my copy of Morris' lengthy tome in the mail
only last week, I shall not read it. Wasting time searching for reasons why a
man like Ronald Reagan was allowed to run a four keg softball game—much
less the most powerful republic on the planet in a time of precarious tension,
while decent men rotted in prisons throughout the third world—is beyond credible rational.

There is an old saying which sites that you can tell a great deal about a man by the company he keeps. The Gipper called Ed Meese friend. Many speak of the terrors the 80s' wrought; but beyond a Tipper Gore rally and Jellybean Benitez, the "Meese stare", as its few remaining survivors referred to it, was a thing of pure evil. Meese was the rabid bite behind the old man's polished bark, and his shadow was long and wide.

The Gipper called Al Haig friend. Not since the Spanish Inquisition was there a Homo Sapian bold enough to cling to the human race while simultaneously gnawing at its weaker strands than the cretin who stood over the prone body of his boss to declare that he was in charge.

The list is longer, but the Gipper was stronger than them all. He couldn't be gunned down by a pathetic loser like John Hinckly. There wasn't an army on this planet that could penetrate the "shining city on a hill" when Rappin' Ronnie was in the big chair. His enemies were many, but his friends all had fangs.

During those dark times anyone caught downwind of the "Reagan People" were not expected to last very long in a flimsy concept like democracy. The Gipper and his lot were mutants of a frightened age brought on by Middle Eastern terrorists and radicals who turned the Carter administration into the laughing stock it begged to be. Ronnie made deals with oil barons for U.S. weapons and lied to congress so blatantly that the hardened boys in the chamber blushed like school boys.

But unlike his pal, Mr. Nixon, The Gipper ran a tight ship. He could not be slowed by a little thing like the constitution—and he sure couldn't be derailed by the lineup of victims the Democrats sent to the alter of his political slaughter. No, the Gipper let that sycophantic uniform, Ollie North take one for the team. If the lieutenant colonel had a lick of John Dean's sense there would have been two Republican presidents taking that helicopter ride from the front lawn to oblivion, but Ollie wasn't in the "habit of questioning" his superiors. "I hear my orders, salute politely, and charge up that hill," Ollie told the dumbfounded at the congressional hearing that by all accounts should have grounded the Gipper for good.

However, let us not forget that although Ronald Reagan was taller than the law, he was a talking mannequin for American Pollyanna in an age of diminishing returns on pride, and, after all, a necessity. The Gipper came riding in on his chariot of slogans from numerous failed attempts at cracking the prize nut of politics to remind us all that the erosion of solidarity would be taking an eight year respite under his watch.

Reagan was a champion for those who were fed up with the images coming in daily from Iran. American flags burning in Baghdad and cheap charlatans like Qaddafi parading his death medals in the face of UN diplomats were like picking off lethargic fish in a tiny barrel for the Gipper. He was the last of the living Red fighters. He hated Communism more than Hollywood. Ironically, these were the two bitch goddesses who made the old man. He learned a thing or two about salesmanship and posturing from Tinsletown—which made him a sideshow act for even those who thought they knew him well. And if not for Russia, with its riddles wrapped in enigmas, there would've been no point to the Reagan presidency.

Instead, Ronald Reagan will be forever linked to the economic implosion of the Soviet Union, a damaged government born on the revulsion of such pertinent concepts as war and profit. The Gipper wanted to be standing when they tore down that wall in Berlin so badly he bet our financial future on it; jamming the national debt up the charts full throttle in a buy-off of weaponry not witnessed in the annals of civilization.

Weep not for the Gipper, he was the political mutation of losers. There would have been no Jimmy Carter if not for Ronnie's friend Mr. Nixon, who gave us all a reason to believe that everyone who ever runs for political office is crooked and mean. Nixon was a crook and Carter was the medicine for a sickened nation. The Gipper was the beneficiary of their failures. He crushed the competition in historic fashion and laughed at their wounds. The Gipper wouldn't allow defeat. He would've fried us all in a vat of crude oil and sesame seeds to prove America was the greatest nation in the world. John Wayne in a three piece suit with one hand on the button and the other giving a peace sign. Memories like that, my poor misguided friend, begin at disturbing and go from there.

11/3/99

SISTERS, WITCHES, & OTHER OCTOBER STORIES

October was a strange month for those of us mired at the Reality Check News and Information Desk. There was little sleep and less sanity. I was deluged with more meaningless campaign mail on and off my computer, and even though I managed credentials for a World Series in which the Yankees stomped Atlanta in the fashion of General Sherman, three hours of shuteye fueled by gallons of tepid Mountain Dew in 48 hours is a pathetic survival routine.

The noisy moles in the electronic media press box out in the right field pavilion reviled me for even suggesting that Pete Rose be drawn and quartered for leaving his house, much less be cheered like a conquering Roman in some garish excuse for a Master Card promotion. And for those keeping score, I took pleasure in shaking Jim Gray's hand for reducing Charlie Hustle to the boorish thug he really is on national television.

Strangely, things calmed considerably for the Halloween weekend. The temps ran straight up and the wife and me followed them north to Syracuse where Hillary Clinton is currently viewed as a terrible mistake of science tantamount to cloned sheep and Thalidomide.

We were hoping for the type of respite her two sisters and their cheerful husbands often provide with good food, wine, and the occasional song. But October was not over, and there was the little matter of a creeping winter solstice and the swirling leave-swept breeze.

Before Saturday was done I'd found myself crammed on aluminum seats in the Carrier Dome between the harried and the caustic faithful to cheer on the doomed Orangeman. To a man, they were sure the home team would meet some interminable fate before the final gun.

Unfortunately for all involved, they were right. There was no way out of that place with a shred of rah-rah dignity left in our considerable pigskin hearts. The chrome under our posteriors was barely warm when the Syracuse head coach was deferring the kickoff and the 19-point underdog, BC Eagles were rambling 102 yards to pay dirt.

Events deteriorated steadily from there.

The fans were sent into a frenzy of rage, and neither gods or monsters could keep those poor souls dressed in orange and blue from baying at the moon by the final quarter. When we left that infernal cage of a stadium the worst part of us still remained. One member of my party spent nearly twenty minutes in the Sheraton downstairs bathroom completing his impending breakdown.The Final: 24-23 Boston College.

The evening held gentler moments. Three couples, ten bottles of wine, and stimulating conversation; for the six of us it was all like a finely crafted cocoon of comfort and gaiety. The music chimed merrily in the background, and the buzz from the Chardonnay settled perfectly into the brain. We were struck by the emotions of our childhoods and the inevitable burrow of the future. This is the adulthood we have chosen in these glaring minutes of clarity, faced with death, jobs, religion, sex, and the strength of friendship. Some of us shed tears, others laughed until it hurt. There was arm wrestling and broken glass. The sisters decided to carve pumpkins, but as I watched my lovely wife slice hard into the top of the orb's squirting skin and scoop out the gummy innards, I succumbed to goulish nightmares.

By the time we arrived home the next day—All Hallows Eve—a message on my machine alerted me to a fax sent from the Circle Network of Wicca located somewhere in Wisconsin. Years ago, I'd written this rather curious sect of paganism requesting an audience with the members of a coven from Poughkeepsie. It was, after all, their Sabbat of Samhain, or summer's end, the Gaelic holiday of shadows and mayhem which came from the shores of Ireland to eventually become the Christianized Halloween. Since Wiccans rarely allow outsiders to observe their holiday ritual, I heeded the voice on the other end which simply said, "In perfect love and perfect trust."

Erin, being a Vegan, wholly in tune with nature, and a rabid opponent of anything with a penis, was further aroused at the notion to join me when she realized the pagan coven in question was of the Dianic order. Well known in the dark circles to repel "male energy" using magic and the vibes of the universe to channel all female pulses, the Dianic's have been known to party.

Arriving at the address given, a park draped in the cool of evening, the ritual had begun with the traditional dances, chants, and the flow of an ancient wine recipe made from honey. No one mentioned the "burning times," or admitted knowing anything about sacrificing babies, but they were lively and festive, dressed in black and garbed in the dress of the ancients. Wiccans do not worry about things like the end of the world or eschatological prophecy. This is the earth we were given. Love for all things in nature, and the revulsion of those who point an accusatory finger, is their golden rule.

It was no place for a man fresh from the World Series and a gut-wrenching loss in the Carrier Dome. The last I saw of my wife was in the shroud of black capes and misty incense. But the Mead wine was flowing, the cauldron bubbling, and midnight beckoned. After all, October's been a strange month.

11/10/99

THE RUSSIAN ELEMENT

Five years ago some dingbat historian stood before a congregation of stoked college graduates on the campus of North Carolina State University and espoused a theory that the world was a freer and far more safer place now that the evil Soviet Union had crumbled beneath the weight of what is good and true. He surmised that this generation would be the first to enjoy an adult life devoid of nuclear fear.

The crowd roared their approval. Of course, in the face of escaping college those desperate children would've cheered the ceremonial burning of their parents; but from my seat in the second balcony of the basketball arena I paused to reflect on this intellectual heresy. For the Soviet Union was merely a symptom of a greater virus already loosed on the unlucky survivors of its demise. Imbedded in the genes and passed on for generations would be the perpetuation of a cultural phenomenon known as the "Russian Element".

Presently, what passes for the Russian military is pounding one of the former Soviet Union's many unstable republics called Chechnya. An "anti-terrorist" campaign ordered by Prime Minister, Vladmir Putin, has been going on for months. Troops continue a steady march to it's burned-out capitol city, Grozny in an attempt to completely crush a rebel contingent said to have been responsible for apartment bombings and brutal slayings throughout the region since the real bloodshed commenced in 1994.

Moscow has clearly stated that it does not care who perishes in this maneuver, despite cries to the contrary by select voices in its fractured parliament. Some even go as far as to wonder where the UN and the United States stand on this sticky issue while thousands of refugees parade across Chechnya's border daily, including a period last week when the numbers reached 100 an hour. The word "Kosovo" comes up often. But other than a reprimand by Madeline Albright and the occasional check-in from British Prime Minister, Tony Blair, there will be no UN relief effort this time. This will be Russia's deal.

Why? Because centuries of social, economic, and political abuse have rendered it so. Whether a godless world power with missiles pointed at Washington or a demented puzzle of broken geographical madness, Mother Russia will be forever at the mercy of the "Russian Element."

I'd first heard it mentioned in a lecture about Arthur Koestler's work during the 80s', when an elderly man with the bravado of someone fast-approaching death was flexing the muscles of the free-world. Ronald Reagan never did comprehend the "Russian Element" as well as he let on. Neither did Jack Kennedy with his imbecilic slap fight with Fidel Castro. But Castro damn-well understood it. So did Churchill, FDR, Hitler, and even that brain-damaged General George S. Patton, who wanted to lead his postwar troops right into its heart and die with his boots on like a good martyred soldier.

The "Russian Element" is something less tangible than an arms race and a freedom issue. It is a state of mind brought on by centuries of slaughter and destruction; something far more horrifying than a flag or blind patriotic duty could ever be. It was a truth told in Joseph Stalin's memoirs and bellowed from the ravaged lungs of those bloody corpses at Leningrad. There would be no more world wars or revolutions, or hand-to-hand trench savagery, no more burning of our homes and torching our land. This time, the "Russian Element" said, if a madman or ideology is felled by force, the sacrifice won't merely include Russia, but the whole world.

Eleven Commonwealth of Independent States stand in the wake of the Soviet Union now. Instead of a common cause to end the planet in the advent of another European lunatic, they claw and fight with the desperation of the ages. Every last one of them have their grubby paws on the same dooms-day buttons that a few rich military monsters once tickled. They have emerged from the wreckage of Communism, just as the revolution 80 years before rose from the ashes of World War I. The unfortunate survivors of that ideological mistake wrought the terror of Stalin's regime. The rest were eradicated by it.

They are the children of those who fought to stem the Nazi tide, like the Kaiser before, and Napoleon before that; not on foreign soil, but their own. Their towns and their families were decimated by war and poverty, brutal winters, and even more brutal leaders lining their pockets with gold at the expense of a war machine bent on cracking the earth in half.

You see, those in attendance that spring day at NC State let that blowhard historian off the hook. One can forgive them for they were jubilant, and most had jobs in waiting the moment their mortarboards hit the hardwood. They knew nothing of what transpired in the wake of the Cold War, when the losers were left to make sense of the social, economic, and religious mess that lay beneath the veneer of independence: the invisible fear of the "Russian Element."

11/17/99

NO REST FOR THE BLEARY: A LATE AUTUMN POLITICAL DIARY

The time for carefully chosen words and snappy leads are over. No one in the gaggle of political writers I ran into at the Bill Bradley fund-raiser in Madison Square Garden last Sunday had the time nor the patience to be creative. New Hampshire creeps ever closer and the incessant staging of events with no grit has gotten to them. Free buffets and polite volunteers leading you from room to room with no word from the candidate must get stale. I only can guess at this, for despite having this preternatural love/hate thing going with American politics, I could not envision spending months of my life following this circus around.

The whole afternoon had a maudlin dirge-like quality. I came only to talk to Joe Namath, but Broadway didn't show. It seems sobriety has a way of dulling the odd plane ride from Florida. He was to join a host of star athletes supporting Dollar Bill in an "on call" capacity former Knicks teammate and hall of famer, Walt "Clyde" Frazier dubbed "a perpetual support group." It was an impressive lineup which ended up fetching up to $1,000 a seat and finally raising over $1.5 million for the campaign. According to the rumpled and ornery media types this now puts Bradley in the financial driver's seat since his opponent has spent nearly 60% of his funds fending him off.

The Bradley people have been very good to me since I sent them a memo which Jennifer and the girls in the P.R. bullpen now call the "pinup letter." The woman laughs every time I talk to her on the phone, and especially loves the part about Al Gore having "the credibility of a street pimp." But none of them were too happy from Press Secretary, Eric Hauser on down when I lead a band of young journalists from Boston down four different corridors trying to wrest a quote from a Gore insurrectionist who infiltrated the event dressed as a chicken and scrambled onto the court just as

Bradley was to speak. He was screaming something about the Senator's failure to meet Gore in a host of debates, but to hear Hauser tell us afterwards, "the Gore people are so frightened now that they will employ Willie Horton if they could find him."

My Demo shrill, Dibbs was not present. He still harbors dreams that Gore will not only shake Dollar Bill, but cut into the imposing national poll numbers, even with John McCain slicing into Bush's once unreachable GOP primary lead. However, Dibbs did admit that the Gore people were behind Chicken Man, and now that Bradley has "entered the ring of ugly politics, it will only be the beginning." If nothing else it was a bold move used to deflect the growing attention paid to Gore's recent phony makeover. His fleeting hope was to regain control of the key party demographics by raising his appeal to women, environmentalists, welfare lifers, and recovering drug addicts. The boys in the press room all agree that the vice president's actions stank of desperation.

Through it all Bradley remains stately. He has that Honest Abe quality, not only in his "I'm a poor boy from Crystal City, Missouri" routine, but his innate ability to appear uncomfortable in suits and political rhetoric. Meanwhile, Gore cannot shake this chilling resemblance to the neighborhood kid who no one likes so he has his parents throw cool parties to procure him a friend. In its wake, Dollar Bill holds fast to the role of outsider, hoping you'll be his pal, but not particularly desperate for your approval.

The last word of the evening from the press corps was that the Bradley people are crossing their fingers for a Hillary Senate run . As this space has been espousing for nearly a year now the presence of Ms. Rodham in New York keeps her and the lame duck president off the national trail. It seems all but certain that by the middle of January their guns will be pointed at the mayor of New York, who told a group of us at the World Series that "his gloves are already off."

The Gore camp has mixed feeling about Ms. Rodham now. He's been systematically separating himself from Big Bill for so long the first lady would be lucky to grab a seat at the back of the campaign's electronic media bus by spring. The vice president is spending less time inside the Beltway these days. That's what his top people have advised. The weekend cry from the latest Gore California jaunt centered around his campaign becoming a "numero uno" priority, and if the national budget hits the Senate next year those poor bastards will have to fend for themselves.

At press time the Bradley camp issued another memo stating that former Clinton Labor Secretary, Robert Reich has ignored convention and endorsed their boy. Reich went on record as saying that although Gore might make a fine president, Bradley is the man for the moment.

It's no secret that since Reich left the administration he's been critical of the president's backtracking on concerns for the growing poverty issue in the face of a booming economy. Bradley's stump story of the little fourth grade girl who told him "it wasn't her turn to eat today" has the diminutive Reich fearing that a Gore presidency might corrupt any system Clinton originally fought for. Reich secretly believes the vice president has always been a closet fiscal conservative whose heritage was earned on big business tobacco farming. Mainly, Reich is pissed for ending up a Clinton comeback causality, and hopes to see Gore reduced to the disingenuous Clintonian suck-ass swine he knows him to be.

12/1/99

THE BELL RINGS

"I'm gonna tell you what we're gonna do. We're going to run the ball. We're gonna pass the ball. We're gonna move right down this field. And we're gonna score!"

- Don Meredith

God bless Dandy Don. He was fearless, insane, and a damn sight better in a bar fight than on a football field. He meant well. It's just that when it came to winning the big one, he made his coach, the venerable, Tom Landry look like a dumb-struck hat check girl at the Hellfire Club. That kind of mindless gumption flies in Texas. There, even the grease monkeys and criminals run for office, and the rest own shotguns and beer cards from Shoney's.

New York is a different breed of feline. Here, we like our danger in pockets of greed and mischief. We like our crazies to have some sheen on them; polished and articulate, with a touch of humor. People will tell you it only happens in the big city, but when you spend more than an afternoon in Albany you get the feeling it runs rampart anywhere you turn in the state.

That's why we never get too excited about political campaigns here. Sure, we expect the odd jab and duck, but it's a subtle pony joust when compared to states like Alabama, Massachusetts, and Texas. Losers of those political races go to places like prison or California, or are expunged from society in way few of us can imagine without the aid of real grade-A embarrassment. The politically wounded speak in Cali and NY, go ask Jerry Brown and Ed Koch.

But that will all change come this summer, because it looks as though we have a real Texas race for Senate heating up in the Empire State. The first lady and the mayor. Political death to the lesser and terminal social disease to anyone with fewer votes. An all out war of words and deeds. Petulant whimpers will rise into bellows of defamatory calls for beheadings and exorcisms. When Uncle Rudy and the Ice Queen from Arkansas are done with the trail only the deaf and the stupid will be fortunate.

Senator Rodham has finally dug into the starting line. The woman whose kept the fuck-happy circus that is the Clinton political machine together for two decades steps out of her cushy Pennsylvania avenue lair to become the public junkyard dog she's allegedly been behind closed doors. In hockey terms, "the gloves are off." Her opponents, the press, and all those left for rotting corpses in the wake of two highly successful presidential runs lie in wait for the darling of the "stand by your man" set. Apologies to longtime Cowboys fans everywhere, but not even Dandy Don had those kind of balls.

This is a woman who never ran for any office making a run in a state she hasn't lived in for one minute. Her track record as a legislator begins at horrendous and drops from there. Her reputation as a litigator is peppered with more alleged maleficence than William & Morris. The best you can say about her is that she is educated and willing to take the most shit from people who claim to love her in a more than clumsy attempt to latch onto something resembling power. No one has sold their soul for a chance at the American political brass ring with more blind gusto since Dick Nixon.

The mere notion that she would choose to endure the personal and professional thrashing that awaits her is baffling. Unless you consider that she is truly a woman scorned. Word out of Washington is she's been making Big Bill pay for every pet he laid on Monica, and the only reason the president ordered the bombing of Kosovo and pardoned those Puerto Rican terrorists was because Mamma Hillary told him so.

And now Senator Rodham has the mighty chip on her shoulder that monster of a father told her she'd never have, but the boys at law school swore was there. They could see it every time she pulled back those ruby red lips and bore her fangs. Big Bill saw those things and married her before sundown.

This would all be a moot point in the realm of real wartime politics if the first lady had a victim sitting in the wings; someone she could badger with attitude and vigor, looking like an arch angel come to slay one of Satan's bad boys. But alas, that little nugget comes packaged in one of the meanest political pit bulls this nation has produced since Lester Maddox.

When Rudy Giuliani finally joins the fray there will be nothing left to the argument that campaigns should be civil exchanges of policy and stance. There is no boxer in Uncle Rudy. He's a puncher. When the mayor gets going on one of his jags he resembles Joe Frazier prior to one of those blood baths with Ali when he told his corner he'd prefer to go in the back alley of Madison Square Garden and settle the fight with bare knuckles and chains.

But Uncle Rudy wouldn't be caught dead baring his knuckles when he can simply bring out the shiny brass ones he's used on everyone whose opposed him since he was district attorney of NY. Not even his friends and colleagues can call him anything less than tyrannical now. He has turned NYC upside down, cleaned the streets and put the swagger back into the police. All the while he's treated the first amendment like a Bazooka Joe comic and bullied the dissenters into looking like radical Commie guerrillas.

The bell rings.

12/8/99

TRAMPS, THUGS, & THE CORPORATE LIE

"The business of America is business."
- Calvin Coolidge

anarchy - a state of society without government or law.
- Random House Dictionary

Fantasy time is over for the psuedo-hippie, radical, cheap fraud street trash who turned a plausible democratic protest into a free-for-all of violence, looting and overall dime-store mania. The union boys and the Friends of the Earth are all packed and headed back to their suburban prisons with their 2.3 burdens and the tax-man moan, and to think the poor bastards over at production for Nightline have to dig harder for topics.

Now that the tear gas has faded and the echoes of rhetoric are left for vacant pedantry, the bright idea to hold the World Trade Organization Convention in the previously utlra-mellow city of Seattle must seem like a bloody public relations abortion to its authors. But it was nothing more than a speed bump on the highway of high profit and the bottom line.

As a public service to those misinformed souls who actually cared about what went down amidst the backdrop of that 60s' revisionism, this space will attempt to strip away the facade and investigate the gooey innards which makes these reactionary sects of humanity dip to the level of the ape for a chance to be psychoanalyzed on the evening news.

Protest is cute, and does occasionally give the impression that the system—whichever one you subscribe to—works. But it is a futile square dance in the face of the brutal law of the jungle: The biggest and baddest have the cash, and they will send us all to the gutter or the grave to hold onto it. Cellular phones are burning our brain cells, fast food is clogging our arteries, pollution is mutating our genes, children are murdering each other for Pokemon cards and Nike sneakers, and if the demonic charlatans in the power ties on the 40th floor could sell you a gun or a cigarette they will run a line of bullshit that would've had Josef Goebbels begging for the blueprint.

No one harboring thoughts of staying in power want to dirty their fingers with anything approaching human rights or environmental issues. This is a nation built on a disgusting stack of mammon earned on the backs of those who might consider a loaf of a bread a feast. Corporate creeps and politicians have ignored the better parts of the Ten Commandments in a king-hell romp from the edge of the industrial revolution to the darkest corners of Wall Street. These are the insatiable vampires of greed who need their slaves and toxic waste. If it cannot be provided south of the Mason Dixon then they will go abroad. We should count ourselves as the lucky ones, for we'll be long dead before they have the resources to rape every inch of this planet.

There wasn't one part of that farce staged in Seattle by the 135 member countries of the WTO, the Kumbaya choral group, and the punks masquerading as police officers, that can serve as evidence for the perpetuation of silly things like hope or fairness in the realm of big business—because in the end it is what runs this nation. Even a spineless geek like Bill Clinton knew the jig was up when he gave his now infamous 180 degree screeching-halt speech to the dumbfounded bloats at the convention while we watched downtown burn under Dan Rather's monotone drawl. The president abandoned his prepared notes to start appeasing the turks out front while trying to defend the idea that most countries would jump at the chance to employ one-legged retarded children at a half a dollar an hour to make it in the black by Christmas.

Then a few fractured groups of unemployed pot heads and masked dip shits started ransacking the Gap and setting fire to Niketown. They called themselves anarchists; achieving precious prime time minutes telling the rest of us puppets about the evils of industry while referring to the sound of breaking glass and crackling flames as orgasmic.

To them it must be said that anarchism is the most misunderstood "ism" left to us. These pusillanimous dupes wouldn't know the meaning of the word if it was spoon fed to their fog-addled brain matter.

Humans need laws. We are weak and stupid and would reduce our quality of life to fossil fragments without them. We have so many laws now it would choke forty civilizations. We cram God and country and all that weepy singsong crap down every throat possible. Yet we continue to reign as the most heinous creatures sucking air.

Anyone scheming a world with no boundaries ought to spend ten minutes on a New York subway train or a Woodstock festival. We talk a good game, but the second our shit is screwed with we run to lawyers and prostrate ourselves to anything resembling the constitution. People are always fond of anarchism when it's someone else's stuff their reducing to twigs. Let us see one of these hard-talking posers take off the mask, drive their corporate-build cars back to their corporate-built condos and start wielding the ax of freedom. Then we'll start seeing a whiz bang hootenanny of anarchism.

But, alas, the phonies have all gone home and the television parasites have moved on to the next flavor of the month. The WTO was hardly shaken and the Chinese will be dutifully trading by spring while joyfully continuing to make an historic mockery of human rights. The "anarchists" are gearing up for the Republican National Convention in the City of Brotherly Love and the environmentalists are gearing up for a world record suck-up by Al Gore.

12/15/99

GEORGETOWN UNLEASHED

"To his dog, every man is Napoleon; hence the constant popularity of dogs."
                                        - Aldous Huxley

Journalism is a despicable trade. I know this because I practice it—but only part-time—because there is no earthy reason to allow one's self to have to live on such painfully wretched means. I have known this as fact for over 20 years now. I knew it when I wrote for my high school newspaper, college newspaper, and every publication since. It's not so much the reporting or writing, or even the act of putting those two talents together to disseminate reasonable information, but the inevitable sycophantic regurgitation of all that is crude and inane.

That may be the harshest definition of anything I've committed to paper, but I stand by every word. I may regret it later, but for now, it breathes new cathartic life into me. It is the only fitting way to begin what will surely be my last conversation of the century with the man who has now taken on legendary status in this space—if not notoriety to those he sells down the river for a few laughs—a man I've seen fit to call Georgetown.

The following conversation took place at several locations in NYC last Saturday night over many drinks at Bars, cafes', restaurants, and finally inside my automobile; cruising along the bevy of cabs rolling down 1st avenue, making every light from Houston to 79th. Something the both of us will take with pride for the rest of our lives. Below are the low lights.

Georgetown - What the fuck is wrong with the people in this town? Are they brain damaged? They better start packing up and heading to somewhere far, far away from this place before that ball hits the ground in two weeks. Do you realize there will be chaos here very shortly? Transit strike, homeless revolt, Hillary campaign, terrorist threats, a full scale riot of epic proportions on New Year's Eve. Times Square will burn. I have that on serious authority!

JC - Be that as it may, what will that do to Uncle Rudy's chances in this Senate campaign he hasn't even declared himself part of yet?

GT - You miserable man, can't you smell the doom in the air? Fucking mayor of charred town, that's what they'll call him. They'll run his corpse against Hillary and win—prop up his rotting remains face down on some rostrum at the debates. I can see her now, complaining about his silence. "But he's dead,

Mrs. Clinton. The Big Apple is but a memory. The survivors hung the mayor's body in effigy on Columbus Circle and spit on him like Mussolini. Yet, he leads in the polls. Can you explain it?" "I am not Mrs. Clinton! I am Ms. Rodham! And I live! A vote for me is a vote for the living! I was nowhere near Times Square when the shit went down. I was on a luxury liner off the Virgin Islands sipping Daiquiris with the Prince of St. Croix!"

JC - Hillary's not beginning well, I'll give you that.

GT - I don't know what that woman is doing, but campaigning to win is not it. Not even that screaming banshee hick, Carville will be able to save her. I'm sick of looking at him bobbing his head like a madman being goosed by a red hot harpoon every goddamn Sunday on that pathetic "Meet the Press." Why didn't she just take a run through the desert and hug Saddam Hussein and mercifully put this abomination to bed?

JC - She's got Rosie O'Donnell in her corner.

GT - I've got news for Rosie, it's probably best she stick to housewives and the mind dead before taking on New York City's homeless problem. Christ! Look at these poor fuckers lying in their own urine, throwing bricks at tourists. Since when is sitting dormant and smelling like digested wine pleasant for the celebrity set? What a witless babbling troll. I see she's pulled out on K-Mart finally. Next year she'll be kicking bums off her lawn.

JC - Between now and New Hampshire, do any of these has-been GOP contenders give you any reason to comment?

GT - Listen, McCain is a great guy. We all love to drink with him and his staff, but he's a loser. He'll lose to Gore or Bradley. He knows it. He wants to be vice president. He says he doesn't, but he says a lot of insane things out there. He's spent all his money in New Hampshire and he's had all the push he's getting. It's over. The numbers will reflect nothing for John come summer. And I wish Forbes would get the fuck out of this thing before he embarrasses us all. That dumb ass flat tax shit is so goddamn off the wall I expect gremlins to start taking his calls from now on. Give it up. The goddamn party needs another stammering rich prick front man like a Drano enema. It's friggin' Disneyland over at his headquarters. He should sell tickets to recoup some of the millions he's dumped into this rotten mess.

JC - I'm going to see Buchanan next month. Any thoughts?

GT - Tell him happy hunting over at the hub of super freaks. What is the Reform Party? They don't even want him. Every time I hear a Jesse Ventura sound bite, he's calling Pat names. He told my golf buddy at State he wants to wring his scrawny neck. And where the hell is Perot? I heard someone beat the dentures out of him in Seattle during the WTO disturbances. You hear that?

JC - I was told he was living with Michael Jackson.

GT - I think George W. is starting to look like Augustus Caesar, but a little dumber.

JC - He's going to be president.

GT- With a cherry on top.

12/22/99

NOTE TO THE NEXT GENERATION TO CLOSE A CENTURY

> *When old age shall this generation waste,*
> *Thou shalt remain, in midst of other woe*
> *Than ours, a friend to man, to whom thou say'st,*
> *"Beauty is truth, truth beauty," —that is all*
> *Ye know on earth, and all ye need to know.*

>   - John Keats
>   "Ode on a Grecian Urn"

Having spent the better part of the last 20 minutes watching my cats eat and lick themselves and search for places to curl up for their obligatory 18 hours of sleep, I have to wonder where the advantages to humanity lie. The Egyptians used to bury cats with their pharaohs. There was a mystic quality to the feline that was attached to most domestic items for Egyptian royalty. They never ignored the true essence of the cat—that it is nature's perfect killing machine. Humans are thinking machines, and if the Egyptians knew anything, it was that anyone considering survival on the next level damn well better have a serious escort.

And while the Egyptians built their pyramids and wrote on their interior walls for generations they never once considered being washed up. The Greeks philosophers didn't see it coming either. They spent countless hours pondering the great questions of the universe between the odd romp in the sack with young boys, but nothing tangible materialized.

The Romans sure didn't think in terms of defeat. They built the roads and formulated the calendar while breaking all records for human misery. They were sure whatever they were doing was gangbusters, but when the Huns came and cleaned out the last bath house, the screeching voices of the last few beautiful people stated emphatically that they weren't ready for the party to end.

The thing is, not too many people know what the hell is going on. Confusion is our legacy. It comes from this curse of thinking; a chip in our brains that manufactures the kind of ego that would make us even consider being made in the image of God without earning a fraction of what such a concept entails. Humans have been building entire civilizations on this incredibly deep barrel of confused logic for centuries.

Confusion is terribly underrated. In fact, it has always been incumbent upon humanity to achieve a greater misunderstanding of life in order to further confuse future generations. Where would we be as a race without it? Confusion keeps the wheels of evolution greased—from the ever-perplexing world of science to the musty arena of religion—it allows the war machine to sing and political madness to thrive. It is the one true element of our being which separates us from the animal.

After all the horrible things we manage to do to each other, humans are still a resilient bunch. We consume our icons and spit out our children, choke reality and ignore mystery. We've perfected the fine art of looking the other way and putting the blame on anyone or anything but us. We argue about color and money and ignore the miracle of every breath. This is what has passed for survival since we figured out our advantage over everything else on the planet.

But, alas, those of us still able to cling to the notion that we belong to anything tangible were taught very early in life that most everything held dear by the people we buried failed in some way. We can trust no one, but have a pristine childlike faith that someone—anyone—is out there just waiting for us to slip up, and that somewhere down the line somebody is paying for this drunken path of power and callous disregard for these brains of ours.

There is, however, one measure of understanding we've achieved: despite our misgivings, stupidity, and collective weakness, we still have a puncher's chance to correct this mess.

You can conquer us, put governments on us, even make us choose one language and swallow this atavistic definition of God. Dump wars and marriage and 500 new ways of screwing our heads up with more "isms" then you can shake a fist at, but we will not be bowed. We've been earth-quaked and storm-fronted and beaten down by everything nature has thrown at us, and made it past another millennium with our knees buckling and our teeth grinding.

When the bell finally rings on this race and there are no more chances, what will the beings that build in our wake have to say about us? Will we be remembered for airplanes, hair transplants, and the Internet? Will they remember that we loved or cared about those who didn't provide for us a cushy existence? Will they mark our greatest achievements as cursory or perennial? Selfish or philanthropic?

Jazz, opera, theater, literature, dance, medicine, technology, drugs, sport, politics, psychology, philosophy, religion, law, reason, humor, compassion, tolerance, regret, sadness, happiness, hate, love; we are capable of so much, and that is what keeps us going.

We like to think that we had the best century ever. But perhaps the 100 years you've just breezed through was that much better. What is your criteria? Who will be your judge?

Yes sir, fine people of earth; you've earned another century, maybe even another thousand years. You're smarter than you've ever been, but are you better? You have conquered the corners of this troubling brain, perfected computer chips to think for yourself so you can forget to smell the flowers and miss the sun set one more time. After all, there'll be more of them. Maybe.

Raise a glass and toast humanity, because it's all we've got.

Acknowledgments

The contributions to *Fear No Art* spiritually, inspirationally, or otherwise, should not go without rousing plaudits and extreme accolade. The list is thus:

My formidable editors, if not for whom my scribble would be mere mental masturbation; Mary Thurmond and Terry Allen.
My good-humored managing editors, if not for whom these terrible musings would go unpaid and unpunished; Dan Davis and Chris Uhl.
My invisible sources and their interminable friends, if not for whom my nights would be quiet and my spite tempered.
My e-mail buddies; if not for whom I would sleep more, but laugh less.
My Check Group; if not for whom I'd feel more alone in this lonely endeavor of satire.
My publisher: if not for whom I'd be groveling at the sanctimonious treachery of moguls and tyrants.
My Family and Friends: if not for whom I'd be nothing more than this wretched character trapped within these pages.
My readers for whom I am eternally grateful.

About the Author

As Chairman of the Reality Check News & Information Desk, James Campion is the leading distiller of meaningless information provided weekly in a column for the Aquarian Weekly. His disdain for deadlines and editors is well documented in the annals of tort . A solitary life of vitriolic whining and caustic blather have been an essential, if not grotesque, part of his work. He still lives on planet earth. This is his second book.

One might wonder about...

One might wonder why this book is brought to you by a frightening web site logo and not a warm and fuzzy traditional "publishing company"?

One might wonder why some people would feel threatened by such things? After all, Why MUST a "publishing company" disseminate literature? Why NOT a web site? Why in this amazing changing world of the internet, can't there be a whole new way to access information, entertainment, ideas, knowledge, soup? Ok, not so much "soup" but maybe soup!?! Yes, perhaps someday even soup will break all the rules and be one with BLAZO!!

One might wonder if someday our children will ask us about "today" the way we asked our parents and grand-parents about the beginning of Television.

BLAZO!! Is an experience reception network for the new millennium! If you are pleasantly irreverent, question authority, sarcastic to the core and find yourself marching to the beat of a drummer with little or no formal musical education... BLAZO!! IS YOUR FRIEND! Remember, a wise man once said... "A little nonsense now and then is relished by the wisest men."

|-------------------------|

If you enjoyed this book and the many "Reality Check" columns it contains you need to visit www.jamescampion.com! There you can find the most recent versions of the columns and stories jc writes for newspapers and magazines around the globe as well as exclusive stories and content found no where else! Visit today and mention code "FNAD" to receive a special discount on all "JAMES CAMPION" books and merchandise like "DEEP TANK JERSEY -- one man's journey into the soul of a New Jersey club band" his critically acclaimed journal of madness live from the Rock N Roll trenches.